AA

Britain's
Best
Hotels

AA Lifestyle Guides

This product includes mapping data licensed from Ordnance Survey® with the permission of the Controller of Her Majesty's Stationery Office. © Crown copyright 2011. All rights reserved. Licence number 100021153.

Maps prepared by the Mapping Services Department of The Automobile Association.

Maps © AA Media Limited 2011.

Advertising Sales:
advertisementsales@theAA.com

Editorial:
lifestyleguides@theAA.com

The contents of this publication are believed correct at the time of printing. Nevertheless, the Publisher cannot be held responsible for any errors or omissions or for changes in the details given in this guide or for the consequences of any reliance on the information provided by the same.

Assessments of AA inspected establishments are based on the experience of the hotel and restaurant inspectors on the occasion of their visit(s) and therefore descriptions given in this guide necessarily dictate an element of subjective opinion which may not reflect or dictate a reader's own opinion on another occasion. We have tried to ensure accuracy in this guide but things do change and we would be grateful if readers would advise us of any inaccuracies they may encounter.

Website addresses are included in some entries and specified by the respective establishment. Such websites are not under the control of AA Media Limited and as such AA Media Limited has no control over them and will not accept any responsibility or liability in respect of any and all matters whatsoever relating to such websites including access, content, material and functionality. By including the addresses of third party websites the AA does not intend to solicit business or offer any security to any person in any country, directly or indirectly.

Typeset by AA Lifestyle Guides

Printed and bound by Graficas, Estella, Spain

Editorial contributor: Philip Bryant

Cover credits
Front Cover: Luckham Park Hotel & Spa
Back Cover: (t) Spread Eagle Hotel & Spa;
(c) Ivy Bush Royal Hotel;
(b) Toravaig House Hotel

A CIP catalogue record for this book is available from the British Library

ISBN: 978-0-7495-6788-0

Published by AA Publishing, which is a trading name of AA Media Limited, whose registered office is:
Fanum House,
Basing View,
Basingstoke,
Hampshire RG21 4EA
Registered number 06112600

theAA.com/shop

A04571

Britain's Best
Hotels

Contents

Welcome

The selection of establishments in Britain's Best Hotels have all been professionally inspected by the AA to ensure the highest standards of hospitality, accommodation and food.

The Best Hotels

This guide covers over 200 town and country houses, small hotels and restaurants with rooms. Every establishment has received a star rating and percentage merit score following a visit by an AA inspector. This indicates that you can expect a friendly welcome, comfortable surroundings, excellent food and a good service. Further details about the AA scheme, inspections and awards and rating system can be found on pages 8–9 of this guide.

Before You Travel

Some places may offer special breaks and facilities not available at the time of going to press. If in doubt, it's always worth calling the hotel before you book. See also the useful information provided on pages 10–11, and visit theAA.com for up-to-date establishment and travel information.

Using the Guide

Britain's Best Hotels has been designed to enable you to find an establishment quickly and efficiently. Each entry provides clear information about the type of accommodation, the facilities available and the local area.

Use the contents (page 3) to browse the main gazetteer section by county and the index to find either a location (page 296) or a specific hotel (page 300) by name.

Finding Your Way

The main section of the guide is divided into four parts, covering England, Channel Islands, Scotland and Wales. The counties within each of these sections are ordered alphabetically as are the town or village locations (shown in capital letters as part of the address) within each county. Finally, the establishments are listed alphabetically under each location name. Town names featured in the guide can also be located in the map section at the back of the guide.

Duisdale House

★★★★ 80% ®® SMALL HOTEL
Address: ISLEORNSAY, Isle of Skye, IV43 8QW
Tel: 01471 833202
Fax: 01471 833404
Email: info@duisdale.com
Website: www.duisdale.com
Map ref: 11, NG71
Directions: 7m S of Bradford on A851 towards Armadale. 7m N of Armadale ferry
Rooms: 18 (1 GF) (1 fmly) **S** £120-£150
D £169-£269 (incl. bkfst) **Facilities:** STV Wi-fi **Parking:** 30 **Notes:** ⊗ ⅏ 5yrs

A romantic hotel in the south of the Isle of Skye with panoramic views across the Sound of Sleat. The sleek bedrooms, including four-poster rooms, have flat-screen TVs, luxury amenities and either sea or garden views. Blazing fires and candlelight create the perfect atmosphere for a romantic evening and there is a well stocked bar and extensive wine list. The chef's skilfully prepared modern Scottish cuisine is based on the freshest island produce. Complimentary Wi-fi is available and daily sailing excursions possible on onboard the hotel's luxury yacht.

Recommended in the area

Talisker Distillery; Dunvegan Castle; Portree Town

---

❶ Stars and symbols

All entries in the guide have been inspected by the AA and, at the time of going to press, belong to the AA hotel scheme. Every establishment in the scheme is classified for quality with a rating of one to five stars (★). Every establishment in Britain's Best Hotels has three, four or five stars and a high merit score (%). The very best hotels in each of these categories have been given red stars (★). Alongside a star rating, each establishment has also been given one of the following descriptive categories:

HOTEL, TOWN HOUSE HOTEL, COUNTRY HOUSE HOTEL, SMALL HOTEL, RESTAURANT WITH ROOMS.

See pages 8–9 for more information on the AA ratings and awards scheme.

Rosette ®: This is the AA's food award (see page 9 for further details). *continued*

❷ Contact Details

The establishment address includes a locator or place name in capitals (e.g. NORWICH). Within each county, entries are ordered alphabetically first by this place name and then by the name of the establishment.

Telephone and fax numbers, and e-mail and website addresses are given where available. See page 10 for information about booking online. The telephone and fax numbers are believed correct at the time of going to press but changes may occur. The latest establishment details are on the Hotel pages at theAA.com.

❸ Map reference

Each establishment in this guide is given a map reference for a location which can be found in the atlas section at the back of the guide. It is composed of the map page number (1–13) and two-figure map reference based on the National Grid.

For example: **Map 05 SU48**
05 refers to the page number of the map section at the back of the guide
SU is the National Grid lettered square (representing 100,000sq metres) in which the location will be found
4 is the figure reading across the top and bottom of the map page
8 is the figure reading down each side of the map page

Maps locating each establishment and a route planner are available at theAA.com.

❹ Directions

Where possible, directions have been given from the nearest motorway or major road.

❺ Room Information

The entries show the number of en suite letting bedrooms available. Bedrooms that have a private bathroom adjacent may be included as en suite. Further details of facilities provided in the rooms are listed in the main entry description (see ❾).

Prices: Prices are per room per night including VAT (unless otherwise specified) and are provided by the hoteliers in good faith. These prices are indications and not firm quotations. Always check before booking.

❻ Facilities

This section lists a selection of facilities offered by the hotel including sports facilities such as indoor and outdoor swimming pools, golf, tennis and gym; options for relaxation such as spa, jacuzzi and solarium, and services such as satellite TV and Wi-fi. Use the key to the symbols on page 7 to help identify what's available at a particular hotel.

Additional facilities, or notes about other services may be listed here. Some hotels have restricted service during quieter months, and at this time some of the listed facilities will not be available. If unsure, contact the hotel before your visit.

Payment

Most hotels now accept credit or debit cards. Credit cards may be subject to a surcharge – check when booking if this is how you intend to pay. Not all hotels accept travellers' cheques.

❼ Parking

This shows the number of parking spaces available. Other types of parking (on road or Park and Ride) may also be possible; check the descriptions for further information.

❽ Notes

This section provides specific details relating to:

Smoking policy: Smoking in public places is now banned in England, Scotland and Wales.

The proprietor can designate one or more bedrooms with ventilation systems where the occupants can smoke, but communal areas must be smoke-free.

Dogs: Although many hotels allow dogs, they may be excluded from some areas of the hotel and some breeds, particularly those requiring an exceptional license, may not be acceptable at all. Under the Disability Discrimination Act 1995 access should be allowed for guide dogs and assistance dogs. Please check the hotel's policy when making your booking.

Children: No children () means children cannot be accommodated, or a minimum age may be specified, e.g. **under 4** means no children under four years old. The main description may also provide details about facilities available for children.

Establishments with special facilities for children may include a babysitting service or baby-intercom system, playroom or playground, laundry facilities, drying and ironing facilities, cots, high chairs and special meals.

❾ Description

This may include specific information about the various facilities offered in the rooms, a brief history of the establishment, notes about special features and descriptions of the food where an award has been given (see page 9).

❿ Recommended in the Area

These listings give local places of interest and potential day trips and activities.

Key to symbols

★	Black stars (see page 8)
★	Red stars (see page 9)
%	Merit score
◉	AA Rosette (see page 9)
3, TQ28	Map reference
S	Single room
D	Double room
GF	Ground floor room
Family	Family room
⊗	No dogs allowed (assist dogs should be allowed)
ⅺ	Children not allowed
Wi-fi	Wireless network
STV	Satellite television
⊛	Indoor heated swimming pool
⌇	Outdoor swimming pool
⌇	Outdoor heated swimming pool

Best Quality

All entries in Britain's Best Hotels have excelled in several categories set by the AA inspection team. Red stars are awarded to the very best establishments in each star category and signify that the hotel offers the finest accommodation available.

High Standards

Hotels recognised by the AA should:

- have high standards of cleanliness
- keep proper records of booking
- give prompt and professional service to guests, assist with luggage on request, accept and deliver messages
- provide a designated area for breakfast and dinner, with drinks available in a bar or lounge
- provide an early morning call on request
- have good quality furniture and fittings
- provide adequate heating and lighting
- undertake proper maintenance

The hotels in Britain's Best Hotels all have a three, four or five black or red star rating. The following is a brief guide to some of the general expectations for each star classification:

★★★ Three Star

- Management and staff smartly and professionally presented and usually wearing a recognisable uniform
- A dedicated receptionist on duty at peak times
- At least one restaurant or dining room open to residents and non-residents for breakfast and dinner whenever the hotel is open
- Last orders for dinner no earlier than 8pm
- Remote-control television, direct-dial phone
- En suite bath or shower and WC

★★★★ Four Star

- A formal, professional staffing structure with smartly presented, uniformed staff anticipating and responding to your needs or requests
- Usually spacious, well-appointed public areas
- Reception staffed 24 hours by well-trained staff
- Express checkout facilities where appropriate
- Porterage available on request
- Night porter available
- At least one restaurant open to residents and non-residents for breakfast and dinner seven days per week, and lunch to be available in a designated eating area
- Last orders for dinner no earlier than 9pm
- En suite bath with fixed overhead shower and WC

★★★★★ Five Star

- Luxurious accommodation and public areas with a range of extra facilities. First time guests shown to their bedroom
- Multilingual service
- Guest accounts well explained and clearly presented

- Porterage offered
- Guests greeted at hotel entrance, full concierge service provided
- At least one restaurant open to residents and non-residents for all meals seven days per week
- Last orders for dinner no earlier than 10pm
- High-quality menu and wine list
- Evening service to turn down the beds
- Remote-control television, direct-dial telephone at bedside and desk, a range of luxury toiletries, bath sheets and robes
- En suite bathroom incorporating fixed overhead shower and WC

★ Inspectors' Choice

Each year the AA selects the best hotels in each rating. These hotels stand out as the very best in the British Isles, regardless of style. The Inspectors' Choice hotels in this guide are identified by red stars.

Types of hotel

The majority of establishments in this guide come under the category of Hotel; other categories are listed below:

Town House Hotel:

A small, individual city or town centre property, which provides a high degree of personal service and privacy.

Country House Hotel:

These are quietly located in a rural area.

Small Hotel:

Has less than 20 bedrooms and is managed by the owner.

Restaurant with rooms:

This category of accommodation is now assessed under the AA's Guest Accommodation scheme. Some of them have been awarded yellow stars, which indicates that they are among the top ten percent of their star rating. Most Restaurants with Rooms have been awarded AA Rosettes for their food.

AA Rosette Awards

Out of the many thousands of restaurants in the UK, the AA identifies some 1,900 as the best. The following is an outline of what to expect from restaurants with AA Rosette Awards. For a more detailed explanation of Rosette criteria please see theAA.com

⊛ Excellent local restaurants serving food prepared with care, understanding and skill, using good quality ingredients.

⊛⊛ The best local restaurants, which aim for and achieve higher standards, better consistency and where a greater precision is apparent in the cooking. There will be obvious attention to the selection of quality ingredients.

⊛⊛⊛ Outstanding restaurants that demand recognition well beyond their local area.

⊛⊛⊛⊛ Amongst the very best restaurants in the British Isles, where the cooking demands national recognition.

⊛⊛⊛⊛⊛ The finest restaurants in the British Isles, where the cooking stands comparison with the best in the world.

Useful Information

If you're unsure about any of the facilities offered, always check with the establishment before you visit or book accommodation.

Hints on booking your stay

It's always worth booking as early as possible, particularly for the peak holiday period from the beginning of June to the end of September. Bear in mind that Easter and other public holidays may be busy too, and in some parts of Scotland, the ski season is a peak holiday period.

Some hotels will ask for a deposit or full payment in advance, especially for one-night bookings. And some hotels charge half-board (bed, breakfast and dinner) whether you require the meals or not, while others may only accept full-board bookings. Not all hotels will accept advance bookings for bed and breakfast, overnight or short stays. Some will not take reservations from mid week.

Once a booking is confirmed, let the hotel know at once if you are unable to keep your reservation. If the hotel cannot re-let your room you may be liable to pay about two-thirds of the room price (a deposit will count towards this payment). In Britain a legally binding contract is made when you accept an offer of accommodation, either in writing or by telephone, and illness is not accepted as a release from this contract. You are advised to take out insurance against possible cancellation, for example AA Single Trip Insurance. Visit theAA.com or call 0845 092 0606 for details.

Booking online

Booking a place to stay can be a very time-consuming process, but you can search quickly and easily online for a place that best suits your needs. Simply visit our website (www.theAA.com/travel) to search for a hotel, then click on Book online on the hotel's own page to check availability.

Prices

The AA encourages the use of the Hotel Industry Voluntary Code of Booking Practice, which aims to ensure that guests know how much they will have to pay and what services and facilities are included, before entering a financially binding agreement. If the price has not previously been confirmed in writing, guests should be given a card stipulating the total obligatory charge when they register at reception.

Facilities for disabled guests

The final stage (Part III) of the Disability Discrimination Act (access to Goods and Services) came into force in October 2004. This means that service providers may have to make permanent adjustments to their premises. For further information, see the government website www.disability.gov.uk

Please note: AA inspectors are not accredited to make inspections under the National Accessibility Scheme. We indicate in the entries if an establishment has ground floor rooms; and if a hotel tells us that they have disabled facilities this is included.

The establishments in this guide should all be aware of their responsibilities under the Act. We recommend that you always phone in advance to ensure that the establishment you have chosen has appropriate facilities.

Licensing Laws

Licensing laws differ in England, Wales, Scotland, the Republic of Ireland, the Isle of Man, the Isles of Scilly and the Channel Islands. Public houses are generally open from mid morning to early afternoon, and from about 6 or 7pm until 11pm, although closing times may be earlier or later and some pubs are open all afternoon. Unless otherwise stated, establishments listed are licensed. Hotel residents can obtain alcoholic drinks at all times, if the licensee is prepared to serve them. Non-residents eating at the hotel restaurant can have drinks with meals. Children under 14 may be excluded from bars where no food is served. Those under 18 may not purchase or consume alcoholic drinks. Club license means that drinks are served to club members only. Forty-eight hours must lapse between joining and ordering.

Fire Safety

The Fire Precautions Act does not apply to the Channel Islands, Republic of Ireland, or the Isle of Man, which have their own rules. As far as we are aware, all hotels listed have applied for and not been refused a fire certificate.

Bank and Public Holidays 2011

New Year's Day	1st January
New Year's Holiday (Scotland)	4th January
Good Friday	22nd April
Easter Monday	25th April
Royal Wedding	29th April
Early May Bank Holiday	2nd May
Spring Bank Holiday	30th May
August Holiday (Scotland)	2nd August
Summer Bank Holiday	29th August
St Andrew's Day (Scotland)	30th November
Christmas Day	25th December
Boxing Day	26th December

theAA.com

- Go to theAA.com to find more AA listed guest houses, hotels, pubs and restaurants – There are around 12,000 establishments on the site.

- The home page leads to the AA's easy-to-use route planner.

- Simply enter your postcode and the establishment postcode given in this guide and click 'Get Route'. You will have a detailed route plan to take you from door-to-door.

- Use the Travel section to search for Hotels & B&Bs or Restaurants & Pubs by location or establishment name. Scroll down the list of results for the interactive map and local routes.

Marlborough, Wiltshire

Thousands of places to stay throughout the UK & Ireland

View information on thousands of AA recognised establishments and other accommodation

Access to online booking facilities for selected establishments

Extensive range and choice of accommodation

Get the most out of your trip with AA Travel

Exclusive discounts for AA Members and eligible customers at participating hotels

Terms and conditions apply

ENGLAND

Forest of Bowland, Lancashire

BEDFORDSHIRE

Luton Hoo

Luton Hoo Hotel, Golf and Spa

★★★★★ 89% ◉◉ HOTEL

Address: The Mansion House, LUTON, LU1 3TQ
Tel: 01582 734437 & 698888
Fax: 01582 485438
Email: reservations@lutonhoo.com
Website: www.lutonhoo.com
Map ref: 3 TL02
Directions: M1 junct 10A, 3rd exit to A1081 towards Harpenden/St Albans. Hotel less than 1m on left
Rooms: 228 (65 GF) (50 fmly) **D** £230-£895 (incl. bkfst) **Facilities:** Wi-fi ⓢ Gym Spa Golf nearby Bird watching Cycling Snooker **Parking:** 316

The Grade I listed mansion house at Luton Hoo has played host to royalty and dignitaries over the centuries. Painstakingly restored to its former glory, the property stands proudly within magnificent grounds. Boasting over 1,000 acres of parkland designed by the celebrated landscape architect 'Capability' Brown, the estate comprises formal gardens, woodland trails, a 50-acre lake, all-weather and Victorian lawn tennis courts, as well as an 18-hole, par 73 golf course. The spa, using Luton Hoo's own organic product range, provides relaxation and calm for all guests. The opulent bedrooms and suites are all beautifully furnished, have individual character and come well equipped; the suites in the mansion are particularly impressive. Exquisite fine dining is offered in the Wernher Restaurant, with rich furnishings and tapestries setting the mood, while the Adam's Brasserie provides a less formal dining option. At the foot of the estate, on the banks of the River Lea, the Warren Weir Suite offers an exclusive use venue for meetings, events and weddings. Ideally situated, the hotel is just 10 minutes' drive from London Luton Airport and has excellent links to the M1 and M25.

Recommended in the area

Whipsnade Wild Animal Park and Tree Cathedral; Berkhamsted Castle; Woburn Abbey

The Inn at Woburn

★★★ 81% ◉◉ HOTEL

Address: George Street, WOBURN, Milton Keynes,
MK17 9PX
Tel: 01525 290441
Fax: 01525 290432
Email: inn@woburn.co.uk
Website: www.woburn.co.uk/inn
Map ref: 3, SP93
Directions: M1 junct 13, left to Woburn, at Woburn
left at T-junct, hotel in village
Rooms: 54 (21 GF) (4 fmly) S £118-£150
D £138-£210 **Parking:** 80

Occupying centre stage in what has been described as 'a Georgian town of village proportions', this former coaching inn is part of the estate belonging to the Duke of Bedford, whose home, Woburn Abbey, has been the family seat for nearly 400 years. The village is noted for its fine architecture, antique and gift shops, tea rooms, restaurants and the parkland that surrounds it. Rooms, from singles to executive king, have satellite TV, radio and direct-dial telephone, trouser press and hot-drinks maker. Across the courtyard are seven cottages, five with their own individual sitting room. Olivier's is the hotel's two AA Rosette-awarded restaurant, where contemporary English and continental cuisine is offered, typified by carpaccio of Woburn venison with roasted beetroot and basil dressing; and daily specials, all of which make extensive use of local produce. Brunch and snack menus, available according to the hour, offer sandwiches, salads, wraps and a 'dish of the day'. The informal Tavistock Bar is a convivial place to relax with a cask-conditioned ale or a fine wine. A concierge service will arrange everything from a restaurant booking to a birthday cake.

Recommended in the area

Woburn Safari Park; Woburn Abbey

BERKSHIRE

Windsor Castle

The Vineyard at Stockcross

★★★★★◉◉◉ HOTEL

Address: Stockcross, NEWBURY, RG20 8JU
Tel: 01635 528770
Fax: 01635 528398
Email: general@the-vineyard.co.uk
Website: www.the-vineyard.co.uk
Map ref: 3, SU36
Directions: M4, A34 signed Newbury, exit at 3rd junct for Speen. Right at rdbt, right at 2nd rdbt
Rooms: 49 (15 GF) Facilities: Wi-fi ☒ Gym Spa Treatment rooms Parking: 100 Notes ☒

Privately owned by Sir Peter Michael, this hotel offers the ultimate in indulgence, from the luxurious accommodation and original artwork to the gourmet dining experience and fine wines. Award-winning executive chef, Daniel Galmiche arrived in late 2009 and has brought his true passion for contemporary French cooking to the restaurant menus; the wine list, always a work in progress, is superb, offering a choice of over 2,000 international wines, including Peter Michael wines, of course. The superb spa has an extensive range of treatments that make it the ideal escape for total relaxation.

Recommended in the area

Highclere Castle; The Watermill Theatre; Newbury Racecourse

Donnington Valley Hotel & Spa

★★★★ 84% ◉◉ HOTEL

Address: Old Oxford Road, Donnington, NEWBURY, RG14 3AG
Tel: 01635 551199
Fax: 01635 551123
Email: general@donningtonvalley.co.uk
Website: www.donningtonvalley.co.uk
Map ref: 3, SU36
Directions: M4 junct 13, A34 signed Newbury. Exit signed Donnington/Services, at rdbt 2nd exit

signed Donnington. Left at next rdbt. Hotel 2m Rooms: 111 (36 GF) (3 fmly) S £99-£240 D £99-£240 Facilities: STV Wi-fi ☒ Gym Spa Golf Sauna Steam room Parking: 150 Notes: ☒ in bedrooms

Set in rolling Berkshire countryside and just minutes from the M4 and the A34, this privately owned hotel boasts its own 18-hole golf course and a sumptuous state-of-the-art health club and spa. The air-conditioned bedrooms are in elegant contemporary style with luxury linens, marble bathrooms and indulgent little extras. The Wine Press restaurant offers imaginative food and a superb wine list.

Recommended in the area

Donnington Castle; The Watermill Theatre; Highclere Castle

Berkshire

Oakley Court Hotel

★★★★ 79% ◉ HOTEL

Address: Windsor Road, Water Oakley, WINDSOR, SL4 5UR
Tel: 01753 609988 & 609900
Fax: 01628 637011
Email: oakley.reservations@principal-hayley.com
Website: www.principal-hayley.com
Map ref: 3, SU97
Directions: M4 junct 6, A355, then A332 towards Windsor, right onto A308 towards Maidenhead. Pass racecourse, hotel 2.5m on right
Rooms: 118 (28 GF) (5 fmly) **Facilities:** Wi-fi ◉ Tennis Gym Spa **Parking:** 120
Notes: ◉ in bedrooms

A distinguished country house built in 1859, Oakley Court is an outstanding example of the Victorian Gothic style of architecture. It sits in 37 acres of landscaped gardens, with extensive lawns flanking a long stretch of the River Thames – a stunning backdrop for weddings and other celebratory events. Sporting and leisure activities are a major attraction, including a 9-hole golf course, tennis courts, a health club with gym and sauna, and opportunities for boating on the river from the hotel's own jetty. All of the bedrooms are spacious, elegant and beautifully furnished, and some have views of the river. The main restaurant, The Dining Room, offers a fine-dining experience and is popular with locals for special-occasion meals. In summer guests have the pleasure of eating out on the terrace. There are also conference facilities for up to 500 delegates, with the option of private dining. In addition, the hotel has a choice of sumptuous lounges in which to relax. The service is efficient, friendly and welcoming, helping to make any stay here a truly memorable one.

Recommended in the area

Legoland; Windsor Castle; Ascot Racecourse

BUCKINGHAMSHIRE

Hambleden Mill

Danesfield House Hotel and Spa

★★★★ 81% ◉◉◉◉ HOTEL

Address: Henley Road, MARLOW-ON-THAMES,
SL7 2EY
Tel: 01628 891010
Fax: 01628 890408
Email: reservations@danesfieldhouse.co.uk
Website: www.danesfieldhouse.co.uk
Map ref: 3, SU88
Directions: 2m from Marlow on A4155 towards
Henley
Rooms: 84 (27 GF) (3 fmly) S £165-£345

D £175-£345 (incl. bkfst) **Facilities:** STV Wi-fi ⊗ Gym Spa Jogging trail Steam room Hydrotherapy
room Treatment rooms **Parking:** 100 **Notes:** ⊗

This magnificent Tudor-style mansion is matched only by its remarkable setting, located as it is in 65
acres of landscaped gardens overlooking the River Thames and beyond towards the Chiltern Hills. The
third building since 1664 to have occupied this site, the current house and gardens were designed and
built at the end of the 19th century. Today, visitors can begin their stay by taking afternoon tea on the
south-facing terrace or in the impressive Grand Hall, before retiring to one of the individually furnished
en suite bedrooms, where comfort is of the essence; all the rooms come well equipped with luxury
bathrobes and Molton Brown toiletries, and valet service is also available. Danesfield Spa, reached by
a connecting bridge and with specially commissioned artwork, has a 20-metre ozone-cleansed pool,
sauna, steam room and spa bath. The award-winning restaurant offers stylish, intimate dining and an
extensive and far-reaching wine list, while those seeking a more informal atmosphere should head for
The Orangery.

Recommended in the area

Windsor Castle; Boutique shopping in Marlow & Henley; Legoland; River Thames trips

Octagon Tower Roof, Ely Cathedral

Bell Inn Hotel

★★★ 79% ◉ HOTEL

Address: Great North Road, STILTON, PE7 3RA
Tel: 01733 241066
Fax: 01733 245173
Email: reception@thebellstilton.co.uk
Website: www.thebellstilton.co.uk
Map ref: 3, TL18
Directions: A1(M) junct 16, follow Stilton signs.
Hotel in village centre **Rooms:** 22 (3 GF) (1 fmly)
S £67-£110 **D** £92-£130 (incl. bkfst)
Facilities: STV Wi-fi **Parking:** 30 **Notes:** ⊗

Just off the Great North Road, this lovely 17th-century coaching inn has served the famous and infamous alike – film star Clark Gable, and highwayman Dick Turpin, for example. The magnificent inn sign is an exact replica of the original and, together with its wrought-iron bracket, weighs an astonishing two and three-quarter tons. Curiously, Stilton cheese has never been made in the village; in coaching days it was extensively sold in the local market, and the name simply stuck. The Bell Inn's en suite bedrooms, including two with four-posters and several with jacuzzis, are arranged around the old courtyard. For dining, guests have a choice – the beamed Galleried Restaurant, with its AA Rosette-awarded menu of modern British cuisine; the softly lit Bistro, offering internationally influenced dishes; and the stone-floored Village Bar, serving bar meals and snacks. Browse over the menus in a comfortable leather armchair in the first-floor Dick Turpin's room, so named because legend says he escaped to his horse, Black Bess, from the window. In favourable weather eat, or just have a drink, in the courtyard.

Recommended in the area

Peterborough Cathedral; Imperial War Museum, Duxford; Flag Fen

Crown Lodge Hotel

★★★ 83% ❀ HOTEL

Address: Downham Road, Outwell, WISBECH,
PE14 8SE
Tel: 01945 773391 & 772206
Fax: 01945 772668
Email: office@thecrownlodgehotel.co.uk
Website: www.thecrownlodgehotel.co.uk
Map ref: 3, TF40
Directions: On A1122/A1101 approx 5m from
Wisbech
Rooms: 10 (10 GF) (1 fmly) **Facilities:** Wi-fi **Parking:** 55

Off the beaten track, yet easily found in the Fenland village of Outwell, Crown Lodge Hotel overlooks the banks of Well Creek, which meanders through Outwell and Upwell. This delightful rural setting belies the contemporary style and state-of-the-art facilities awaiting you. Bedrooms are smart, well-equipped and comfortable. There's a brasserie-style restaurant, an open-plan bar and a comfortable lounge where you can relax while choosing your freshly prepared meal, sourced largely from local suppliers.

Recommended in the area

Ely Cathedral; Welney Wildfowl and Wetlands Trust; Wicken Fen National Nature Reserve

Wicken Fen, Cambridgeshire

CHESHIRE

The Cheshire Plain

Alderley Edge Hotel

★★★ 86% ☺☺☺ HOTEL

Address: Macclesfield Road, ALDERLEY EDGE,
SK9 7BJ
Tel: 01625 583033
Fax: 01625 586343
Email: sales@alderleyedgehotel.com
Website: www.alderleyedgehotel.com
Map ref: 6, SJ87
Directions: Off A34 in Alderley Edge onto B5087
towards Macclesfield. Hotel 200yds on right
Rooms: 50 (6 GF) **S** £89.50-£130 **D** £125-£400 **Facilities:** STV Wi-fi **Parking:** 90 **Notes:** ⊗

Standing in charming, wooded grounds in a commanding position with panoramic views over the Cheshire Plain and Derbyshire countryside, this hotel offers a relaxed and inviting atmosphere. It was built in 1850 for one of the region's wealthy 'cotton kings' and was very much considered to be a grand mansion. Since that time it has been home to a doctor and then to American servicemen in the Second World War. Today there is easy access to central Manchester and transport networks, and the hotel makes a great base for exploring this interesting area. The attractively furnished bedrooms and suites offer excellent quality and comfort; all have good facilities including internet access and some have splendid views. The Presidential Suite also has a lounge, dressing room and en suite bathroom with walk-in shower. The welcoming bar and adjacent lounge lead into the light and airy, award-winning conservatory restaurant where imaginative and memorable food is showcased on menus of modern British dishes. The Gourmet Tasting menu demonstrates the chef's talents perfectly and, for a real treat, should not be missed. Throughout the hotel the friendly, attentive service is noteworthy and makes any stay one to remember.

Recommended in the area

Jodrell Bank; Tatton Park; Gawsworth Hall

Crowne Plaza Chester

★★★★ 79% HOTEL

Address: Trinity Street, CHESTER, CH1 2BD
Tel: 0870 442 1081 & 01244 899988
Fax: 01244 316118
Email: cpchester@qmh-hotels.com
Website: www.crowneplaza.co.uk
Map ref: 5, SJ46 **Directions:** M53 junct 12, A56
onto St Martins Way, under footbridge, left at lights,
1st right, hotel on right
Facilities: STV Wi-fi 🕲 Gym Spa **Parking:** 80

Within the city's old walls and no distance at all from the famous covered galleries known as The Rows, this modern hotel covers all bases with particularly well-appointed, air-conditioned bedrooms, a leisure club with indoor pool, a choice of meeting rooms and the horse-racing themed Silks restaurant. With the hills of Wales visible in the distance across the Dee, dine on traditionally British fillet of poached salmon, or beer-battered cod, followed by the kitchen's signature dish of frangipane-flavoured Chester tart. In such a tourist honeypot as Chester, it's a real bonus being able to use the hotel's own car park.

Recommended in the area

Chester Cathedral; Roman Amphitheatre; Chester Zoo

Mere Court Hotel & Conference Centre

★★★★ 77% ⊛ HOTEL

Address: Warrington Road, Mere, KNUTSFORD,
WA16 0RW
Tel: 01565 831000 **Fax:** 01565 831001
Email: sales@merecourt.co.uk
Website: www.merecourt.co.uk
Map ref: 6, SJ77 **Directions:** A50, 1m W of junct
with A556, on right **Rooms:** 34 (12 GF) (24 fmly)
S £75-£105 **D** £85-£155 (incl. bkfst) **Facilities:** STV Wi-fi **Parking:** 150

Built in 1903 as a wedding present, this country house hotel in seven acres of grounds has been lovingly restored as a tribute to the Arts and Crafts movement. Individually designed and furnished bedrooms in the original part include two with four-posters, while the newer Lakeside rooms all sport a king-size bed and spa bath. Overlooking the ornamental lake and proud of its AA Rosette, the oak-panelled Arboreum Restaurant offers weekly changing menus, all essentially traditional English but Mediterranean influences are also evident.

Recommended in the area

Tatton Park (NT); Lion Salt Works; Anderton Boat Lift

CORNWALL

Sennen Cove

Falcon Hotel

★★★ 79% HOTEL

Address: Breakwater Road, BUDE, EX23 8SD
Tel: 01288 352005
Fax: 01288 356359
Email: reception@falconhotel.com
Website: www.falconhotel.com
Map ref: 1, SS20
Directions: Off A39 into Bude, follow road to
Widemouth Bay. Hotel on right over canal bridge
Rooms: 29 (7 fmly) S £55-£68.50 D £110-£137
(incl. bkfst) Facilities: STV Wi-fi Parking: 40 Notes: ⊗

The Falcon, the oldest coaching house in north Cornwall, was once the headquarters for the four-horse coaches running between Bideford, Bude, Boscastle, Tintagel and Newquay. Travellers have been welcomed here for more than 200 years and the warm and friendly atmosphere is still apparent as you walk through the front door. Overlooking the picturesque and historic Bude Canal, and with beautiful walled gardens, the hotel occupies a delightful setting. The well-appointed bedrooms are traditionally furnished with co-ordinated fabrics and have spacious modern bathrooms, irons, trouser presses, hairdryers, direct dial telephones, tea- and coffee-making facilities, guest controlled heating and flat-screen TVs with Freeview and Sky. Guests can also choose one of the four-poster bedrooms with a luxury spa bath, or the Summerleaze Suite, for a memorable occasion. The bar and restaurant offer a wide range of good quality, modern dishes, and the Garden Room, residents' lounge, Carriage Room and Acland Suite are all licensed for civil ceremonies so hotel can easily cater for both small and large wedding receptions. Wi-fi is freely available throughout.

Recommended in the area

Clovelly; Tintagel; Boscastle; Port Isaac; Padstow

Royal Duchy Hotel

★★★★ 79% ◉◉ HOTEL
Address: Cliff Road, FALMOUTH, TR11 4NX
Tel: 01326 313042
Fax: 01326 319420
Email: info@royalduchy.com
Website: www.royalduchy.com
Map ref: 1, SW83
Directions: On Cliff Rd, along Falmouth seafront
Rooms: 43 (1 GF) (6 fmly) **S** £95-£115
D £170-£300 (incl. bkfst) **Facilities:** Wi-fi ⓧ
Parking: 50 **Notes:** ⓧ in bedrooms

It could so easily be the Med. Stretching away to the horizon is an azure bay, to the left a castle stands high on a headland, above your head palm fronds quiver in the gentle breeze, while on the umbrellashaded table your chilled cocktails await. Actually, this is the Gulf Stream-warmed English Channel on Cornwall's southern coast, and the view is that from the hotel terrace. A short stroll away are the beaches, alleyways and quaint streets of Falmouth, a town that seems content to run at a gentler pace than most, and where you can lose yourself in centuries of maritime history. With so much to see, how useful it is to have binoculars provided in the bedrooms, along with bathrobes, slippers, hairdryer, TV, radio, telephone, and tea and coffee tray. In the Terrace Restaurant a talented team of chefs brings diners an appealing variety of AA Rosette-awarded, classical signature dishes, created from top Cornish produce. And from the bar it's but a few steps to the sun lounge where light snacks, lunches and cream teas are served.

Recommended in the area

Lizard Peninsula; Trelissick Garden; St Michael's Mount

Old Quay House Hotel

★★ ◉◉ HOTEL

Address: 28 Fore Street, FOWEY, PL23 1AQ
Tel: 01726 833302
Fax: 01726 833668
Email: info@theoldquayhouse.com
Website: www.theoldquayhouse.com
Map ref: 1, SX15
Directions: M5 junct 31 onto A30 to Bodmin. Then A389 through town, then B3269 to Fowey
Rooms: 11 **Facilities:** STV Wi-fi
Notes: ❧ 12yrs ⊗

Occupying a perfect waterfront location, this boutique hotel's interior combines traditional architecture and 21st-century styling with the sort of flair that one expects in, say, London. How refreshing then to find here an eclectic assembly of 'island-styled' and classic European furnishings and ornaments characterising the bedrooms, seven of which survey the Fowey estuary through floor-to-ceiling glass doors, and bathrooms that feature high quality fittings and luxury amenities. The theme continues downstairs where, from the entrance, your eyes are drawn through to 'Q', the restaurant, and the glittering water beyond. Q's two AA Rosettes and clutch of gushing media reviews are testament to the creativity of head chef Ben Bass, whose modern European menus, complemented by daily specials, and a carefully selected wine list, have made it one of 'the' places to eat in these parts. The Old Quay House has a full wedding and civil ceremony licence and is available for receptions and functions. As the hotel does not have parking facilities, summer season guests should drop off their bags and collect a permit for the Harbour Commissioner's car park about 800 yards further on. Winter guests may use a long term pay-and-display car park about 700 yards away.

Recommended in the area

The Eden Project; Lost Gardens of Heligan; Lanhydrock House (NT)

The Well House Hotel

★★ 85% HOTEL

Address: St Keyne, Liskeard, LOOE, PL14 4RN
Tel: 01579 342001
Fax: 01579 343891
Email: enquiries@wellhouse.co.uk
Website: www.wellhouse.co.uk
Map ref: 1, SX25
Directions: From Liskeard on A38 take B3254 to St Keyne (3m). At church fork left, hotel 0.5m down hill on left **Rooms:** 9 (2 GF) (1 fmly) S £90-£130 D £130-£215 (incl. bkfst) **Facilities:** ⚓ **Parking:** 30 **Notes:** ⊗

This luxurious country house hotel sits in impressive grounds within easy reach of many of Cornwall's best attractions, not least its magnificent coastline. The Well House Hotel is privately owned, with an emphasis on providing a quiet and relaxing haven and the highest levels of comfort and care. Guests can have a drink in the intimate bar before enjoying a meal in the elegant restaurant, prepared with great skill by the kitchen team.*As we went to press there was a change of head chef and the Rosette award was suspended.

Recommended in the area

Eden Project; Coastal walks, moors and tors; Looe, Polperro and Fowey

Mount Haven Hotel

★★★ 84% ◉◉ HOTEL

Address: Turnpike Road, MARAZION, TR17 0DQ
Tel: 01736 710249
Fax: 01736 711658
Email: reception@mounthaven.co.uk
Website: www.mounthaven.co.uk
Map ref: 1, SW44
Directions: From A30 towards Penzance. At rdbt take exit for Helston onto A394. Next rdbt right into Marazion, hotel on left **Rooms:** 18 (6 GF) (1 fmly) S £85-£105 D £120-£210 (incl. bkfst) **Facilities:** Wi-fi Spa **Parking:** 30 **Notes:** ⊗ in bedrooms

St Michael's Mount rises dramatically from the bay just a stone's throw from the terrace at this lovely boutique hotel. The Mount Haven's chic and contemporary design is a fusion of western comfort and eastern culture. Try the double deluxe or one of the four-poster rooms with balconies for a particularly romantic break, and don't miss dinner in the St Michael's Restaurant. A team of dedicated holistic therapists are available to sort out any remnants of stress.

Recommended in the area

West Cornwall beaches; St Michael's Mount, Minack Theatre, coastal walks

Hotel Penzance

★★★ 85% ◉◉ HOTEL

Address: Britons Hill, PENZANCE, TR18 3AE
Tel: 01736 363117
Fax: 01736 350970
Email: reception@hotelpenzance.com
Website: www.hotelpenzance.com
Map ref: 1, SW43
Directions: From A30 pass heliport on right, left at next rdbt for town centre. 3rd right onto Britons Hill. Hotel on right

Rooms: 25 (2 GF) S £80-£90 D £120-£190 (incl. bkfst) **Facilities:** Wi-fi ⊀ **Parking:** 12

Converted from two Edwardian merchants' houses in the 1920s, this boutique hotel stands in a Mediterranean-style garden perched high above the town's rooftops, overlooking the waterfront activity below. Many of the individually styled rooms enjoy sea views. In the restaurant, the seasonally changing menu takes full advantage of local produce in peak condition – fish from Newlyn, meats and dairy produce from nearby farms, plus some Cornish wines.

Recommended in the area

St Michael's Mount; Minack Theatre; Tate St Ives

St Michael's Mount

The Lugger Hotel

★ ★ ★ 81% ◉ HOTEL

Address: PORTLOE, Truro, TR2 5RD
Tel: 01872 501322
Fax: 01872 501691
Email: reservations.lugger@ohiml.com
Website: www.oxfordhotelsandinns.com
Map ref: 1, SW93
Directions: A390 to Truro, B3287 to Tregony,
A3078 (St Mawes Rd), left for Veryan, left for Portloe
Rooms: 22 (1 GF) **Facilities:** Wi-fi Spa
Parking: 26 **Notes:** ⊗ in bedrooms

The very Cornish harbour of Portloe, its picturesque cove familiar perhaps from that childhood jigsaw puzzle, was once popular with smugglers. They would meet in this 17th-century inn to share out their contraband, but it all came to an end in the 1890s, when the landlord was hanged for complicity, the liquor licence was withdrawn and boat builder used it as a shed for the next half century. Today's bijou luxury hotel has spread into adjoining cottages with modern, en suite bedrooms featuring bleached Portuguese woods and crisp white linens. A sun terrace overlooking the harbour is the perfect place for a drink, but when the waves are crashing against the rocks the open fireplaces in the beamed sitting room may become a more appealing proposition. Taking full advantage of its location, the restaurant specialises in locally sourced produce, particularly straight-off-the boat seafood, such as megrim sole served lightly grilled with crab and shellfish linguine; and baked fillet of hake that comes with a lemon and herb crust. Other options include roasted duck breast with root vegetable casserole; roasted rump of Cornish lamb; and Mediterranean vegetable gateau topped with Cornish cheese.

Recommended in the area

The Eden Project; Lost Gardens of Heligan; National Maritime Museum Cornwall

Driftwood

★★★ ◎◎◎ HOTEL

Address: Rosevine, PORTSCATHO, TR2 5EW
Tel: 01872 580644
Fax: 01872 580801
Email: info@driftwoodhotel.co.uk
Website: www.driftwoodhotel.co.uk
Map ref: 1, SW83
Directions: A390 towards St Mawes. On A3078 turn left to Rosevine at Trewithian
Rooms: 15 (1 GF) (3 fmly) **S** £157-£216
D £165-£255 (incl. bkfst) **Facilities:** Wi-fi **Parking:** 30 **Notes:** ⊗

In seven acres of cliffside gardens, with panoramic views of Gerrans Bay, stands this peaceful and secluded hotel. Walk down a wooded path to your own little cove and look out across the very waters that will provide your dinner lobster or crab. Head indoors to find stylishly contemporary sitting rooms stocked with books, magazines and board games. There's even a small games room for the children. Comfortable, uncluttered bedrooms are decorated in soft shades reminiscent of the seashore. Ground floor rooms have their own decked terrace, while tucked away, overlooking the sea, is a restored weatherboarded cabin with two bedrooms and a sitting room. A large deck in the sheltered terraced garden is strewn with steamer chairs for taking in the unbroken sea view. On warm evenings hurricane lamps are lit for pre-dinner drinks and after-dinner coffee. The three AA Rosette awarded restaurant (from which, no surprise, you can again see the sea) serves fresh, locally sourced food – and not just fish. Yes, there's John Dory or monkfish, for example, but the menu will also feature dishes such as roasted Terras Farm duck breast, pastilla of duck leg, endives and orange and port jus.

Recommended in the area

Falmouth Maritime Museum; Lost Gardens of Heligan; Tate Gallery St Ives

The Carlyon Bay Hotel, Spa & Golf Resort

★★★★ 77% ® HOTEL

Address: Sea Road, Carlyon Bay, ST AUSTELL,
PL25 3RD
Tel: 01726 812304 & 811006
Fax: 01726 814938
Email: reservations@carlyonbay.com
Website: www.carlyonbay.com
Map ref: 1, SX05 **Directions:** From St Austell,
follow signs for Charlestown. Carlyon Bay signed on left
Rooms: 86 (14 fmly) **S** £95-£300 **D** £145-£300 **Facilities:** Wi-fi ③ ⅂ Gym Spa Sauna **Parking:** 100

From the air, this sprawling, creeper-covered hotel points like an arrowhead across some of its 250 clifftop acres of secluded gardens and grounds, part of which is taken up by a championship 18-hole golf course. Nearby, you'll find a 10-acre practice ground, putting lawns and a nine-hole approach course. If none of that appeals, you can swim in both outdoor and indoor pools, play tennis, enjoy all the benefits of the spa, or take it relatively easy with a game of snooker. Bedrooms are well equipped and maintained, and many have marvellous views across St Austell Bay. So too, as the name rather suggests, does the AA Rosette Bay View restaurant, where a four-course dinner menu makes full use of the best local produce, including fresh day-boat fish and seafood. Must-eat main courses to try include saddle of spring lamb with crushed peas and fève beans; English Rose veal with white truffle pumpkin and golden raisins; pan-fried bass with lobster fumet; or mascarpone tart with tomato and cardamom. Alternative dining options are Fusion, which offers Asian cuisine, and the Green Bar and Terrace for traditional grills and light bar snacks in the evening. During school holidays there's a supervised nursery.

Recommended in the area

The Eden Project; Georgian Charlestown; Lanhydrock Park (NT)

The Nare Hotel

★★★★ ◉ COUNTRY HOUSE HOTEL

Address: Carne Beach, VERYAN-IN-ROSELAND,
TR2 5PF
Tel: 01872 501111
Fax: 01872 501856
Email: office@narehotel.co.uk
Website: www.narehotel.co.uk
Map ref: 1, SW93
Directions: From Tregony take A3078, approx 1.5m.
Left at Veryan sign, through village towards sea &
hotel **Rooms:** 37 (7 GF) (7 fmly) **S** £130-£248 **D** £250-£466 (incl. bkfst) **Facilities:** Wi-fi ⊗ ⅞ Gym
Spa Health & beauty clinic Steam room Sauna **Parking:** 80

Overlooking a superb beach, The Nare is the only four-red-star hotel in Cornwall. It has a delightful country-house ambience and is now in its third generation of family ownership. Those guests looking for total relaxation will certainly find it here, from the comfy sofas in the lounge to the spa treatments and hot tub overlooking the sea. More active types can enjoy a good range of leisure activities including tennis courts, croquet, billiards, two swimming pools, a gym and even a 22-foot yacht for charter. The owners have shied away from the trend for designer hotels, preferring to individually style their rooms in a more traditional but equally luxurious style. Most are spacious and many have a balcony or terrace with wonderful sea views. Suites have a separate lounge and one has a kitchen, too. All rooms enjoy the valet service, including 24-hour room service. For dinner there's a choice of two eating options – the more formal Dining Room and the casual Quarterdeck. Whichever you go for, expect to enjoy plenty of first-class Cornish ingredients, including locally reared beef, seafood from local fishermen, and lots of fresh seasonal vegetables and fruit. The Nare also boasts an extensive wine cellar.

Recommended in the area

Eden Project; Lost Gardens of Heligan; Caerhays Castle

CUMBRIA

Dewentwater, Lake District National Park

Rothay Manor

★★★ 83% ☺ HOTEL

Address: Rothay Bridge, AMBLESIDE, LA22 0EH
Tel: 015394 33605
Fax: 015394 33607
Email: hotel@rothaymanor.co.uk
Website: www.rothaymanor.co.uk/aa
Map ref: 5, NY30
Directions: In Ambleside follow signs for Coniston (A593). Hotel 0.25m SW of Ambleside opposite rugby pitch **Rooms:** 19 (3 GF) (7 fmly) **S** £100-£160 **D** £150-£240 (incl. bkfst) **Facilities:** STV Wi-fi **Parking:** 45 **Notes:** ⊗

This traditional Regency country house hotel was built in 1825 and lies in the heart of the Lake District, just a quarter of a mile from Lake Windermere, making it ideally situated for walking, cycling or exploring the local towns and villages. Set in its own landscaped gardens, it offers guests the perfect opportunity to relax and recharge their batteries. Owned and run by the Nixon family for over 40 years, it has a long-standing reputation for its relaxed, comfortable and friendly atmosphere, as well as its excellent food and wine. All the bedrooms are en suite and include a number of suites, family rooms and rooms with balconies, from which to enjoy fine views of the fells. For added privacy, two suites are located in a separate building close to the main hotel. All the guest rooms are comfortably equipped and furnished to a very high standard, with TV and tea- and coffee-making facilities supplied. Public areas include a choice of lounges, a spacious restaurant with an imaginative menu making much use of fresh, local produce, and conference facilities. Guests can also enjoy free use of the Low Wood leisure club, which has an indoor heated pool and is located 1.5 miles from the hotel.

Recommended in the area

Cruises on the Lakes; Hill Top (Beatrix Potter); Holker Hall and Gardens

The Pheasant

★★★ 83% ⚘ HOTEL

Address: BASSENTHWAITE, Cockermouth,
CA13 9YE
Tel: 017687 76234
Fax: 017687 76002
Email: info@the-pheasant.co.uk
Website: www.the-pheasant.co.uk
Map ref: 5, NY23
Directions: Midway between Keswick &
Cockermouth, signed from A66 Facilities: Wi-fi
Parking: 40 Notes: ✶12yrs

Dating back over 500 years, this historic coaching inn, in the unspoilt northern end of the Lake District, was further enhanced in 2010 by the creation of a fine-dining restaurant that overlooks the well-tended gardens and the fells beyond. One of 19th-century regulars was the famous huntsman John ('With his hounds and his horn in the morning') Peel, who recounted his exploits in the tap room, now the hotel bar. This oak-panelled room with exposed beams, polished parquet flooring and log fires remains more or less as it was then, although it now offers 60 malt whiskies, 12 vodkas, 12 gins, 12 wines by the glass and three draught ales on hand pump; it also displays two water colours by renowned Cumbrian artist Edward W Thompson who exchanged them for beer. The Pheasant has a reputation for high quality cuisine, using the best local produce whether in the restaurant or the more informal bistro; lighter lunches and afternoon teas are served in the lounges and bar. The individually decorated bedrooms have been appointed to a high standard with en suite bathrooms offering both bath and power shower, and all equipped with phone, tea tray and flat-screen TV.

Recommended in the area

Muncaster Castle; Wordsworth House; Rheged Discovery Centre

Borrowdale Gates Country House Hotel

★★★ 79% COUNTRY HOUSE HOTEL

Address: GRANGE-IN-BORROWDALE, Keswick,
CA12 5UQ
Tel: 017687 77204
Fax: 017687 77195
Email: hotel@borrowdale-gates.com
Website: www.borrowdale-gates.com
Map ref: 5, NY21
Directions: From A66 follow B5289 for approx 4m. Turn right over bridge, hotel 0.25m beyond village
Rooms: 27 (10 GF) **S** £75-£135 **D** £150-£240 (incl. bkfst & dinner) **Facilities:** Wi-fi **Parking:** 29

Surrounded by first-class fell-walking country and set in two acres of peaceful, wooded grounds, this delightful hotel, is close to the shores of Derwentwater, with the many attractions of Keswick nearby. This Victorian country house is a real home-from-home with log fires, Lakeland-inspired cooking and updated and stylish accommodation. Rooms with views might be considered a speciality here - the cosy bar and beamed lounges look out over the gardens to the valley beyond and each bedroom has picture-perfect views whether bathed in glorious sunshine or shimmering with a wintery frost. The dining room looks onto green pastures where Herdwick sheep graze, and is a wonderful place to linger over a Cumbrian breakfast or candlelit dinner. Each of the bedrooms comes complete with crisp cotton sheets, feather pillows (unless you prefer a different kind), fluffy white towels and a tray of morning tea and coffee. All are individually designed and some boast a decked balcony or French doors opening onto the gardens. Contemporary country-house cooking with a lightness of touch is the mainstay of the kitchen, with menus making the most of superb Lake District produce.

Recommended in the area

Keswick's Theatre by the Lake; Honister Slate Mine; lakeside and fell walks

Clare House

★ ❀ HOTEL

Address: Park Road, GRANGE-OVER-SANDS,
LA11 7HQ
Tel: 015395 33026 & 34253
Fax: 015395 34310
Email: info@clarehousehotel.co.uk
Website: www.clarehousehotel.co.uk
Map ref: 5, SD47
Directions: Off A590 onto B5277, through Lindale
into Grange, keep left, hotel 0.5m on left past Crown
Hill & St Paul's Church **Rooms:** 18 (4 GF) **S** £84-£89 **D** £168-£178 (incl. bkfst & dinner)
Facilities: Wi-fi **Parking:** 18 **Notes:** ⊗ in bedrooms

A family-run hotel, with Morecambe Bay to the south and the Lake District to the north; most rooms
enjoy a view over the bay. They are all well equipped and some have balconies. A full English breakfast
is the ideal start to the day, before setting off along the mile-long promenade at the foot of the garden.
Return for a light lunch or skilfully prepared dinner chosen from the British and French menu.
Recommended in the area
Holker Hall; Windermere Steamboat Centre; Cumberland Pencil Museum

Dewent colouring pencils

Rothay Garden Hotel

★★★★ 80% ◉◉ HOTEL

Address: Broadgate, GRASMERE, LA22 9RJ
Tel: 015394 35334
Fax: 015394 35723
Email: stay@rothaygarden.com
Website: www.rothaygarden.com
Map ref: 5, NY31
Directions: Off A591, opposite Swan Hotel, into Grasmere, 300yds on left
Rooms: 30 (8 GF) (3 fmly) **S** £109-£182
D £138-£284 (incl. bkfst) **Facilities:** Wi-fi **Parking:** 38 **Notes:** ⚫ 5yrs

Situated on the edge of picturesque Grasmere village, and nestling in two acres of riverside gardens surrounded by majestic fells, this privately-run and delightful hotel provides luxurious comfort, quality and peace and quiet that so many visitors to the Lake District look for. There are 25 beautiful bedrooms, as well as five stylish loft suites. Relax in the chic lounge bar before dining in the elegant candlelit conservatory restaurant overlooking the gardens. Masterchef Andrew Burton serves a modern European menu which takes fine Lakeland produce as its starting point. Rothay Garden has been owned and operated by Chris Carss for 20 years, and he and his dedicated team will do their utmost to make sure your stay is memorable for all the right reasons. Of course, the beauty of the Lake District is right on the doorstep and Wordsworth's Grasmere really is the 'jewel of the Lakes'; the hotel is ideally situated for visiting Ambleside, Windermere, Keswick and Kendal. Rothay Garden offers special short getaways and holidays all year, including seasonal weekend breaks, four-night midweek value breaks, traditional Christmas and New Year breaks, and a specialist food and wine programme during March and November.

Recommended in the area

Dove Cottage and Wordsworth Museum; Grasmere Gingerbread Shop; Lake Windermere Steamers

Gilpin Hotel & Lake House

★★★★ @@@ HOTEL

Address: Crook Road, WINDERMERE, LA23 3NE
Tel: 015394 88818
Fax: 015394 88058
Email: hotel@gilpinlodge.co.uk
Website: www.gilpinlodge.co.uk
Map ref: 6, SD49
Directions: M6 junct 36, take A590/A591 to rdbt north of Kendal, take B5284, hotel 5m on right
Rooms: 26 (12 GF) S £180-£525 D £290-£575 (incl. bkfst & dinner) **Parking:** 40 **Notes:** ⊗ in bedrooms ♯7yrs

An elegant, friendly hotel in 20 tranquil acres of gardens, moors and woodland, owned and run by two generations of the Cunliffe family. The en suite bedrooms all have bath and shower, luxury toiletries and bathrobes. Individually and stylishly decorated to a high standard, they are quiet, with delightful views. Each room has a sitting area, TV, direct-dial phone, radio, hairdryer, and beverage tray with homemade biscuits; some rooms also have a trouser press. The Garden Suites have enormous beds, walk-in dressing areas, large sofas, modern fireplaces, flat-screen TVs and sensual bathrooms; glass-fronted lounge areas lead to individual gardens with cedarwood hot tubs. Food is important at Gilpin Lodge. The chefs are passionate about using the finest local ingredients as extensively as possible. It's hard to put a label on the food – classically based, yes, yet thoroughly modern and imaginative, without being too experimental. Tables have fresh flowers, candles at night, crisp white linen, fine china and glass, and gleaming silver. The walk-in wine cellar, featuring over 300 wines from 13 countries, reflects real interest rather than a desire to sell high priced vintages. Residents have free use of a local leisure club, although on-call spa therapists will visit guest rooms.

Recommended in the area

Lake Windermere; Beatrix Potter Gallery; Dove Cottage and Wordsworth Museum

Washington Central Hotel

★★★ 83% HOTEL

Address: Washington Street, WORKINGTON,
CA14 3AY
Tel: 01900 65772
Fax: 01900 68770
Email: kawildwchotel@aol.com
Website: www.washingtoncentralhotelworkington.
com
Map ref: 5, NY02
Directions: M6 junct 40, A66 to Workington. Left at
lights, hotel on right
Rooms: 46 (4 fmly) S £95-£105 D £140-£220 (incl. bkfst) **Facilities:** Wi-fi ⓢ Gym Sauna
Steam room Jacuzzi Sunbed **Parking:** 21 **Notes:** ⊗

Enjoying a prominent town centre location, this distinctive red-brick hotel is within walking distance of most amenities, including shops, cinema and parks, while only a little further afield are the delights of the Lake District National Park. Public areas include several lounges, a spacious bar, a popular coffee shop and Caesar's leisure club, which has a 20-metre swimming pool surrounded by frescoes. The well-maintained and comfortable en suite bedrooms are equipped with TV, safe, hairdryer, trouser press, work desk, and tea- and coffee-making facilities. The executive accommodation includes a four-poster suite with hi-fi system and luxurious lounge. In the wood-panelled Carlton Restaurant the best local ingredients are used in dishes such as rack of Lakeland fell-bred lamb on rosemary crushed potatoes, and Solway sea bass. For special occasions, book the eight-cover Clock Tower Restaurant, not just for the food, but for views towards Scotland.

Recommended in the area

Western Lakes; Scafell and Wasdale; Keswick; Solway Firth; Cockermouth

DERBYSHIRE

Peak District National Park

The Peacock at Rowsley

★★★ ◉◉◉ HOTEL

Address: Bakewell Road, ROWSLEY, Bakewell,
DE4 2EB
Tel: 01629 733518
Fax: 01629 732671
Email: reception@thepeacockatrowsley.com
Website: www.thepeacockatrowsley.com
Map ref: 7, SK26
Directions: A6, 3m from Bakewell, 6m from Matlock
towards Bakewell **Rooms:** 16 (5 fmly) **Facilities:**
Wi-fi **Parking:** 25 **Notes:** ✕10yrs

Within Britain's oldest national park, this is a perfect base for taking exhilarating walks across lonely moorland, for exploring beautiful secluded valleys and pretty villages, and for fishing – the hotel owns fly fishing rights on the Wye and Derwent, the latter flowing through the garden. Some years ago Keira Knightley, Matthew Macfadyen and other actors and crew stayed here while filming *Pride and Prejudice* at Haddon Hall. The bedrooms are luxurious, most with king or super king-size beds, and each has been styled by the international designer, India Mahdavi, who has blended antique furniture with contemporary decor. One room has a four-poster bed, another has an antique bed from Belvoir Castle. Modern facilities include Wi-fi, and there are soft drinks as well as tea- and coffee-making supplies. The main restaurant overlooks the garden and has an interesting menu that might include starters like duck liver ballotine with hazelnuts and figs, or smoked eel with apple purée, celeriac remoulade and a quail's egg. Main courses are equally imaginative, perhaps shoulder of lamb with roast sweetbread, black olive gnocchi, fennel and goats' cheese. There's also a cosy bar, with an open fire and stone walls, serving real ales, cocktails and simple dishes.

Recommended in the area

Haddon Hall; Chatsworth House; Peak District National Park

DEVON

Lyme Regis harbour

The Imperial

★★★★ 77% HOTEL

Address: Taw Vale Parade, BARNSTAPLE,
EX32 8NB
Tel: 01271 345861
Fax: 01271 324448
Email: info@brend-imperial.co.uk
Website: www.brend-imperial.co.uk
Map ref: 2, SS53 **Directions:** M5 junct 27/A361 to
Barnstaple. Follow town centre signs, passing Tesco.
Straight on at next 2 rdbts. Hotel on right **Rooms:** 63
(4 GF) (7 fmly) **S** £87-£225 **D** £97-£185 **Facilities:** Wi-fi **Parking:** 80

In the heart of Barnstaple, the River Taw runs right past the manicured gardens and sun terrace of
this traditional Victorian hotel. Public areas feature specially commissioned paintings by local artists
of North Devon scenes, and pieces from the town's Brannam Pottery. The en suite bedrooms, many
overlooking the river and some with balconies, are furnished and equipped to a high standard, perhaps
none more so than the State Rooms, offering fresh flowers and 42" digital plasma TV. Both traditional
and contemporary food is served in the air-conditioned Arlington restaurant, whose set menu offers
duo of haddock with Parma ham, creamed cabbage and fennel; Dover sole meunière with herb butter
and garlic prawns; galette of pork medallions, black pudding, caramelised peach and scrumpy cider
reduction; and Moroccan spiced vegetable and feta b'stilla with mango, pawpaw and mint chutney.
For a lighter meal, Colours Lounge Bar has an appetising snack menu and is also good for an aperitif
or after-dinner port. Guests may use the heated indoor and outdoor pools free at sister hotel, the
Barnstaple; normal member rates apply to the solarium, sauna and other facilities. Banqueting and
conference suites are available for businesses.

Recommended in the area

Clovelly; Arlington Court (NT); RHS Garden Rosemoor

Northcote Manor

★★★ ◉◉ COUNTRY HOUSE HOTEL

Address: BURRINGTON, Umberleigh, EX37 9LZ
Tel: 01769 560501
Fax: 01769 560770
Email: rest@northcotemanor.co.uk
Website: www.northcotemanor.co.uk
Map ref: 2, SS61
Directions: Off A377 opposite Portsmouth Arms, into
hotel drive. (NB. Do not enter Burrington village)
Rooms: 11 S £110-£170 D £160-£260 (incl. bkfst)
Facilities: Wi-fi Tennis Croquet **Parking:** 30

This beautiful early 18th-century hotel stands in 20 acres of mature grounds and woodlands. Bedrooms exude comfort and style and have luxurious touches, from designer bath products to fluffy bathrobes, creating a haven of tranquillity. The restaurant's seasonal menu offers well-prepared, locally sourced dishes such as Ruby Red beef and Exmoor lamb with exceptional wines to accompany each course.

Recommended in the area

Rosemoor RHS garden; Dartington Crystal; North Devon coast

Clovelly, Devon

Langstone Cliff

★★★ 78% HOTEL

Address: Dawlish Warren, DAWLISH, EX7 0NA
Tel: 01626 868000
Fax: 01626 868006
Email: reception@langstone-hotel.co.uk
Website: www.langstone-hotel.co.uk
Map ref: 2, SX97
Directions: 1.5m NE off A379 (Exeter road) to
Dawlish Warren **Rooms:** 66 (10 GF) (52 fmly)
S £78-£92 **D** £122-£166 (incl. bkfst)
Facilities: STV Wi-fi ⓡ ⤙ Gym **Parking:** 200

It was the Rogers family who welcomed the first guests here in 1947. They're still here – although it's generations two and three running the show now – and some of those original guests are still coming. Such loyalty is understandable: the views of the sea from the lawn, veranda and lounges are breathtaking, and a two-mile stretch of beach is five minutes' walk away. The service is attentive, the public rooms spacious, the lounges are comfortable and the bars friendly. Bedrooms are frequently refurbished and all are en suite, with TV, radio, baby-listening, phone and other amenities. Many are designed as family rooms and some have balconies. The extensive breakfast menu in the Lincoln Restaurant gets guests off to a good start, and during the day everything from pastries and light snacks through to full meals are available. Dinner is chosen from a fixed price menu or the carvery, and many of the sensibly priced wines are available by the glass. There are indoor and outdoor heated pools, a hard tennis court, compact leisure centre and full-size snooker table. The hotel has taken corporate membership at the nearby Dawlish Warren Golf Course, giving one four ball each day, free of charge. Contact the reception for further details.

Recommended in the area

Paignton Zoo; Powderham Castle; Miniature Pony Centre

The Horn of Plenty

★★★ 85% ◉◉ HOTEL

Address: GULWORTHY, Tavistock, PL19 8JD
Tel: 01822 832528
Fax: 01822 834390
Email: enquiries@thehornofplenty.co.uk
Website: www.thehornofplenty.co.uk
Map ref: 1, SX47
Directions: From Tavistock take A390 W for 3m.
Right at Gulworthy Cross. In 400yds turn left, hotel in
400yds on right
Rooms: 10 (4 GF) (3 fmly)
Parking: 25

The Horn of Plenty, a beautiful country house hotel, continues to provide award-winning food and excellent accommodation in a glorious location. Surrounded by a designated Area of Outstanding Natural Beauty and boasting stunning views of the Tamar Valley, the hotel is located just off the western edge of Dartmoor which provides walkers, holidaymakers and food lovers with many choices. Food features high on the agenda here, with local produce providing interesting and memorable dining. A dinner menu might include a starter of sautéed Falmouth bay scallops, confit chicken, artichoke and Madeira butter, followed by a main course of English rose veal with creamed cabbage and bacon, turnip purée and a red wine sauce. A signature dessert is warm hazelnut cake with stout ice cream. The bedrooms are luxurious and well equipped, with Vi-spring mattress beds, fresh flowers, bottled water, towelling robes and quality toiletries. Bedrooms in the main house are large and traditionally furnished while those in the coach house are more contemporary; most rooms have balconies overlooking the gardens and the valley.

Recommended in the area

Cotehele (NT); Buckland Abbey (NT); Plymouth; The Garden House, Buckland Monachorum

Combe House - Devon

★ ★ ★ ◉◉ COUNTRY HOUSE HOTEL

Address: Gittisham, HONITON, EX14 3AD
Tel: 01404 540400
Fax: 01404 46004
Email: stay@combehousedevon.com
Website: www.combehousedevon.com
Map ref: 2, ST10
Directions: Off A30 1m S of Honiton, follow
Gittisham Heathpark signs. From M5 exit 29 for
Honiton. Exit Pattasons Cross

Rooms: 16 (1 fmly) **S** £159-£379 **D** £179-£399 (incl. bkfst) **Facilities:** Wi-fi **Parking:** 38

This privately run Grade I, Elizabethan manor is set in 3,500 acres of Devon estate. It has a lovely, relaxed atmosphere, almost like staying in the country home of good friends. The reception rooms are warm and welcoming with huge open fires, while all the spacious bedrooms have been refurbished. The staff service and food are the big attractions; the two Master Chefs of Great Britain create modern British dishes using local produce and ingredients from Combe's own Victorian kitchen garden, so the hotel talks of 'food metres not food miles'.

Recommended in the area

Southwest coast (Sidmouth to Lyme Regis); National Trust houses and gardens; Honiton Antiques

Best Western The White Hart Hotel

★ ★ ★ 81% ◉ HOTEL

Address: The Square, MORETONHAMPSTEAD,
TQ13 8NQ
Tel: 01647 441340
Fax: 01647 441341
Email: enquiries@whitehartdartmoor.co.uk
Website: www.whitehartdartmoor.co.uk
Map ref: 2, SX78
Directions: A30 towards Okehampton. At Whiddon Down take
A382 **Rooms:** 28 (4 GF) (6 fmly)

This hotel has been standing at the heart of Moretonhampstead – gateway to the Dartmoor National Park– since 1639. These days it's a perfect blend of contemporary style and old-world charm. The beautifully furnished bedrooms all have bags of character, while the brasserie is a warm and welcoming setting for some fine British and European cooking. Meals can also be taken in the cosy bar, washed down, perhaps, by a pint of local real ale.

Recommended in the area

Cathedral city of Exeter; Becky Falls; Drago Castle

Tides Reach Hotel

★★★ 82% ❀ HOTEL
Address: South Sands, SALCOMBE, TQ8 8LJ
Tel: 01548 843466
Fax: 01548 843954
Email: enquire@tidesreach.com
Website: www.tidesreach.com
Map ref: 2, SX73
Directions: Off A38 at Buckfastleigh to Totnes. Then A381 to Salcombe, follow signs to South Sands
Rooms: 32 S £82-£156 D £70-£162 (incl. bkfst & dinner) **Facilities:** STV Wi-fi ⊗ Gym Spa **Parking:** 100 **Notes:** ❦ 8yrs

This hotel sits in an idyllic spot overlooking a quiet, sandy cove on the shores of the beautiful Salcombe Estuary. The views from the public rooms and the bedrooms are fabulous, but you needn't merely look out across the water – there are plenty of opportunities to get out on the water. A short walk or ferry ride along the estuary will bring you to the picturesque sailing resort of Salcombe, while right in front of the hotel you can enjoy safe swimming and various watersports. The hotel has been owned by the Edwards family for three generations, which probably has a lot to do with its friendly, homely atmosphere. The accommodation is tastefully furnished and there are several different room types, including many with balconies. The conservatory-style Garden Room Restaurant offers a daily-changing modern British menu featuring top-quality Devon produce, especially fish and seafood. Expect the likes of hand-picked Salcombe crab or Bigbury Bay mussels to begin, followed by line-caught Salcombe sea bass or rib of prime South Devon beef. During your stay make sure you find time to visit the spa, take a dip in the indoor pool and relax in the peaceful garden with its centrepiece ornamental lake.

Recommended in the area

Overbeck's Museum & Gardens (NT); Dartmoor National Park; South West Coastal Path

Saunton Sands

★★★★ 79% HOTEL

Address: SAUNTON, EX33 1LQ
Tel: 01271 890212 & 892001
Fax: 01271 890145
Email: reservations@sauntonsands.com
Website: www.sauntonsands.com
Map ref: 1, SS43
Directions: Off A361 at Braunton, signed Croyde B3231, hotel 2m on left
Rooms: 92 (39 fmly) S £95-£150 D £95-£150 (incl. bkfst) Facilities: Wi-fi ⊗ ↖ Gym Spa Parking: 140 Notes: ⊗

From the front of this majestic hotel, high above Braunton Burrows, three things account for what you can see – sea, sand and sky, stretching far into the distance. It's an inspiring view, probably best savoured from a seat on the terrace, while inside other moods may be satisfied in one of the public rooms – a quiet corner in which to read or snooze maybe, or the bar for freshly ground coffee, or perhaps a peaty malt. Imagine then the views from the many bedrooms that face the beach and the sometimes gentle, sometimes roaring Atlantic Ocean. Wherever your room, it will be equipped to the standard expected from a luxury hotel. In the restaurant, daily changing dinner menus make the most of seasonal local produce, while the Terrace Lounge offers snacks, hot and cold meals throughout the day, and traditional afternoon cream teas. At night these areas become the social heart of the hotel, with live music and entertainment. Just below the hotel is The Sands Café Bar, a more relaxed place for a daytime drink or light bite, or freshly cooked pastas and grills in the evening.

Recommended in the area

Exmoor National Park; Tarka Trail; Hartland Heritage Coast

Victoria Hotel

★★★★ 83% ❀ HOTEL
Address: The Esplanade, SIDMOUTH, EX10 8RY
Tel: 01395 512651
Fax: 01395 579154
Email: info@victoriahotel.co.uk
Website: www.victoriahotel.co.uk
Map ref: 2, SY18
Directions: On seafront
Rooms: 65 (6 fmly) S £135-£290 D £175-£290
Facilities: Wi-fi ⓧ ⍁ Spa Sauna
Parking: 100

In its architectural sense the word 'imposing' can be a cliché; not, however, in this case, for here is a truly splendid pile built in the early 1900s that lords it not just over its five acres of landscaped grounds, but over Sidmouth and its bay too. Its dignified period style is just as evident inside, where high ceilings and fancy plasterwork provide just the right setting for a dress code that requires men to wear a jacket and tie for dinner in the elegant, AA Rosette restaurant, and where a resident orchestra or pianist may strike up. Equally in tune is the kitchen, devising menus that may well partner trout mousse and rillettes with horseradish cream, followed by guinea fowl breast with bacon, peas and fondant potato, and finally a more contemporary dessert which partners trio of passion fruit jelly with sorbet and cheesecake. The en suite bedrooms, most facing the English Channel, and many with private balconies, are beautifully furnished. The sun lounge is the place for morning coffee, traditional Devonshire cream tea, and a fireside after-dinner liqueur. Other ways of passing the time include swimming in the indoor or outdoor heated pool, relaxing in the spa and tennis.

Recommended in the area

Exeter Cathedral; Crealy Adventure Park; Knightshayes Court (NT)

Riviera Hotel

★★★★ 82% ◉ HOTEL

Address: The Esplanade, SIDMOUTH, EX10 8AY
Tel: 01395 515201
Fax: 01395 577775
Email: enquiries@hotelriviera.co.uk
Website: www.hotelriviera.co.uk
Map ref: 2, SY18
Directions: M5 junct 30 & follow A3052
Rooms: 26 (6 fmly) **S** £119-£185 **D** £218-£350
(incl. bkfst & dinner) **Facilities:** Wi-fi
Parking: 27

The Riviera Hotel, with its fine Regency façade and alluring blend of old-fashioned service and present day comforts, is splendidly positioned at the centre of Sidmouth's esplanade, overlooking Lyme Bay. With its mild climate and the beach just on the doorstep, the setting echoes the south of France and is ideal for those in search of relaxation and quieter pleasures. Glorious sea views can be enjoyed from bedrooms, all of which are fully appointed and have many thoughtful extras. In the elegant bay-view dining room guests are offered a fine choice of dishes from extensive menus, with local seafood being a particular speciality. Wedding parties and business conferences can be accommodated, and the hotel can arrange sporting activities in the area, including golfing with concessionary fees at the nearby Sidmouth Golf Club and Woodbury Park Golf and Country Club. Arrangements can also be made for riding, and pheasant and duck shooting on local estates. The hotel has a long tradition of hospitality and is perfect for unforgettable holidays, long weekends, or a memorable Christmas break.

Recommended in the area

Bicton Gardens; Killerton House and Gardens; Exeter Cathedral

Belmont Hotel

★★★★ 75% HOTEL

Address: The Esplanade, SIDMOUTH, EX10 8RX
Tel: 01395 512555
Fax: 01395 579101
Email: reservations@belmont-hotel.co.uk
Website: www.belmont-hotel.co.uk
Map ref: 2, SY18
Directions: On seafront
Rooms: 50 (2 GF) (4 fmly) S £115–£225
D £145–£225 Facilities: STV Wi-fi
Parking: 45

With plenty of land available, the Victorians cherry-picked the best building plots for their seafront houses and hotels. At the western end of Sidmouth's Regency esplanade, the Belmont is a case in point. Although just minutes from the town centre, you could be a world away as you enjoy a light lunch or cream tea on the hotel terrace. Fresh flowers greet guests on opening the door to their en suite bedroom, most of which have a sea view. Dinner is a reverential occasion, with men expected to wear a jacket and tie in the lounges and dining rooms, where traditional and contemporary dishes are exemplified by carved fillet of beef Wellington with rich Madeira sauce; sautéed mignons of pork with port and sage jus; and poached délice of salmon with vermouth and scallop velouté. On hand is a sommelier to help you navigate the extensive wine list. For indoor relaxation there's a spa with sauna and hot stone therapy beds, while outdoor activities include swimming (children can use a smaller pool), an 18-hole putting green, tennis court and five acres of grounds in which to walk. A drink in the Pavilion Bar will then, no doubt, be most welcome.

Recommended in the area

Killerton House (NT); Powderham Castle; Lyme Regis

Westcliff Hotel

★★★ 79% HOTEL

Address: Manor Road, SIDMOUTH, EX10 8RU
Tel: 01395 513252
Fax: 01395 578203
Email: stay@westcliffhotel.co.uk
Website: www.westcliffhotel.co.uk
Map ref: 2, SY18
Directions: Exit A3052 to Sidmouth then to seafront & esplanade, turn right, hotel directly ahead
Facilities: Wi-fi ⚲ **Parking:** 40

The privately-owned Westcliff Hotel is set in two beautiful acres of lawns and gardens, right in the middle of the Jurassic Coast, a World Heritage Site. In fact, the Westcliff's position gives it a natural advantage, sheltering it from every wind but the south. Regency Sidmouth is known as the 'Jewel of the West Country' and its town centre, promenade and beaches are just a short walk away. Locally renowned for excellent food and courteous and efficient service, this hotel offers elegant lounges and a cocktail bar opening onto the heated outdoor swimming pool (June to September). The different types of bedroom are well proportioned, tastefully furnished and equipped with all the usual amenities. Most have sea views, some from their own private balconies. In fact, only a few of the single and standard rooms do not face the sea. The Harding's restaurant offers a tempting choice of both carte and fixed price menus, and views of the red cliffs for which this part of Devon is famous. The Westcliff Hotel is open all year round.

Recommended in the area

Bicton Gardens; Otterton Mill; The Jurassic Coast

Orestone Manor Hotel & Restaurant

★★★ 87% ◉◉ HOTEL

Address: Rockhouse Lane, Maidencombe,
TORQUAY, TQ1 4SX
Tel: 01803 328098
Fax: 01803 328336
Email: info@orestonemanor.com
Website: www.orestonemanor.com
Map ref: 2, SX96
Directions: A38 onto A380 then B3192
Rooms: 12 (1 GF) (3 fmly) **S** £90-£149 **D** £135-£225 (incl. bkfst) **Facilities:** Wi-fi ₹ **Parking:** 40

With stunning views of the Torbay coastline and set in lovely rolling countryside near Torquay, Orestone Manor was the home of painter John Calcott Horsley, RA, best known for painting the first Christmas card and whose celebrated portrait of his brother-in-law, Isambard Kingdom Brunel, hangs in the National Gallery. Located in landscaped gardens, this Edwardian house has a colonial theme running throughout the public areas with wooden floors, wicker furniture and palms setting the style. There's an elegant sitting room and bar with an adjoining conservatory leading up to a terrace which overlooks the manicured gardens and the sea; it makes the perfect place for a relaxing drink or alfresco dining in the warmer weather. The elegant, individually decorated bedrooms, including a deluxe four-poster retreat, have flat-screen TVs, tea- and coffee-making facilities, home-made biscuits, bathrobes and luxury toiletries to ensure a comfortable and pampered stay.

Recommended in the area

Dartmoor; South Devon Railway; Berry Pomeroy Castle

Corbyn Head Hotel & Orchid Restaurant

★★★ 77% ◉◉◉ HOTEL

Address:	Torbay Road, Sea Front, TORQUAY, TQ2 6RH
Tel:	01803 213611
Fax:	01803 296152
Email:	info@corbynhead.com
Website:	www.corbynhead.com

Map ref: 2, SX96 **Directions:** Follow signs to Torquay seafront, turn right on seafront.

Rooms: 45 (9 GF) (4 fmly) **S** £30-£85 **D** £60-£172 (incl. bkfst) **Facilities:** Wi-fi ₹ Gym **Parking:** 50

This hotel is sited in a fantastic setting on the waterfront just a minute's leisurely walk to Livermead Beach. Most of the bedrooms have sea views, and many have private balconies. The air-conditioned Orchid Restaurant offers fine dining on the top floor, with magnificent views over Torbay. The traditional English cuisine of the Harbour View Restaurant is constantly changing, while the Regency Lounge and the Continental Coffee Bar open onto the Poolside Terrace.

Recommended in the area

Paignton Zoo; Kent's Cavern, Torquay; Babbacombe Model Village

Harbour Bridge, Torquay

DORSET

Poole Quay

BridgeHouse

★★★ 80% ◉ HOTEL

Address: 3 Prout Bridge, BEAMINSTER, DT8 3AY
Tel: 01308 862200
Fax: 01308 863700
Email: enquiries@bridge-house.co.uk
Website: www.bridge-house.co.uk
Map ref: 2, SY40
Directions: Off A3066, 100yds from town square
Rooms: 13 (4 GF) (2 fmly) **Facilities:** Wi-fi
Parking: 20

Sitting beside a bridge, this small hotel offers the perfect blend of historic charm and 21st-century luxury. The building is medieval but its interior has been sympathetically updated by owners Mark and Joanna Donovan, so expect beautiful public areas that are full of character, excellent bathrooms for each of the stylish bedrooms, and all the latest technology. There are several areas for enjoying the top-notch Dorset produce offered on the seasonal menus – the stylish brasserie, the sun room conservatory overlooking the beautiful walled garden, and alfresco when the weather permits.

Recommended in the area
The Jurassic Coast; Abbotsbury Swannery; Mapperton House and Gardens

---

Chine Hotel

★★★ 81% ◉ HOTEL

Address: Boscombe Spa Road, BOURNEMOUTH,
BH5 1AX
Tel: 01202 396234 & 0845 337 1550
Fax: 01202 391737
Email: reservations@fjbhotels.co.uk
Website: www.fjbhotels.co.uk
Map ref: 3, SZ19 **Directions:** Follow BIC signs to St Pauls rdbt. 1st exit. At next rdbt, 2nd exit signed Eastcliff/Boscombe/S'bourne. Next rdbt, 1st exit. Right at 2nd lights **Rooms:** 88 (8 GF) (16 fmly) **S** £60-£110 **D** £120-£220 (incl. bkfst & dinner) **Facilities:** STV Wi-fi ⊗ ⊰ Gym **Parking:** 55 **Notes:** ⊗

The Chine sits in three acres of secluded, mature gardens with magnificent sea views. A short walk through the gardens quickly brings you to miles of sandy beaches, but if it's not beach weather, you can always escape to the Roman Spa. The guest rooms, many with balconies include interconnecting family rooms and some have Wi-fi and internet access. For dining, choose between the Sea View restaurant, overlooking Poole Bay, or the Gallery Brasserie.

Recommended in the area Bournemouth shopping centre; Poole Quay; New Forest National Park

Best Western Connaught Hotel

★★★ 83% ◉ HOTEL

Address: West Hill Road, West Cliff,
BOURNEMOUTH, BH2 5PH
Tel: 01202 298020
Fax: 01202 298028
Email: reception@theconnaught.co.uk
Website: www.theconnaught.co.uk
Map ref: 3, SZ19
Directions: Follow Town Centre West & BIC signs
Rooms: 83 (10 fmly) S £50-£70 D £110-£170
(incl. bkfst) **Facilities:** STV Wi-fi ⊗ Gym Spa Sauna **Parking:** 66 **Notes:** ⊗

Built around 1850 as a gentleman's residence, this award-winning, environmentally-friendly hotel is centrally located on the West Cliff in an acre of grounds. All of the attractions of the town centre are less than five minutes' walk away, as are the beach and the Bournemouth International Centre with its busy programme of concerts and events. Accommodation is stylish and well equipped, with a variety of rooms and suites, including family suites, available in the main hotel as well as in the neighbouring Connaught Lodge. All rooms are en suite, most have Wi-fi and some have private balconies or terraces overlooking the private garden terrace. The Spa with its 18-metre pool, sauna, aroma steam room and massage therapy room adds to the relaxation factor, while for those feeling more energetic there are two gyms. It was the first hotel in the town to be awarded a silver shield through the Green Tourism Business Scheme for its commitment to the environment. 'Green' activities include recycling as much waste as possible, switching to low energy lighting and using local ingredients in the AA Rosetted Blakes restaurant. The restaurant now has a garden terrace for alfresco dining.

Recommended in the area

Bournemouth Pier; Lower Gardens; Bournemouth Oceanarium

Captain's Club Hotel and Spa

★★★★ 81% ◉◉ HOTEL

Address: Wick Ferry, Wick Lane, CHRISTCHURCH, BH23 1HU

Tel: 01202 475111

Fax: 01202 490111

Email: enquiries@captainsclubhotel.com

Website: www.captainsclubhotel.com

Map ref: 3, SZ19

Directions: B3073 to Christchurch. On Fountain rdbt take 5th exit (Sopers Ln) 2nd left (St Margarets Ave) 1st right onto Wick Ln

Rooms: 29 (12 fmly) S £179-£209 D £179-£239 (incl. bkfst) **Facilities:** STV Wi-fi Spa Sauna

Parking: 41

Sleek, smooth and ultra modern, Captain's Club Hotel is a testament to designer flair. This strikingly contemporary boutique hotel resides on the banks of the River Stour, just a short walk from the centre of historic Christchurch. There are many relaxing and fun ways to spend your time here – amongst them enjoying a soothing spa treatment, a trip across the bay aboard the hotel's 34-foot luxury motor cruiser, a stroll along the quayside to Christchurch Priory (which boasts choir stalls older than those in Westminster Abbey), or simply sitting back in a so-comfortable armchair to drink in the superb vista through floor-to-ceiling windows. All 29 bedrooms and suites have a contemporary maritime theme and are light and airy with stunning riverside views, air-conditioning, flat-screen TV, DVD player and free Wi-fi. The modern maritime theme and fabulous river views continue in Tides Restaurant, where the cuisine reflects the feel of the hotel: uncomplicated, fresh, innovative and ultimately satisfying.

Recommended in the area

Christchurch Priory and harbour; Isle of Wight; New Forest National Park

Harbour Heights Hotel

★★★★ 80% ◉◉ HOTEL

Address:	73 Haven Road, Sandbanks, POOLE, BH13 7LW
Tel:	01202 707272 & 0845 337 1550
Fax:	01202 708594
Email:	reservations@fjbhotels.co.uk
Website:	www.fjbhotels.co.uk
Map ref:	3, SZ09

Directions: Follow signs for Sandbanks, hotel on left after Canford Cliffs

Rooms: 38 (2 fmly) S £110-£220 D £220-£440 (incl. bkfst & dinner) Facilities: STV Wi-fi Parking: 50 Notes: ⊗

The hotel was built in 1920 and completely renovated in 2003, and offers contemporary elegance with a classic Rhode Island twist. The two-AA Rosette Harbar bistro offers an impressive menu using local produce wherever possible. The bar and restaurant extend onto a tiered landscaped terrace with panoramic views over Poole Harbour. The hotel is ideally situated for the many local attractions.

Recommended in the area

Tank Museum; Swanage Railway; Purbeck Heritage Coast

Sandbanks Hotel

★★★★ 76% ◉ HOTEL

Address:	15 Banks Road, Sandbanks, POOLE, BH13 7PS
Tel:	01202 707377 & 0845 337 1550
Fax:	01202 708885
Email:	reservations@fjbhotels.co.uk
Website:	www.fjbhotels.co.uk
Map ref:	3, SZ09

Directions: A338 from Bournemouth onto Wessex Way, to Liverpool Victoria rdbt. Left, then 2nd exit onto B3965. Hotel on left

Rooms: 110 (4 GF) (31 fmly) S £95-£170 D £190-£340 (incl. bkfst) Facilities: STV Wi-fi ⓧ Gym Spa Parking: 120 Notes: ⊗

The Sandbanks is situated on a Blue Flag beach, looking across Poole Bay to the famous Old Harry Rocks. The view can be enjoyed from the terrace, the lounges, the Seaview Restaurant and many of the bedrooms. Depending on the time of year several watersports are offered. Experienced staff are available to assist with all aspects of business or social events.

Recommended in the area

Poole Quay; Alice in Wonderland Park; Jurassic Coastal Path

Haven Hotel

★★★★ 76% ◉◉ HOTEL

Address: Banks Road, Sandbanks, POOLE, BH13 7QL
Tel: 01202 707333 & 0845 337 1550
Fax: 01202 708796
Email: reservations@fjbhotels.co.uk
Website: www.fjbhotels.co.uk
Map ref: 3, SZ09
Directions: B3965 towards Poole Bay, left onto the Peninsula. Hotel 1.5m on left adjacent to Swanage Toll Ferry **Rooms:** 77 (4 fmly) **S** £110-£220 **D** £220-£440 (incl. bkfst & dinner) **Facilities:** STV Wi-fi ⊗ ⋠ Gym Spa Sauna **Parking:** 160 **Notes:** ⊗

The Haven is idyllically located at the very tip of the exclusive Sandbanks peninsular with uninterrupted views of Poole Harbour. Most rooms have balconies and views across to the Purbeck Hills, Studland Beach or Brownsea Island. The waterside La Roche restaurant showcases some of Dorset's finest produce on its seasonally changing menus.

Recommended in the area

Jurassic Coast; Brownsea Island; Purbeck Hills; Compton Acres; Corfe Castle

Early morning mist, Corfe Castle

COUNTY DURHAM

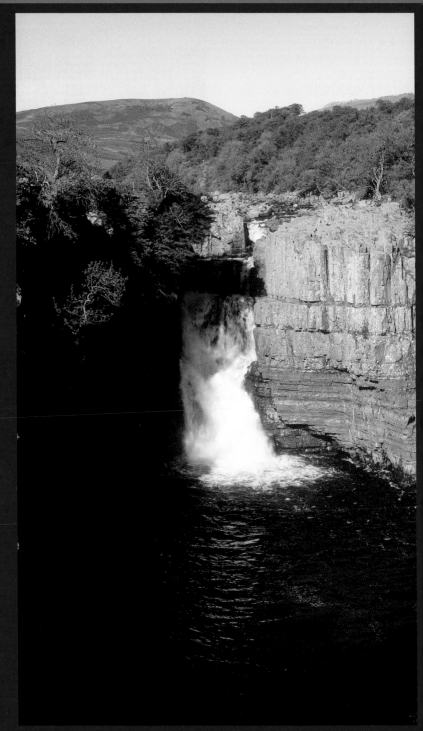

High Force Waterfall, Forest-in-Teesdale

Headlam Hall

★★★★ 75% ◉ HOTEL

Address: Headlam, Gainford, DARLINGTON,
DL2 3HA

Tel: 01325 730238

Fax: 01325 730790

Email: admin@headlamhall.co.uk

Website: www.headlamhall.co.uk

Map ref: 6, NZ21

Directions: 2m N of A67 between Piercebridge &
Gainford Rooms: 40 (10 GF) (4 fmly) S £95-£120
D £120-£195 (incl. bkfst) Facilities: STV Wi-fi ⓧ Gym Spa Parking: 80

A fine 17th-century mansion set amid beautiful grounds and gardens in a tranquil part of Teesdale. A glorious haven for anyone conducting business in the Middlesbrough-Stockton-Darlington conurbation to the east, it is also perfect for exploring rural County Durham and the Yorkshire Dales. There is also the option of taking in a round of golf on the hotel's own nine-hole course, a dip in its spacious indoor pool with water-jet feature, a work-out in the gym or a pampering spa treatment. The spa also has a sauna, steam room and air-conditioned exercise studio. The bedrooms come in a variety of sizes, some with elegant period furniture, others are more comtemporary. All have modern facilities including Sky TV and free Wi-fi. The public areas are richly decorated and include a cocktail bar and the elegant drawing room overlooking the main lawn. The restaurant, spread across four very different dining areas, serves modern British cuisine along the lines of pan-fried rib-eye beef with roasted root vegetables, horseradish mash and red wine sauce; pan-seared sea bass with sautéed new potatoes, cauliflower purée, couscous and lemon butter sauce. There is a strong emphasis on locally sourced ingredients including produce from the hall's own gardens.

Recommended in the area

Raby Castle; Bowes Museum; High Force waterfall

Best Western Parkmore Hotel

★★★ 79% HOTEL

Address: 636 Yarm Road, Eaglescliffe,
STOCKTON-ON-TEES, TS16 0DH
Tel: 01642 786815
Fax: 01642 790485
Email: enquiries@parkmorehotel.co.uk
Website: www.parkmorehotel.co.uk
Map ref: 8, NZ41
Directions: Exit A19 at Crathorne, A67 to Yarm.
Through Yarm, right onto A135 to Stockton. Hotel 1m
on left **Rooms:** 55 (9 GF) (8 fmly) **S** £55-£84.50 **D** £75-£104.50
Facilities: STV Wi-fi 🕸 Gym Spa **Parking:** 90

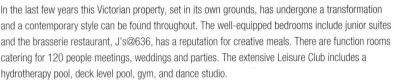

In the last few years this Victorian property, set in its own grounds, has undergone a transformation
and a contemporary style can be found throughout. The well-equipped bedrooms include junior suites
and the brasserie restaurant, J's@636, has a reputation for creative meals. There are function rooms
catering for 120 people meetings, weddings and parties. The extensive Leisure Club includes a
hydrotherapy pool, deck level pool, gym, and dance studio.

Recommended in the area

Billingham Beck Valley: Head of Steam, Darlington Railway Museum; RSPB Saltholme

Raby Castle

Beth Chatto Gardens, Elmstead Market

milsoms

★★★ 78% 🌑 SMALL HOTEL
Address: Stratford Road, Dedham, COLCHESTER,
CO7 6HW
Tel: 01206 322795
Fax: 01206 323689
Email: milsoms@milsomhotels.com
Website: www.milsomhotels.com
Map ref: 4, TM03 **Directions:** 6m N of Colchester
off A12, follow Stratford St Mary/Dedham signs. Turn
right over A12, hotel on left
Rooms: 15 (4 GF) (3 fmly) **S** £95-£115 **D** £115-£150 **Facilities:** STV Wi-fi **Parking:** 90

Ssituated in the heart of Constable country in the Dedham Vale, milsoms makes a perfect base for exploring the countryside on the north Essex/Suffolk border. The hub of milsoms is the contemporary bar and brasserie, where food is served all day and the whole carte menu is available from noon until late. The restaurant spills out onto the terrace which is covered with a huge architectural sail. Fifteen stylish, individually designed en suite bedrooms complete the milsoms picture.

Recommended in the area

The Painters Trail - Constable, Gainsborough & Munnings; Suffolk Heritage Coast; Stour Valley

The Pier at Harwich

★★★ 87% 🌑🌑 HOTEL
Address: The Quay, HARWICH, CO12 3HH
Tel: 01255 241212
Fax: 01255 551922
Email: pier@milsomhotels.com
Website: www.milsomhotels.com
Map ref: 4, TM23
Directions: From A12, take A120 to Quay. Hotel
opposite lifeboat station
Rooms: 14 (1 GF) (5 fmly) **S** £85-£140
D £110-£190 (incl. bkfst) **Facilities:** STV Wi-fi **Parking:** 10 **Notes:** ⊗ in bedrooms
Beside the quay in Harwich old town and located in two historic buildings, The Pier enjoys spectacular views of the ever-changing scenery of the east coast's busiest harbour. Bedrooms are stylish with many individual touches and all have private bathrooms, satellite TV, minibars and tea and coffee tray. There are two fabulous restaurants, the first-floor Harbourside, with views of the Stour and Orwell estuaries and the harbour below, specialises in locally caught seafood while the Ha'penny Bistro offers relaxed brasserie-style food. The hotel can arrange sailing days on a renovated traditional fishing smack.

Recommended in the area

Sailing; Ha'penny Pier and Museum; Redoubt Fort; Martello Tower

Maison Talbooth

★ ★ ★ ◉◉ COUNTRY HOUSE HOTEL

Address: Stratford Road, DEDHAM, CO7 6HN
Tel: 01206 322367
Fax: 01206 322752
Email: maison@milsomhotels.co.uk
Website: www.milsomhotels.com
Map ref: 4, TM03
Directions: A12 towards Ipswich, 1st turn signed Dedham, follow to left bend, turn right. Hotel 1m on right

Rooms: 12 (5 GF) (1 fmly) **S** £150-£285 **D** £190-£395 (incl. bkfst) **Facilities:** STV Wi-fi ⚊ Tennis Spa **Parking:** 40 **Notes:** ⊗ in bedrooms

This impressive Victorian country house sits in a peaceful rural location in the heart of Constable country, amid pretty landscaped grounds overlooking the River Stour. It boasts three principal suites, each with its own hot tub on a private terrace. All the spacious en suite bedrooms are individually decorated, with tasteful furnishings, co-ordinated fabrics and thoughtful extras such as super-king-size beds, goose-feather duvets, fluffy towels and mini-bars; many rooms have fine views over Dedham Vale. The hotel features a day spa with three treatment rooms, plus an outdoor hot tub. In the Pool House there's a dining area complete with kitchen, which can be used for house parties and meetings, while other public areas include a comfortable drawing room where guests may take afternoon tea or snacks. The Garden Room Restaurant is a light and airy room with a high-vaulted ceiling and large windows. Here, guests can enjoy everything from breakfast to a light lunch through to dinner, and even dancing if the house is booked for exclusive use. It's no wonder the hotel is a popular venue for weddings.

Recommended in the area

Sir Alfred Munnings Museum; Beth Chatto Gardens; Colchester Castle

GLOUCESTERSHIRE

Arlington Row, Bibury

Swan Hotel

★★★ 82% ❀ HOTEL

Address: BIBURY, GL7 5NW
Tel: 01285 740695
Fax: 01285 740473
Email: info@swanhotel.co.uk
Website: www.cotswold-inns-hotels.co.uk/swan
Map ref: 3, SP10
Directions: 9m S of Burford A40 onto B4425. 6m N
of Cirencester A4179 onto B4425
Rooms: 22 (1 fmly) D £155-£195 (incl. bkfst)
Facilities: Wi-fi Parking: 22

With beautifully landscaped gardens bisected by the River Coln, within one of England's prettiest villages, the picturesque, ivy-clad Swan Hotel truly presents a Cotswolds idyll. Starting life as coaching inn in the 17th century, it is now furnished in country-house style to create a relaxing atmosphere and its ornamental garden is surrounded by a crystal-clear moat. The cosy lounges, decorated in country house style, offer a peaceful place to relax, each having a feature fireplace, and the convivial bar serves real ales. There's a touch of eccentricity about the bedrooms, most of which have river views; each is individually styled and all boast a lavish bathroom, perhaps with a large hot-tub bath. There are also some two-storey self-contained suites a short walk from the main building, with separate sitting rooms and a private garden. The Whooper Suite, in a Cotswold stone cottage, offers the ultimate luxury and stunning views. The Gallery Restaurant serves modern European-style cuisine in a romantic setting, with original oil paintings by a Dartmoor artist on the walls. The freshest local produce goes into dishes such as roast venison and baby turnips, with a pancetta and thyme port glaze, or brill poached in red wine shallots and rosemary, with sweet potato purée and goats' cheese ravioli.

Recommended in the area

Cirencester; Cotswold Wildlife Park; Chedworth Roman Villa

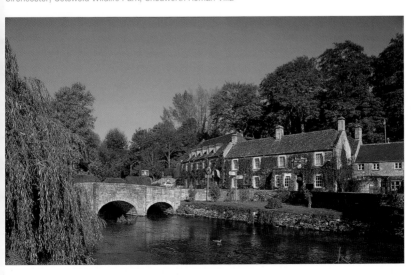

Manor House Hotel

★★★★ 75% ◉◉ HOTEL
Address: High Street, MORETON-IN-MARSH,
GL56 0LJ
Tel: 01608 650501
Fax: 01608 651481
Email: info@manorhousehotel.info
Website: www.cotswold-inns-hotels.co.uk/manor
Map ref: 3, SP23
Directions: Off A429 at south end of town. Take East
St off High St, hotel car park 3rd on right
Rooms: 35 (1 GF) (3 fmly) **D** £145-£185 (incl. bkfst) **Facilities:** Wi-fi **Parking:** 24

The Manor House was bequeathed to the Dean and Chapter of Westminster in 1539 by Henry VIII, when it was a traditional coaching inn at the heart of the busy market town of Moreton-in-Marsh. Today the attractive Cotswold stone building retains plenty of 16th-century character, blending seamlessly with 21st-century style and technology. The bedrooms, including four-poster rooms and suites, are elegantly furnished with a country-house look, and have lots of period features such as open fireplaces and window seats. Each comes with flat-screen TV, tea- and coffee-making facilities and luxurious Molton Brown toiletries in the bathroom. There's also a one-bedroom cottage in the grounds with its own private garden and terrace with hot tub – perfect for longer stays or a truly indulgent escape. The cooking in the Mulberry Restaurant is modern British and takes its lead from fresh, seasonal, local produce. Dinner might begin with peppered Cerney goats' cheese with carpaccio of beetroot and beetroot sorbet for example, followed, perhaps, by belly of pork and tenderloin with Scotch egg, French beans and celeriac. The Beagle Bar & Brasserie offers a more informal dining option, as well as serving afternoon tea and cocktails.

Recommended in the area

Royal Shakespeare Company, Stratford-upon-Avon; Batsford Arboretum; Hidcote Manor Gardens

Cotswolds88 Hotel

★★★★ 80% ◉◉ SMALL HOTEL

Address: Kemps Lane, PAINSWICK, GL6 6YB
Tel: 01452 813688
Fax: 01452 814059
Email: reservations@cotswolds88hotel.com
Website: www.cotswolds88hotel.com
Map ref: 2, SO80
Directions: From Stroud towards Cheltenham on A46, in Painswick centre right at St Marys Church into Victoria St. Left into St Marys St, right into Tibbiwell St, right into Kemps Lane

Rooms: 17 (2 fmly) **Facilities:** Wi-fi **Parking:** 17 **Notes:** ⊗ in bedrooms

Built on an ancient Roman site, this late-Palladian mansion is a fine example of its style, although various later architects have left their mark, including Arts and Crafts impresario, Detmar Blow. The interior is – to use the hotel's own word – funky, blending off-the-wall vintage pieces and splashes of colour with touches of psychedelia. Some of the individually styled, en suite bedrooms are decorated with limited-edition wallpaper inspired by Leigh Bowery, one-time model of Lucian Freud; most have good views of the surrounding hills. Abstract images of the hotel and grounds by internationally renowned photo-artist David Hiscock feature throughout the building in various forms. The 88Room restaurant sprawls across the ground floor, offering from its contemporary menu slow-braised shoulder of lamb and roasted rump, mashed potato and Provençal sauce; potato-wrapped fillet of halibut with creamed leeks, sautéed trompette mushrooms and red wine jus; and risotto with sliced black truffle and poached egg yolk. The terrace is also a good place to eat. The intimate bar serves signature cocktails, while residents may relax with tea and homemade scones in the private lounge and library, or on the balcony. Would-be kitchen supremos can book a master class with head chef, Lee Scott.

Recommended in the area

Painswick Rococo Garden; City of Bath; Cheltenham Racecourse

Lords of the Manor

★★★★ ◉◉◉ COUNTRY HOUSE HOTEL
Address: UPPER SLAUGHTER, GL54 2JD
Tel: 01451 820243
Fax: 01451 820696
Email: enquiries@lordsofthemanor.com
Website: www.lordsofthemanor.com
Map ref: 3, SP12
Directions: 2m W of A429. Exit A40 onto A429, take 'The Slaughters' turn. Through Lower Slaughter for 1m to Upper Slaughter. Hotel on right
Rooms: 26 (9 GF) (4 fmly) S £195–£370 D £195–£370 (incl. bkfst) **Facilities:** Wi-fi **Parking:** 40

A 17th-century honey-coloured rectory in eight acres of gardens and parkland, the Lords is the next best thing to a private retreat. Reception rooms have been preserved with style and character, their log fires blazing throughout the winter, and French windows thrown open to the terrace in summer. Some of the bedrooms overlook the gardens and lake, others the Victorian courtyard. Room extras include DVD player and luxury toiletries. The restaurant serves some of the county's finest food.

Recommended in the area

Bourton Model Village; Cotswold Farm Park; Broadway

Cotswold Farm Park, Guiting Power

GREATER MANCHESTER

The Town Hall, Albert Square, Manchester

Egerton House Hotel

★★★ 79% HOTEL

Address: Blackburn Road, Egerton, BOLTON,
BL7 9SB
Tel: 01204 307171
Fax: 01204 593030
Email: reservation@egertonhouse-hotel.co.uk
Website: www.egertonhouse-hotel.co.uk
Map ref: 6, SD70
Directions: M61, A666 (Bolton road), pass ASDA on
right. Hotel 2m on just passed war memorial on right
Rooms: 29 (7 fmly) **S** £69-£75 **D** £79-£98 (incl. bkfst) **Facilities:** Wi-fi **Parking:** 135
Notes: ⊗ in bedrooms

This beautiful privately-owned country-house hotel enjoys a secluded location in three acres of developed gardens just three miles away from Bolton. A family home for over 200 years, Egerton House has a warm and welcoming feel and plenty of character, making it a delightful retreat with the beauty of the Lancashire Hills right on the doorstep. Indeed, once you've settled into the cosy lounge with its open fire and lovely views of the grounds, it would be easy to forget the outside world exists. All 29 en suite rooms are non-smoking and come with flat-screen TV with Freeview, tea- and coffee-making facilities, iron and ironing board and trouser press. Wi-fi access is available in the lounge. Dinner and Sunday lunch are served in The Dining Room, a smart and contemporary space where the focus of the set menu is high-quality regional produce put to use in classic English and French dishes. Whether you're staying for business or pleasure, you can expect first-class, friendly service from a dedicated team. The hotel is an ideal venue for meetings, private gatherings and weddings.

Recommended in the area

Bolton Museum, Art Gallery & Aquarium; Smithills Hall; Trafford Centre

The Saddleworth Hotel

★★★★ 80% ◉◉ COUNTRY HOUSE HOTEL

Address: Huddersfield Road, DELPH, Saddleworth, OL3 5LX

Tel: 01457 871888

Fax: 01457 871889

Email: enquiries@thesaddleworthhotel.co.uk

Website: www.thesaddleworthhotel.co.uk

Map ref: 7, SE00

Directions: M62 junct 21, A640 towards Huddersfield. At Junction Inn take A6052 towards Delph; at White Lion left onto unclassified road; in 0.5m left on A62 towards Huddersfield. Hotel 0.5m on right

Facilities: STV Wi-fi ↖ **Parking:** 140 **Notes:** ⊗ in bedrooms

Once a coaching station on one of the busiest routes across the Pennine Hills, the Saddleworth Hotel sits in nine acres of beautiful gardens and woodland in the picturesque Castleshaw Valley. The house was built in the 17th century and has been lovingly restored and sympathetically updated by the live-in owners. There are many interesting period features, including the panelling and fireplace in the Great Hall which were taken from historic Weasenham Hall in East Anglia, and the wrought iron French doors leading to the garden which date back to 1795 and were recovered from a Newmarket stud, but originally came from a château in Bordeaux. All the bedrooms have their own individual character and are elegantly furnished and equipped with all the latest technology, while the luxury continues in the en suite marble bathrooms. The Saddleworth Hotel is a popular venue for parties, weddings, fine dining and afternoon tea. The restaurant serves a combination of traditional English and continental cuisine, complemented by a choice of over 100 fine wines.

Recommended in the area

Roman fortress; Standedge Tunnel; Pennine Way

The Lowry Hotel

★★★★★ 81% ◉◉ HOTEL

Address: 50 Dearmans Place, Chapel Wharf,
Salford, MANCHESTER, M3 5LH
Tel: 0161 827 4000 **Fax:** 0161 827 4001
Email: enquiries.lowry@roccofortecollection.com
Website: www.roccofortecollection.com
Map ref: 6, SJ89 **Directions:** M6 junct 19, A556/
M56/A5103. A57(M) to lights, right onto Water St.
Left to New Quay St/Trinity Way. At lights right onto
Chapel St **Rooms:** 165 (7 fmly) **S** £119-£350

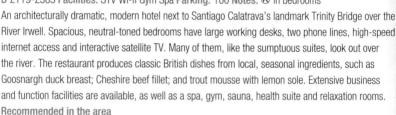

D £119-£385 **Facilities:** STV Wi-fi Gym Spa **Parking:** 100 **Notes:** ⊗ in bedrooms

An architecturally dramatic, modern hotel next to Santiago Calatrava's landmark Trinity Bridge over the River Irwell. Spacious, neutral-toned bedrooms have large working desks, two phone lines, high-speed internet access and interactive satellite TV. Many of them, like the sumptuous suites, look out over the river. The restaurant produces classic British dishes from local, seasonal ingredients, such as Goosnargh duck breast; Cheshire beef fillet; and trout mousse with lemon sole. Extensive business and function facilities are available, as well as a spa, gym, sauna, health suite and relaxation rooms.

Recommended in the area

The Lowry; Chinatown; Museum of Science & Industry

Piccadilly Gardens, Manchester

HAMPSHIRE

Cycling track, Brockenhurst

Esseborne Manor

★★★ 80% ◉ HOTEL

Address: Hurstbourne Tarrant, ANDOVER, SP11 0ER
Tel: 01264 736444
Fax: 01264 736725
Email: info@esseborne-manor.co.uk
Website: www.esseborne-manor.co.uk
Map ref: 3, SU34
Directions: Halfway between Andover & Newbury on A343, just 1m N of Hurstbourne Tarrant
Rooms: 19 (6 GF) (2 fmly) **S** £110-£130
D £125-£180 (incl. bkfst) **Facilities:** STV Wi-fi Tennis **Parking:** 50

A long drive leads to this privately-owned Victorian country-house hotel, set in three acres of gardens high on the hill above the lovely Bourne Valley. The surrounding high downland makes this a perfect spot for country walks, with lots of delightful village pubs for refreshment along the way. All the bedrooms, overlooking the gardens and farmlands beyond, are individually decorated, and some have jacuzzis and four-poster beds. Feature rooms include Lymington, with a luxurious Victorian bath overlooking the croquet lawn; Ferndown, with a canopy bed and a private patio; and the Honeymoon Suite, with a separate lounge and rococo-style king-size bed. The Dining Room, with its fabric-lined walls, provides a warm and elegant setting for the chef's fine English cuisine, using local produce and herbs from the hotel's own gardens. A choice of fixed-price menus is offered, including a Menu du Vin that includes a specially selected glass of wine with each course. There's also an extensive wine list should you prefer to select your own. The dinner menu might include such main courses as slow-roast pheasant, steak and Guinness pie with pot-au-feu vegetables, and fillet of cod with crushed new potato and tomato fondue.

Recommended in the Area
Highclere Castle; Winchester; Broadlands

Oakley Hall Hotel

★★★★ 81% ◉ COUNTRY HOUSE HOTEL
Address: Rectory Road, BASINGSTOKE, RG23 7EL
Tel: 01256 783350
Fax: 01256 783351
Email: enquiries@oakleyhall-park.com
Website: www.oakleyhall-park.com
Map ref: 3, SU65 **Directions:** M3 junct 7
Basingstoke signs. 500yds before lights left onto
A30 towards Oakley, right onto unclass road towards
Oakley. 3m, left into Rectory Rd. Left onto B3400.
Hotel signed 1st on left **Rooms:** 18 (18 GF) (8 fmly) **Facilities:** Wi-fi **Parking:** 100

An impressive drive leads to this country house hotel, built in 1795 and once owned by the Bramstons, close friends of Jane Austen, whose father was rector at nearby Steventon. It has been beautifully, indeed expensively, restored and offers luxury rooms and a swish contemporary restaurant with classy mirrors, leather seats, well-dressed tables and a striking striped carpet. The views across the rolling north Hampshire countryside are delightful - no wonder it's a popular wedding venue. In the AA Rosette Winchester restaurant the broadly modern European cuisine typically includes spiced monkfish tail with pak choi, basmati rice and coriander beurre blanc; pan-fried fillet of organic Laverstoke pork (from the 2,500-acre farm down the road run by 1979 Formula One champion, Jody Scheckter) in pancetta with grain mustard mash, black pudding and roast root vegetables; and rösti with mushroom and spinach mille-feuille, artichoke, pumpkin purée and balsamic and tomato dressing. Afternoon tea is served either on the Garden Terrace or in the Library. The bedrooms, many located around the courtyard, are spacious and well equipped; others are tucked away in an 18th-century, gingerbread-style cottage beneath the trees on the rear lawns. Within the main house are nine elegant meeting rooms.

Recommended in the area

Milestones; Basing House; The Vyne (NT)

Cloud Hotel

★★ 84% SMALL HOTEL

Address: Meerut Road, BROCKENHURST, SO42 7TD

Tel: 01590 622165 & 622354

Fax: 01590 622818

Email: enquiries@cloudhotel.co.uk

Website: www.cloudhotel.co.uk

Map ref: 3, SU30

Directions: M27 junct 1 signed New Forest, A337 through Lyndhurst to Brockenhurst. On entering Brockenhurst 1st right. Hotel 300mtrs

Rooms: 18 (2 GF) (1 fmly) S £108–£112 D £170–£224 (incl. bkfst & dinner)

Facilities: Wi-fi **Parking:** 20 **Notes:** ⊗ in bedrooms ✶ 8yrs

The famous New Forest ponies can often be seen near the entrance to this award-winning hotel, owned for 35 years by acclaimed businesswoman, international speaker and charity fundraiser Avril Owton. She was once one of the famous Tiller Girls dance troupe, which now gives its name to the bar. Avril's stage days are also recalled by heaps of high-kicking memorabilia on display around the hotel. The rooms, all en suite, are decorated in an up-to-date style and the majority, including the one with a four-poster, have either uninterrupted views of the forest, or of the garden. The forest is again to hand through the windows of Encore Restaurant, now sporting a new, less chintzy look, where largely traditional English food includes roast lamb with stuffing and honey mint sauce; chargrilled sirloin steak with red onion and port sauce; poached supreme of salmon with mushroom fish sauce; and roast vegetable lasagne. After lunch or dinner take coffee in the conservatory and admire the well-maintained gardens, where, in summer, you may have something to eat. The hotel is open to non-residents for lunch, dinner and cream teas; in fact, traditional tea parties are proving popular for all sorts of celebrations.

Recommended in the area

Exbury Gardens; Beaulieu Motor Museum; New Forest Safaris

Bell Inn

★★★ 80% ◉◉ HOTEL

Address: BROOK, SO43 7HE
Tel: 023 8081 2214
Fax: 023 8081 3958
Email: bell@bramshaw.co.uk
Website: www.bellinnbramshaw.co.uk
Map ref: 3, SU21 **Directions:** M27 junct 1 onto
B3079, hotel 1.5m on right **Rooms:** 27 (8 GF)
(1 fmly) **S** £45-£70 **D** £90-£140 (incl. bkfst)
Facilities: Wi-fi **Parking:** 150

Although part of Bramshaw Golf Club, a stay at this 18th-century hotel on the edge of the New Forest doesn't warrant packing a chipping iron, or even knowing what one is. Nevertheless, for those who do it remains the perfect '19th hole', after a round on one of the three 18-hole courses. Period features have been retained in the bar and the award-winning Briscoe's fine dining restaurant. Bedrooms are light, spacious and spotlessly maintained and include redesigned Superior rooms and two that have their own entrance. Businesses make good use of the hotel for presentations and conferences.

Recommended in the area

Beaulieu Abbey; Paulton's Park; Buckler's Hard

Westover Hall Hotel

★★★ 88% ◉◉ COUNTRY HOUSE HOTEL
Address: Park Lane, MILFORD ON SEA, SO41 OPT
Tel: 01590 643044
Fax: 01590 644490
Email: info@westoverhallhotel.com
Website: www.westoverhallhotel.com
Map ref: 3, SZ29
Directions: M3 & M27 W onto A337 to Lymington,
follow signs to Milford on Sea onto B3058, hotel
outside village centre towards cliff

Rooms: 15 (2 GF) (2 fmly) **S** £90-£140 **D** £160-£310 (incl. bkfst & dinner) **Facilities:** Wi-fi
Parking: 50

A beautiful, Grade II listed Victorian country house hotel, 150 metres from the beach, with views of the Isle of Wight and The Needles. Bedrooms have private bathrooms, tasteful furnishings and luxury Italian bed linen. There is also a 'Beach Retreat' adjacent to the hotel with two suites. Top quality New Forest produce is used to great effect in Westover Hall's fine dining restaurant, One Park Lane, as well as in the more informal Vista Bistro.

Recommended in the area

Beaulieu Palace & Motor Museum; Hurst Castle; Hengistbury Head

Chewton Glen Hotel & Spa

★★★★★ ⊛⊛⊛ COUNTRY HOUSE HOTEL

Address: Christchurch Road, NEW MILTON,
BH25 5QS
Tel: 01425 275341
Fax: 01425 272310
Email: reservations@chewtonglen.com
Website: www.chewtonglen.com
Map ref: 3, SZ29
Directions: A35 from Lyndhurst for 10m, left at
staggered junct. Follow tourist sign for hotel through
Walkford, take 2nd left
Rooms: 58 (9 GF) **Facilities:** Wi-fi ⊗ ↘ Tennis Gym Spa Sauna **Parking:** 100
Notes: ⊗ in bedrooms

The sea is just 10 minutes' walk from this superb 18th-century country-house hotel. Bedrooms are individually styled with luxurious fabrics and furnishings. All bedrooms enjoy the benefits of air conditioning, satellite TV, radio, DVD and CD players, and direct-dial telephone. There are also a number of suites, some duplex, and all with secluded private gardens. Guests can enjoy the health and beauty treatments, both traditional and modern, of the elegant high-tech spa, where everything from a massage to a facial or a body polish is available. The restaurant offers a wide variety of cuisines, using as much fresh local produce as possible and vegetarian and low-calorie dishes can be provided. The nearby New Forest offers wild mushrooms, vegetables and game; seafood may come from Christchurch and Lymington nearby. The wine list is drawn from a cellar of over 600 bins. Short residential packages are available including: Gourmet Dining Breaks, Spa Breaks and Celebration Breaks. Children of all ages are welcome at the hotel.

Recommended in the area

New Forest National Park; National Motor Museum, Beaulieu; Buckler's Hard historic village

Tylney Hall Hotel

★★★★ ◎◎ HOTEL

Address: ROTHERWICK, Hook, RG27 9AZ
Tel: 01256 764881
Fax: 01256 768141
Email: sales@tylneyhall.com
Website: www.tylneyhall.com
Map ref: 3, SU75
Directions: M3 junct 5, A287 to Basingstoke, over junct with A30, over rail bridge, towards Newnham. Right at Newnham Green. Hotel 1m on left

Rooms: 112 (40 GF) (1 fmly) **D** £220-£500 (incl. bkfst) **Facilities:** STV Wi-fi ⑨ ➤ Tennis Gym Spa
Parking: 120

A grand, Victorian Grade II listed house, Tylney Hall sits peacefully in 66 acres of rich, rolling Hampshire countryside, with the tree-lined approach setting the scene for this idyllic destination. This sense of calm is echoed throughout the grounds, where the lake, manicured lawns and magnificently restored water gardens were originally laid out by the famous gardener Gertrude Jekyll. The level of comfort is typified by 112 bedrooms and suites, all individually furnished and meticulously maintained. Palatial lounges offer the perfect location to enjoy a quiet drink or afternoon tea overlooking the grounds. Award-winning cuisine is served in the Oak Room Restaurant, where a modern cooking style with classic hallmarks combines with the best local produce. Rest and relaxation is never far away, with the luxurious health spa offering the latest treatments in tranquil surroundings, plus a gym, saunas, and indoor and outdoor pools. There is also an 18-hole golf course close by. With a range of private function rooms, including the self-contained Hampshire Suite, Tylney Hall is a popular venue for weddings, meetings and events. Tylney Hall's storybook setting is at odds with its convenient location, close to the M25, 40 minutes from Heathrow Airport and with good links into London.

Recommended in the area

Jane Austen's House; Milestones Museum; Watercress Line, heritage steam railway line

Ross-on-Wye at dusk

Bridge at Wilton

★★★★ ⊛⊛ RESTAURANT WITH ROOMS
Address: Wilton, ROSS-ON-WYE, HR9 6AA
Tel: 01989 562655
Fax: 01989 567652
Email: info@bridge-house-hotel.com
Website: www.bridge-house-hotel.com
Map ref: 2, SO52 **Directions:** Off junct A40 &
A49 into Ross-on-Wye, 300yds on left. Hotel on right
Rooms: 8 S £75-£80 D £100-£120 **Facilities:** Wi-fi
Parking: 30 **Notes:** ⊗ in bedrooms ⚲ under 14 yrs

There are eight attractively furnished en suite bedrooms at this smart Georgian country house beside a medieval bridge. It's a delightful spot, with well established gardens stretching down to the banks of the River Wye, but it's the food – served in the rustic chic dining room – that's the star attraction here. The modern British cooking is founded on top-quality local produce, including vegetables and herbs from the garden. Typical dishes include twice-baked Hereford hop soufflé with rhubarb compôte and beetroot vinaigrette, and loin of Gorsley lamb with crab tortellini, curried parsnip nage and mint oil.

Recommended in the area

Ross-on-Wye shopping; Symonds Yat; Goodrich Castle

High Street, Ross-on-Wye

HERTFORDSHIRE

Knebworth House

The Grove

★★★★★ 87% ❀❀❀ HOTEL

Address: Chandler's Cross, RICKMANSWORTH, WD3 4TG
Tel: 01923 807807
Fax: 01923 221008
Email: info@thegrove.co.uk
Website: www.thegrove.co.uk
Map ref: 3, TQ09
Directions: M25 junct 19, A411 towards Watford. Hotel on right **Rooms:** 227 (35 GF) (32 fmly)
Facilities: STV Wi-fi ❀ ❀ Gym Spa Sauna Tennis **Parking:** 400 **Notes:** ❀ in bedrooms

The history of The Grove, a magnificent 18th-century stately home set within 300 acres of park and woodland, is rich and interesting. In its heyday, having been the seat of the Earls of Clarendon, it was a venue for lavish country house parties, which royalty attended. Today, the hotel calls its mix of traditional elegance with hip, contemporary design, 'groovy grand'. The guest rooms range from the merely luxurious in the West Wing, to the positively palatial in the individually designed Mansion suites, many with fireplaces and four-poster beds. There is a choice of three dining venues, each with an outdoor terrace. Head for three-Rosette Colette's for fine dining in elegant surroundings, The Glasshouse for a gourmet buffet, or The Stables for simply presented, contemporary twists on British classics. The award-winning Sequoia spa is a tranquil sanctuary - a place to retreat, rest, workout and re-energise. The 18-hole golf course is playable all year and has been host to the World Championships. Although in the heart of the Hertfordshire countryside The Grove is just 17 minutes by train from London Euston, and three minutes from the M25, making it the perfect venue for a weekend escape with the family.

Recommended in the area

Whipsnade Wild Animal Park; St Albans Cathedral; Knebworth House

KENT

Canterbury Cathedral

Eastwell Manor

★★★★ ◉◉ HOTEL

Address: Eastwell Park, Boughton Lees, ASHFORD,
TN25 4HR
Tel: 01233 213000
Fax: 01233 635530
Email: enquiries@eastwellmanor.co.uk
Website: www.eastwellmanor.co.uk
Map ref: 4, TR04
Directions: On A251, 200yds on left when entering
Boughton Aluph **Rooms:** 62 (10 GF) (2 fmly)
S £125-£415 **D** £125-£445 (incl. bkfst) **Facilities:** STV Wi-fi ⊗ ⌇ Tennis Golf Gym Spa
Parking: 200 **Notes:** ⊗ in bedrooms

Eastwell Manor, dating back to the Norman Conquest, lies in 62 acres of grounds, including a formal
Italian garden, lawns and parkland. In the 16th century Richard Plantagenet lived here, and Queen
Victoria and King Edward VII were frequent visitors. Its age is apparent in the lounges, restaurant and
bar, with their original fireplaces, carved panelling and fine antiques. Twenty-three individually designed
bedrooms are named after previous owners. The luxury mews cottages in the grounds have been
converted from Victorian stables; each has a kitchen, sitting room and dining facilities and are available
on a self-catering basis. Complimentary Wi-fi is available throughout. The informal, all-day brasserie
in The Pavilion looks out across the countryside, while the more formal dining destination is the Manor
Restaurant with a French and modern British menu. The Pavilion Spa houses a 20-metre pool in a
Roman baths-style setting, hydrotherapy pool, sauna, jacuzzi, steam room and technogym. The beauty
and therapy area, Dreams, pampers both men and women. There is also a 20-metre outdoor heated
pool, all-weather tennis court and the 'Eastwell 9' Golf Course (2,132 yards, par 32).

Recommended in the area

Canterbury Cathedral; Sissinghurst Castle; Leeds Castle; Godinton House

LANCASHIRE

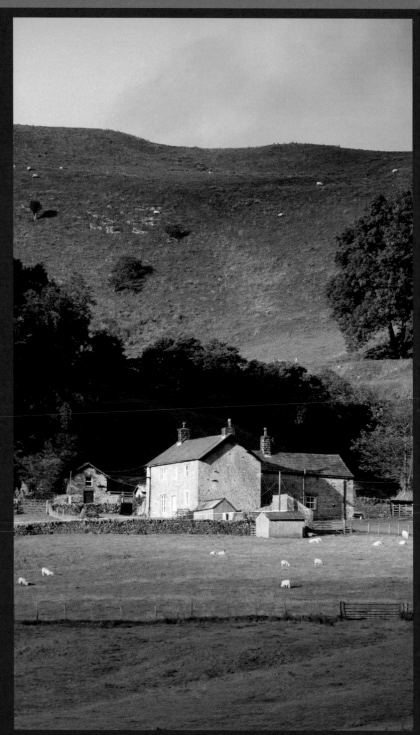

Laund Hill. Forest of Bowland

Northcote

★★★★ 84% ◎◎◎◎ SMALL HOTEL

Address: Northcote Road, LANGHO, Blackburn, BB6 8BE

Tel: 01254 240555

Fax: 01254 246568

Email: reception@northcote.com

Website: www.northcote.com

Map ref: 6, SD73

Directions: M6 junct 31, 9m to Northcote. Follow Clitheroe (A59) signs, Hotel on left before rdbt

Rooms: 14 (4 GF) (2 fmly) S £175-£210 D £200-£260 (incl. bkfst)

Facilities: STV Wi-fi **Parking:** 50 **Notes:** ⊗ in bedrooms

Built in the 1880s, Northcote still has the ambience of a Victorian family home and the focus is on eating well, as, no doubt, it was when it belonged to a textile baron. Its former ownership explains its proximity to Lancashire's industrial heartland to the south, but stretching northwards across the River Ribble is Longridge Fell and the Forest of Bowland. The excellent road network also makes it easy to reach the Yorkshire Dales. Proprietors Nigel Haworth and Craig Bancroft describe their hotel as a restaurant with rooms, and the food is certainly a very good reason to come here. Nigel is a staunch supporter of the county's many artisan food producers and, with their ingredients and organic fruit, vegetables and herbs from the hotel's own gardens, creates memorable culinary delights. The bedrooms have individual, contemporary decor that is stunning in its originality and the quality of the fabrics and wall coverings. Each room has a high-tech sound system with iPod connector, TV with 200 satellite channels, DVD and CD player and complimentary Wi-fi. Cosy bathrobes are provided, along with Molton Brown hair and skin-care products.

Recommended in the area

Clitheroe; Ribble Valley; Gawthorpe Hall (NT)

Whitewell, Forest of Bowland

Bedford Hotel

★★★ 80% HOTEL

Address: 307-313 Clifton Drive South,
LYTHAM ST ANNES, FY8 1HN
Tel: 01253 724636
Fax: 01253 729244
Email: reservations@bedford-hotel.com
Website: www.bedford-hotel.com
Map ref: 5, SD32
Directions: M55, follow airport signs to last lights.
Left through 2 sets of lights. Hotel 300yds on left
Rooms: 45 (6 GF) **Facilities:** Wi-fi Gym **Parking:** 25 **Notes:** ⊗

This popular family-run hotel is close to the town centre and the seafront, with its safe sandy beach and Victorian pier. Bedrooms vary in size and style and are elegantly appointed. Public areas include a choice of lounges, a coffee shop, fitness facilities with hydrotherapy spa pool and an impressive ballroom. The Bedford Hotel enjoys a fabulous location on the beautiful Fylde Coast, with four championship golf courses nearby.

Recommended in the area

Beach, pier and promenade; Royal Lytham and St Annes Golf Club; Blackpool

Blackpool Tower

The Town Hall, Leicester

Sketchley Grange Hotel

★★★★ 81% ◉◉ HOTEL

Address: Sketchley Lane, Burbage, HINCKLEY,
LE10 3HU
Tel: 01455 251133
Fax: 01455 631384
Email: info@sketchleygrange.co.uk
Website: www.sketchleygrange.co.uk
Map ref: 3, SP49 **Directions:** SE of town, off A5/
M69 junct 1, take B4109 to Hinckley. Left at 2nd
rdbt. 1st right onto Sketchley Lane **Rooms:** 94 (6 GF)
(9 fmly) **Facilities:** STV Wi-fi ⊗ Gym Spa Sauna **Parking:** 270 **Notes:** ⊗ in bedrooms

Motorway connections are not far away, not that you'd know from the unexpectedly tranquil location of this Mock Tudor-style hotel, surrounded by beautiful willow gardens and open country. Rooms range from luxurious Master suites, spacious enough to comfortably accommodate an emperor-size bed, to the Classic Collection of traditionally decorated en suite doubles, twins, triples and family rooms. Easily accessible ground-floor rooms with a wheel-in shower are set aside for less able guests. The honour of holding two AA Rosettes goes to The Dining Room, the elegant fine-dining restaurant serving, for example, sautéed fillet of Ayrshire beef, and poached wild turbot. The more contemporary 52° North, overlooking the beautiful gardens, has a more cosmopolitan menu, represented by Thai red chicken curry, and wild mushroom and leek tagliatelle. Here on Sundays a table magician provides entertainment. For a cappuccino or a quick bite between meetings, head for the Terrace Bistro & Bar. All overnight guests enjoy complimentary use of Romans Health and Leisure Club, which houses a 17-metre swimming pool, sauna and steam room, gym, outdoor hot tub, beauty therapy suites, hair salon and crèche. The largest of the meeting and event rooms can accommodate up to 300 delegates.

Recommended in the area

Warwick Castle; Twycross Zoo; Bosworth Battlefield Heritage Centre and Country Park

Belmont Hotel

★★★ 81% HOTEL

Address: De Montfort Street, LEICESTER, LE1 7GR
Tel: 0116 254 4773
Fax: 0116 247 0804
Email: info@belmonthotel.co.uk
Website: www.belmonthotel.co.uk
Map ref: 3, SK50
Directions: From A6 take 1st right after rail station. Hotel 200yds on left
Rooms: 75 (9 GF) (7 fmly) **Facilities:** Wi-fi Gym
Parking: 70

Owned by the Bowie family for over 70 years, this well-established, elegant town house hotel stands in the city's green and tranquil New Walk conservation area. Yet the main shops and railway station are only minutes away via a tree-lined walkway laid out in 1785 to connect the town with Victoria Park, once a racecourse. Over the years many changes have been made to the fabric of the building, but always with a sympathetic eye to its past. Individually designed, well-equipped bedrooms offer Wi-fi, TV with Freeview, radio, hospitality tray, hairdryer, direct-dial telephone, modem point and ironing facilities. The Executive rooms additionally offer a business desk, second phone and a more spacious bathroom. From the kitchen, making use of the freshest, highest quality ingredients, comes good British and continental cuisine, served in Cherry's Restaurant. In the hotel's own words, though, its 'heart' is Jamie's Lounge Bar, where you can order a lighter meal, or just have a coffee or glass of wine from a comprehensively international wine list. The Belmont is much in demand for weddings and business meetings; the largest of the nine conference rooms holds 175 delegates.

Recommended in the area

Rockingham Castle; National Space Centre; Foxton Locks; Highcross shopping quarter; Curve Theatre

Stapleford Park

★★★★ ◉◉ COUNTRY HOUSE HOTEL

Address: Stapleford, MELTON MOWBRAY,
LE14 2EF
Tel: 01572 787000
Fax: 01572 787651
Email: information@stapleford.co.uk
Website: www.staplefordpark.com
Map ref: 3, SK71
Directions: 1m SW of B676, 4m E of Melton
Mowbray & 9m W of Colsterworth

Rooms: 55 (10 fmly) **S** From £210 (incl. bkfst) **Facilities:** STV Wi-fi ⊛ Tennis Gym Spa **Parking:** 120
Sitting in 500 acres of 'Capability' Brown-designed parkland, Stapleford Park is one of England's finest
stately homes. Despite the grandeur of the 17th-century building, the hotel has a wonderfully homely
feel. Eat in the either the fine-dining award-winning Grinling Gibbons dining room or from the more
informal menu available throughout the house. There's no shortage of things to do – the Donald Steel-
designed golf course, a falconry school and clay pigeon shooting, plus archery, tennis, seven Clarins
treatment rooms, a swimming pool and gym.

Recommended in the area

Rutland Water; Burghley House; Belvoir Castle; Rockingham Castle

Belvoir Castle

Kilworth House Hotel

★★★★ ◉◉ HOTEL

Address: Lutterworth Road, NORTH KILWORTH,
LE17 6JE
Tel: 01858 880058
Fax: 01858 880349
Email: info@kilworthhouse.co.uk
Website: www.kilworthhouse.co.uk
Map ref: 3, SP68
Directions: A4304 towards Market Harborough,
after Walcote, hotel 1.5m on right
Rooms: 44 (13 GF) (2 fmly) **Facilities:** Wi-fi Fitness room **Parking:** 140 **Notes:** assist dogs only in bedrooms

This grand, Grade II listed country house sits amid 38 acres of landscaped parkland. It's an enchanting place – a blend of Victorian opulence and contemporary luxury with a warm and welcoming atmosphere. There are 11 bedrooms on the first floor of the house, including two with four-poster beds, all furnished with a mixture of antiques, rich fabrics and the latest technology. Across the knot garden courtyard are a further 33 rooms, all individually designed in an elegant, country-house style. The two-Rosette Wordsworth Restaurant, with its double oak and stained glass doors, domed ceiling, glittering chandeliers, open fireplaces and views over the knot garden, is a gloriously ornate setting for some fine modern British cuisine. For a less formal alternative, or perhaps, for morning coffee or afternoon tea take a seat in the beautifully restored Victorian Orangery, which has a special ambience both day and night. With its modern conference facilities, private dining rooms, attentive staff, beauty therapy suite, fitness room and vast grounds where Muntjac deer dart across woodland trails, and the lake is well-stocked with fish, it's no wonder Kilworth House draws in business and leisure guests in equal measure.
Recommended in the area
Kilworth Springs Golf Club; Stanford Hall; Rutland Water; Foxton Locks

LONDON

Waterloo Bridge and the South Bank

ANdAZ Liverpool Street

★★★★★ 82% ☺☺☺ HOTEL

Address: 40 Liverpool Street, LONDON, EC2M 7QN
Tel: 020 7961 1234
Fax: 020 7961 1235
Email: info.londonliv@andaz.com
Website: www.andaz.com
Map ref: 3, TQ38 **Directions:** On corner of
Liverpool St & Bishopsgate, adjacent to Liverpool St
station **Rooms:** 267 **Facilities:** STV Wi-fi Gym

Pioneer of Hyatt's new funky, fashionable and sophisticated ANdAZ concept, this City of London hotel has been carved out of the late-Victorian, former Great Eastern Hotel. The interior, however, is cutting-edge modern. Bedroom decoration and furnishings are truly different; all room rates include Wi-fi, local landline calls, a non-alcoholic mini-bar and health club access. As for dining, it would be a picky customer who shunned all five appealing options: modern British in 1901 Restaurant; Japanese in Miyako; fresh seafood in Catch Restaurant & Champagne Bar; brasserie style in Eastway; and hearty meals and real ales in the George Pub.

Recommended in the area

Spitalfields Market; St. Paul's Cathedral; Whitechapel Art Gallery

Fountain in Regent's Park

The Landmark London

★★★★★ ◉◉ HOTEL

Address: 222 Marylebone Road, LONDON, NW1 6JQ

Tel: 020 7631 8000

Fax: 020 7631 8080

Email: reservations@thelandmark.co.uk

Website: www.landmarklondon.co.uk

Map ref: 3, TQ38 **Directions:** Adjacent to Marylebone Station **Rooms:** 300 (64 fmly) Superior Room £239-£550; Deluxe Room £269-£600

Facilities: STV Wi-fi ⓦ Gym Spa Sauna **Notes:** ⊗

The Landmark London ranks among the finest of the capital's grand dame hotels. Built in 1899, it personifies classic Victorian opulence, and is perfectly located in one of London's most upmarket districts, close to all of the capital's main attractions. The guest rooms are some of the largest in London, averaging 55 square metres, and all 300 have an executive desk, private bar, high-speed internet access as well as a marble bathroom. The Landmark's spectacular Winter Garden restaurant is situated beneath the soaring eight-storey glass atrium and offers seasonal modern British cuisine, and is also popular for brunch and afternoon tea. For a more informal setting, the twotwentytwo restaurant and bar fits the bill, offering a relaxing place to meet, eat and drink. Meanwhile for late-night drinks, champagne and cocktails, the Mirror Bar is the place to head for. The exclusive Landmark Spa and Health Club offers a complete wellbeing experience; it features a 15-metre chlorine-free swimming pool, a heat therapy sanarium, a steam room, whirlpool, a state-of-the-art gym and four lavish treatment rooms. For pure indulgence, try one of the ESPA or VOYA spa treatments.

Recommended in the area

Marylebone High Street; Regent's Park; London Zoo; Wembley Stadium

Meliá White House

★★★★ 80% ◉◉ HOTEL

Address: Albany Street, Regents Park, LONDON, NW1 3UP
Tel: 020 7391 3000
Fax: 020 7388 0091
Email: melia.white.house@solmelia.com
Website: www.melia-whitehouse.com
Map ref: 3, TQ38
Directions: Opp Gt Portland St tube station
Rooms: 581 (7 fmly) **Facilities:** STV Wi-fi Gym Spa
Notes: ⊗ in bedrooms

Managed by the Spanish Solmelia company, this impressive art deco property is located just to the south of Regents Park, and only a few blocks north of Oxford Street. Spacious public areas offer a high degree of comfort and include an elegant cocktail bar. The en suite bedrooms come in a variety of sizes and are comfortable, stylish and well equipped with air-conditioning, hairdryer, magnifying mirror, tea and coffee tray, safe, trouser press, satellite TV, radio, direct-dial phone, and high-speed Wi-fi connection via laptop or TV. Room service is available 24 hours a day. Diners looking for somewhere fashionable to eat will approve of L'Albufera, an elegant, award-winning Spanish restaurant; for greater informality, The Place Brasserie offers buffet breakfast, lunch and dinner, with an emphasis on Mediterranean cuisine. Relax in comfortable Longfords Bar, while listening to live music (from Wednesdays to Saturdays). Among the hotel's other amenities are an air-conditioned gym with the latest cardiovascular equipment, and a modern therapy room full of treatments that 'alleviate and rejuvenate'. For those looking to stay longer in the capital, there are various apartments to choose from. The hotel also has a business centre and eight conference and banqueting or meeting rooms.

Recommended in the area

Madame Tussaud's; Regent's Park; Oxford Street; Camden Town

York & Albany

★★★★★ 🏵🏵🏵 🔔

RESTAURANT WITH ROOMS

Address: 127-129 Parkway, LONDON, NW1 7PS
Tel: 020 7387 5700
Fax: 020 7255 9250
E-mail: yandareception@gordonramsay.com
Web: www.gordonramsay.com
Map ref: 4, TQ38
Directions: overlooking Regent's Park
Rooms: 10 D £205-£675 (room only)
Facilities: STV Wi-fi **Notes:** ⊗ in bedrooms

In the early 19th century, architect John Nash designed this majestic building on the edge of Regents Park as part of his area master plan of elegant crescents, terraces and villas. In September 2008, Gordon Ramsay and his then protégé Angela Hartnett arrived to transform what had been a pub into a stunning restaurant over two floors, a vibrant bar, an enticing deli called Nonna's, and highly appointed bedrooms and suites, where period antiques share space with the latest technology and guest goodies. Using produce from overall kitchen supremo Hartnett's favourite suppliers, head chef Colin Buchan creates seasonal, modern European dishes that have helped the restaurant earn three AA Rosettes. By way of example, you can expect pan-fried grey mullet with celeriac fondant, mushroom forestière and pancetta lardons; osso bucco with wet polenta and glazed Chantenay carrots; and roasted partridge with smoked garlic pommes purée, spinach and baby artichokes. The bar menu includes wood-fired pizzas, and if you detect other Italian influences bear in mind that Hartnett's Italian grandmother taught her how to make the country's classic dishes. You can, of course, expect a very good wine selection. Two private dining rooms can be turned into reception and meeting rooms.

Recommended in the area

London Zoo; British Museum; Regent Street

Plaza on the River - Club & Residence

★★★★★ 82% TOWN HOUSE HOTEL

Address: 18 Albert Embankment, LONDON, SE1 7TJ
Tel: 020 7769 2525 **Fax:** 020 7769 2524
Email: sales@plazaontheriver.co.uk
Website: www.plazaontheriver.co.uk
Map ref: 3, TQ38 **Directions:** From Houses of Parliament
onto Millbank, left, Lambeth Bridge. At rdbt 3rd exit onto Albert
Embankment **Rooms:** 65 **Facilities:** STV Wi-fi Gym
Parking: 10
Notes: ⊗ in bedrooms

For outstanding views of the River Thames, Tate Britain, the Houses of Parliament and the London Eye you can hardly better those from this modern South Bank hotel. Fully air-conditioned studios, and one and two-bedroom suites have all been finished to a very high standard, and all benefit from an inclusive kitchen area, plasma TV, CD and DVD player and high-speed Wi-fi. The restaurant, Chino Latino Brasserie, serves modern Pan-Asian cuisine, such as sirloin steak on hot rocks with soya, mirin and garlic; monkfish tail with yuzu kusho dressing; and tofu with crispy bonito and spring onion. Dishes are brought in stages to the table to be shared. Light meals are served in the Latino part, which is essentially a cocktail bar and lounge. The hotel has also joined forces with Fakhreldine, a famous Piccadilly restaurant that will provide traditional Lebanese food for a business lunch or private dinner. You might, however, prefer to arrange for your fridge to be pre-stocked with groceries from Fortnum & Mason before you arrive, make use of 24-hour room service, or even arrange a private chef and butler. Residents may use the Fitness Suite and Malina Aveda Lifestyle Spa & Salon.

Recommended in the area

Westminster Abbey; Imperial War Museum; Buckingham Palace

London Bridge Hotel

★★★★ 79% HOTEL

Address: 8-18 London Bridge Street, LONDON, SE1 9SG

Tel: 020 7855 2200

Fax: 020 7855 2233

Email: sales@londonbridgehotel.com

Website: www.londonbridgehotel.com

Map ref: 3, TQ38

Directions: Access through London Bridge Station (bus/taxi yard), into London Bridge St (one-way). Hotel on left, 50yds from station

Rooms: 138 (12 fmly) **S** £112-£289 **D** £112-£289 **Facilities:** STV Wi-fi Gym **Notes:** ⊗ in bedrooms

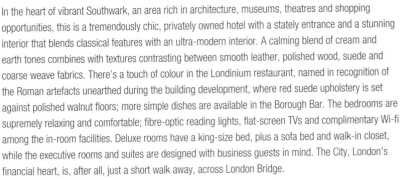

In the heart of vibrant Southwark, an area rich in architecture, museums, theatres and shopping opportunities, this is a tremendously chic, privately owned hotel with a stately entrance and a stunning interior that blends classical features with an ultra-modern interior. A calming blend of cream and earth tones combines with textures contrasting between smooth leather, polished wood, suede and coarse weave fabrics. There's a touch of colour in the Londinium restaurant, named in recognition of the Roman artefacts unearthed during the building development, where red suede upholstery is set against polished walnut floors; more simple dishes are available in the Borough Bar. The bedrooms are supremely relaxing and comfortable; fibre-optic reading lights, flat-screen TVs and complimentary Wi-fi among the in-room facilities. Deluxe rooms have a king-size bed, plus a sofa bed and walk-in closet, while the executive rooms and suites are designed with business guests in mind. The City, London's financial heart, is, after all, just a short walk away, across London Bridge.

Recommended in the area

Tate Modern; Shakespeare's Globe Theatre The London Dungeon

Park Plaza County Hall

★★★★ 79% HOTEL

Address: 1 Addington Street, LONDON, SE1 7RY
Tel: 020 7021 1800
Fax: 020 7021 1801
Email: ppchsales@pphe.com
Website: www.parkplazacountyhall.com
Map ref: 3, TQ38
Directions: From Houses of Parliament cross
Westminster Bridge (A302). At rdbt turn left. 1st right
into Addington St. Hotel on left

Rooms: 398 (303 fmly) **S** £99-£1000 **D** £99-£1000 **Facilities:** STV Wi-fi Gym Spa Sauna **Parking:** 3

A bowler-hatted attendant greets guests arriving at this contemporary, design-led hotel just south of Westminster Bridge, handy for Waterloo mainline and underground stations. These days, this part of the South Bank has a lot going for it, not least the street market in Lower Marsh round the corner and The Old Vic theatre at its far end. In fact, to describe this once lacklustre area as lively would be no exaggeration. The hotel's air-conditioned bedrooms, studio apartments and suites, most with kitchenettes, have a plasma-screen TV and interactive entertainment systems providing music and movies on demand. The views over the rooftops are fantastic, especially at night. Spectrum Restaurant, on the mezzanine floor, underneath the 14-storey atrium, basks in daylight from its stunning glass front; its outside tables make dining on a British, Mediterranean or classic dish even more enjoyable. Spectrum Bar and Café serves a hearty breakfast, coffee during the day and lunchtime favourites, then in the evening it transforms into a chic after-work cocktail bar, where you can also find speciality European beers. There are six meeting rooms, the largest accommodating up to 100 guests, an executive lounge and a fully-equipped spa and fitness centre.

Recommended in the area

London Aquarium; National Theatre; Big Ben

Park Plaza Riverbank London

★★★★ 77% ☺ HOTEL

Address: 18 Albert Embankment, LONDON,
SE1 7SP

Tel: 020 7958 8000

Fax: 020 7769 2400

Email: rppres@pphe.com

Website: www.parkplazariverbank.com

Map ref: 3, TQ38

Directions: From Houses of Parliament onto
Millbank, at rdbt left onto Lambeth Bridge. At rdbt 3rd
exit onto Albert Embankment **Rooms:** 394 S £79.35-£228.85 D £79.35-£228.85

Facilities: Wi-fi Gym **Parking:** 10

"Any time you're Lambeth way..." So begins the song from a 1937 musical that brought fame to Lambeth Walk, the little street that runs a couple of blocks behind this modern Thames-side hotel. Sadly, it was flattened in the Blitz and its post-war successor doesn't have quite the same working-class charisma, so unless you're very curious, you will most likely focus your attention on the other side of the river, Tate Britain, and to its right, the Houses of Parliament. Views of these iconic buildings come at no extra charge from some of the efficiently designed, air-conditioned rooms and suites, all of which have a flat-screen TV and large work desk. On the ground floor is Chino Latino, the hotel's East-meets-West brasserie, whose fusion cuisine has earned it a much-coveted AA Rosette. Fresh sushi and seafood abound, with other options represented by soft shell crab and crispy avocado nigiri; black cod in miso; 28-day mature Casterbridge rib-eye steak; daily specials and children's meals. A bento-box menu is served at lunchtime, while the Latino Bar & Lounge serves modern European food in surroundings that can't fail to impress. Other facilities include Wi-fi throughout, high-tech conference rooms, business centre, and fitness centre.

Recommended in the area

Westminster Abbey; National Gallery; Southbank Centre

The Halkin Hotel

★★★★★ ◉◉◉ TOWN HOUSE HOTEL
Address: Halkin Street, Belgravia, LONDON,
SW1X 7DJ
Tel: 020 7333 1000
Fax: 020 7333 1100
Email: res@halkin.como.bz
Website: www.halkin.como.bz
Map ref: 3, TQ38
Directions: Between Belgrave Sq & Grosvenor Place.
Via Chapel St into Headfort Place, left into Halkin St

Rooms: 41 **D** £282-£528.75 **Facilities:** STV Wi-fi Gym **Notes:** ⊗ in bedrooms

Behind the Georgian-style façade is one of London's smartest hotels. Discreetly situated in a quiet street, The Halkin is surrounded by elegant buildings, smart shops, and is just a short stroll from Hyde Park Corner, Knightsbridge and Buckingham Palace. Inside, the style is contemporary Italian, much of the impact being derived from the use of luxury textiles in cool shades of taupe and cream. The bedrooms and suites are equipped to the highest standard with smart, all marble bathrooms – among the largest in London – and many extras, including three dual-line phones with voice mail and modem connection, high-speed internet, fax, interactive cable TV with CD and DVD services, air conditioning and personal bar. Each floor has been designed thematically – earth, wind, fire, water and the universe. Public areas include a lounge, an airy bar for light meals, drinks and cocktails, and then there's Nahm, David Thompson's award-winning Thai restaurant. Service from Armani-clad staff is attentive and friendly. Guests may use the gym or enjoy the COMO Shambhala Health Club at The Halkin's sister hotel, The Metropolitan.

Recommended in the area

Buckingham Palace; Harrods & Harvey Nichols, Knightsbridge; Hyde Park

Jumeirah Carlton Tower

★★★★★ ◉◉ HOTEL

Address: Cadogan Place, LONDON, SW1X 9PY
Tel: 020 7235 1234
Fax: 020 7235 9129
Email: jctinfo@jumeirah.com
Website: www.jumeirahcarltontower.com
Map ref: 3, TQ38
Directions: A4 towards Knightsbridge, right onto Sloane St. Hotel on left before Cadogan Place
Facilities: STV Wi-fi ⌖ Gym Spa **Parking:** 85
Notes: ⊗

The Jumeirah Carlton Tower is situated in fashionable Knightsbridge, only moments away from Harrods, Harvey Nichols and Sloane Street's exclusive boutiques. The hotel features bedrooms and luxury suites with panoramic views over London's skyline. There is a wide choice of excellent dining options, including the Chinoiserie, popular for afternoon tea, and the renowned, award-winning Rib Room. At the 9th-floor health club and spa, members can benefit from the gym, state-of-the-art golf simulator, aerobics studio, sauna, steam room, 20-metre pool and a full range of beauty treatments.

Recommended in the area

Hyde Park; Buckingham Palace; Science Museum

Changing the guard at Buckingham Palace

Sofitel London St James

★★★★★ 86% ◉ HOTEL

Address: 6 Waterloo Place, LONDON, SW1Y 4AN
Tel: 020 7747 2200
Fax: 020 7747 2210
Email: H3144@sofitel.com
Website: www.sofitel.com
Map ref: 3, TQ38
Directions: 3 mins walk from Piccadilly Circus and Trafalgar Square
Rooms: 185 (98 fmly) **S** £200-£300 **D** £220-£320
Facilities: STV Wi-fi Gym Spa

A hidden gem in the centre of London, Sofitel London St James lies discreetly at the heart of the prestigious area of St James, moments away from Piccadilly Circus, Trafalgar Square and theatreland. Created in a magnificent Grade II listed building, the hotel's contemporary and luxurious bedrooms and suites are equipped to the highest standard, with world-class MyBed beds, interactive high definition TVs, media hubs, laptop safes, hairdryers, ironing boards and tea- and coffee-making facilities. In addition to the restaurant, St James bar, with its wide range of champagnes and cocktails, provides the ideal meeting place before dinner, after a show or just for a nightcap. The unique and exceptional Rose Lounge is feminine, warm and cosy with its cream and pink colour scheme – the perfect setting to enjoy a traditional afternoon tea to a backdrop of music from the hotel's resident harpist. Should you wish to unwind some more, head to the award-winning So SPA by Sofitel, with its five contemporary treatment rooms as well as a hammam. The hotel also offers advanced fitness and wellness equipment in the gym, So FIT by Sofitel. For business and functions there are 12 dining and meeting rooms featuring state-of-the-art technology.

Recommended in the area

St James's Park; Buckingham Palace; Trafalgar Square

Cavendish London

★★★★ 81% ◉ HOTEL

Address: 81 Jermyn Street, LONDON, SW1Y 6JF
Tel: 020 7930 2111
Fax: 020 7839 2125
Email: info@thecavendishlondon.com
Website: www.thecavendishlondon.com
Map ref: 3, TQ38
Directions: From Piccadilly, (pass The Ritz), 1st right into Dukes St before Fortnum & Mason
Rooms: 230 (12 fmly) **Facilities:** STV Wi-fi
Parking: 50 **Notes:** ⊗ in bedrooms

Situated on the prestigious Jermyn Street, in the heart of Piccadilly, the smart Cavendish Hotel offers guests the ultimate in luxury. Although the location makes it ideal for sampling the thrill of both London's theatres and its renowned shopping opportunities, it also provides a chance to escape the hustle and bustle of the city. It was run in Edwardian times by Rosa Lewis, the 'Duchess of Duke Street', famous for her hospitality and cooking, and the tradition continues to this day. Inside, however, the hotel now features cutting-edge design, carried through from the public areas to the bedrooms, which have some of the best views in London. All guest rooms – including spacious executive rooms and suites – boast elegant furnishings, subtle lighting and clean, uncluttered lines, complemented by Villeroy and Boch bathrooms. Each comes fully equipped with the latest technology, including flat-screen LCD TV with over 600 channels and high-speed broadband. The AA Rosette-awarded David Britton at The Cavendish Restaurant serves an indulgent breakfast, as well as informal lunches and dinners, and the emphasis is on British cuisine using sustainably sourced ingredients. The monthly changing menus feature the best of seasonal and regional produce.

Recommended in the area

Fortnum & Mason; Buckingham Palace; Piccadilly Circus

Park Plaza Victoria London

★★★★ 78% ◉ HOTEL

Address: 239 Vauxhall Bridge Road, LONDON,
SW1V 1EQ
Tel: 020 7769 9999 & 7769 9800
Fax: 020 7769 9998
Email: info@victoriaparkplaza.com
Website: www.parkplaza.com
Map ref: 3, TQ38
Directions: Turn right from Victoria Station
Rooms: 299 Facilities: STV Wi-fi Gym Spa Sauna
Parking: 36

A smart, modern hotel two minutes from Victoria mainline railway station, from which frequent services run to London Gatwick airport and much of south-east England. From the associated underground station tube trains serve most parts of the capital, while down the road is Victoria coach station, with extensive nationwide connections. The hotel's minimalist-styled lobby leads to public areas including an elegant bar, with live music mid-week, a popular coffee lounge and the AA Rosette-awarded JB's restaurant, which follows the contemporary theme with floor-to-ceiling windows and a lengthy, cosmopolitan menu of both classic and modern European cuisine. Thus dinner could comprise seared duck with watercress and pea-shoot salad; followed by veal cutlet with spinach purée, caramelised shallots and anchovies; and, finally, apple tart with cinnamon ice cream. Guest rooms are divided into superior, executive and studio; in addition there are spacious one-and two-bedroom serviced apartments on two dedicated floors. All rooms feature a large comfortable bed with soft linen, and a marble-and-glass bathroom with bath and shower. The Fitness Suite, brimming with weights, resistance machines, cardiovascular equipment, sauna, steam room, and beauty treatments should keep the health-conscious off the streets (although there's plenty to do for those who do go out).

Recommended in the area

Buckingham Palace; Hyde Park; West End theatres and shops

The Draycott Hotel

★★★★★ 81% TOWN HOUSE HOTEL

Address: 26 Cadogan Gardens, LONDON, SW3 2RP

Tel: 020 7730 6466

Fax: 020 7730 0236

Email: reservations@draycotthotel.com

Website: www.draycotthotel.com

Map ref: 3, TQ38

Directions: From Sloane Sq station towards Peter Jones, keep to left. At Kings Rd take 1st right into Cadogan Gdns, 2nd right, hotel on left

Rooms: 35 (2GF) (9 fmly) **Facilities:** STV Wi-fi

Combining Edwardian grandeur with the feel of a private residence, albeit a luxurious one, the hotel is a skilful conversion of three elegant town houses. It is part of the Cadogan estate, built by the eponymous peer around Sloane Square, the hub of this ever-fashionable district. The bedrooms all have high ceilings, fireplaces and carefully selected antiques. Each is named after a theatrical personality and decorated around a print, poster or other memento associated with that character. More practical considerations include a well-proportioned en suite bathroom, air conditioning, satellite TV and CD music system, and Sea Island sheets covering the specially made large beds with some rooms looking out over the garden. Start the day in the Breakfast Room, adorned with masks of famous artistes, such as Dame Kiri Te Kanawa, and framed programmes of plays performed at the nearby Royal Court Theatre. Although there is no formal restaurant, a 24-hour room service menu offers a selection of seasonal meals and snacks. There is also a private dining room that combines the decadence of The Draycott Hotel with the cosiness of a private home. The fully air-conditioned, oak-panelled Donald Wolfit Suite is a conference room with its own private garden square.

Recommended in the area

Harrods; Hyde Park; Kensington Gardens Serpentine Gallery; Natural History Museum; V&A Museum

The Capital

★★★★★ TOWN HOUSE HOTEL

Address: Basil Street, Knightsbridge, LONDON, SW3 1AT

Tel: 020 7589 5171

Fax: 020 7225 0011

Email: reservations@capitalhotel.co.uk

Website: www.capitalhotel.co.uk

Map ref: 3, TQ38

Directions: 20yds from Harrods & Knightsbridge tube station

Rooms: 49 S from £240 D from £320 **Facilities:** STV Wi-fi **Notes:** ⊗

Just yards from Harrods, Harvey Nichols and Sloane Street, and within easy reach of the West End, this Hotel offers luxury accommodation and personal service in the heart of one of London's most prestigious neighbourhoods. Opened in 1971 by David Levin, it is to this day privately owned and run by the Levin family. Muted tones characterise the chic decor, which combines contemporary and antique furniture. The Capital's 49 bedrooms and suites come in a variety of styles, but each has a luxurious marble bathroom and an interactive television system with satellite TV, email and movies on demand. All the suites and double rooms have super-king-size beds with handmade mattresses and Egyptian cotton bedding. The Capital Restaurant has long held a reputation for being one of the finest in the country, and that looks set to continue with the appointment of award-winning French chef Jérôme Ponchelle (the AA Rosette award was not confirmed at the time of going to press). Afternoon tea is served in The Capital's elegant lounge, and cocktails are a speciality in the stylish bar.

Recommended in the area

Harrods; Buckingham Palace; Hyde Park

The Levin

★★★★ TOWN HOUSE HOTEL

Address: 28 Basil Street, Knightsbridge, LONDON, SW3 1AS
Tel: 020 7589 6286
Fax: 020 7823 7826
Email: reservations@thelevin.co.uk
Website: www.thelevinhotel.co.uk
Map ref: 3, TQ38
Directions: 20yds from Harrods & Knightsbridge tube station
Rooms: 12 (1 GF) **S** from £255 **D** from £285 (incl. bkfst) **Facilities:** STV Wi-fi
Notes: ⊗

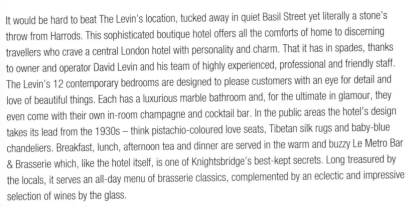

It would be hard to beat The Levin's location, tucked away in quiet Basil Street yet literally a stone's throw from Harrods. This sophisticated boutique hotel offers all the comforts of home to discerning travellers who crave a central London hotel with personality and charm. That it has in spades, thanks to owner and operator David Levin and his team of highly experienced, professional and friendly staff. The Levin's 12 contemporary bedrooms are designed to please customers with an eye for detail and love of beautiful things. Each has a luxurious marble bathroom and, for the ultimate in glamour, they even come with their own in-room champagne and cocktail bar. In the public areas the hotel's design takes its lead from the 1930s – think pistachio-coloured love seats, Tibetan silk rugs and baby-blue chandeliers. Breakfast, lunch, afternoon tea and dinner are served in the warm and buzzy Le Metro Bar & Brasserie which, like the hotel itself, is one of Knightsbridge's best-kept secrets. Long treasured by the locals, it serves an all-day menu of brasserie classics, complemented by an eclectic and impressive selection of wines by the glass.

Recommended in the area

Harrods; Hyde Park; South Kensington museums

Cannizaro House

★★★★ 80% ◎◎ COUNTRY HOUSE HOTEL

Address: West Side, Wimbledon Common,
LONDON, SW19 4UE
Tel: 020 8879 1464
Fax: 020 8879 7338
Email: info@cannizarohouse.com
Website: www.cannizarohouse.com
Map ref: 3, TQ38
Directions: From A3 follow A219 signed Wimbledon
into Parkside, right onto Cannizaro Rd, sharp right
onto Westside Common **Rooms:** 46 (5 GF) (10 fmly) **Facilities:** STV Wi-fi **Parking:** 95

Cannizaro House, an 18th-century Georgian mansion, is a true little gem tucked away in an idyllic location in SW19. The hotel sits just on the edge of Cannizaro Park and Wimbledon Common, and has beautifully designed bedrooms plus six meeting rooms, two with their own terrace, making it a perfect destination for business and pleasure. The two-Rosette restaurant serves imaginative modern European food, while the bar offers an extensive cocktail selection and drinks list.

Recommended in the area

Hampton Court; Chessington World of Adventures; Wimbledon Lawn Tennis Museum

Brown's Hotel

★★★★★ ◎◎◎ HOTEL

Address: Albemarle Street, Mayfair,
LONDON, W1S 4BP
Tel: 020 7493 6020
Fax: 020 7493 9381
Email: reservations.browns@roccofortecollection.com
Website: www.roccofortecollection.com
Map ref: 3, TQ38
Directions: Nearest tube Station: Green Park
Rooms: 117 S £240-£425 D £280-£3200
Facilities: STV Wi-fi Gym Spa **Notes:** ⊗

Brown's has a fascinating history and has hosted many distinguished guests since it opened as London's first hotel in 1837. This legendary establishment blends a traditional English style with an elegant contemporary twist to create a chic and sophisticated atmosphere together with intuitive service. All the luxurious guest rooms and suites are equipped with the latest technology. HIX at The Albemarle offers classic British cuisine; The Donovan Bar is a fashionable London meeting place, while the English Tea Room is the perfect place for afternoon tea.

Recommended in the area

Bond Street shopping; the West End; Green Park

124

The Langham, London

★★★★★ 85% HOTEL

Address: Portland Place, LONDON, W1B 1JA
Tel: 020 7636 1000
Fax: 020 7323 2340
Email: lon.info@langhamhotels.com
Website: www.langhamlondon.com
Map ref: 3, TQ38
Directions: N of Regent St, left opposite All Soul's Church
Rooms: 380 (5 fmly) **S** £185-£7000 **D** £185-£7000
Facilities: STV Wi-fi ⓣ Gym Spa Sauna **Notes:** ⊗

The Langham, London has been enchanting guests since it opened as Europe's first 'grand hotel' in 1865. From the grandeur of its elegant entrance to the timeless style of its public rooms and bedrooms, this certainly ranks among London's top luxury hotels. All 380 exquisitely appointed guest rooms evoke a warm, residential feel. Choose from the modern and elegant Grand rooms or the traditionally styled Classic rooms. For breakfast, lunch and dinner. Roux at The Landau offers classically constructed French dishes together with some classic British dishes. The chic and glamorous bar, Artesian, serves imaginative cocktails and houses a selection of over 70 rums. Afternoon tea is served in the dazzling Palm Court which was awarded London's Top Afternoon Tea 2010 by the Tea Guild. Choose from either the Wonderland traditional afternoon tea or the unique Bijoux Tea, inspired by the collections of top jewellery designers. The luxury Chuan Spa offers rejuvinating treatments based on the philosophies of Traditional Chinese Medicine. The hotel also features a state-of-the-art gym, 16-metre pool, men and women's saunas, steam rooms and solarium.

Recommended in the area

The Wallace Collection; Hyde Park; Trafalgar Square

Hyatt Regency London - The Churchill

★★★★★ 82% ◉◉◉ HOTEL

Address: 30 Portman Square, LONDON, W1H 7BH
Tel: 020 7486 5800
Fax: 020 7486 1255
Email: london.churchill@hyatt.com
Website: www.london.churchill.hyatt.com
Map ref: 3, TQ38
Directions: From Marble Arch rdbt, follow signs for Oxford Circus onto Oxford St. Left turn after 2nd lights onto Portman St. Hotel on left **Rooms:** 444 S £218-£470 D £218-£470 **Facilities:** STV Wi-fi Tennis Gym **Notes:** ⊗

In the heart of the West End, this hotel is perfectly placed for London's main attractions. Elegant bedrooms and suites offer extreme comfort and many thoughtful extras. Dining experiences include seasonal dishes in the The Montagu and top-notch Italian cuisine in the Locanda Locatelli restaurant.

Recommended in the area

Buckingham Palace; Hyde Park; Theatreland

The Albert Memorial, Hyde Park

Park Plaza Sherlock Holmes London

★★★★ 76% ◉ HOTEL

Address: 108 Baker Street, LONDON, W1U 6LJ
Tel: 020 7486 6161 **Fax:** 020 7958 5211
Email: info@sherlockholmeshotel.com
Website: www.sherlockholmeshotel.com
Map ref: 3,TQ38 **Directions:** From Marylebone Flyover onto Marylebone Rd. At Baker St right for hotel on left **Rooms:** 119 (20 fmly)
Facilities: STV Wi-fi Gym

Well placed for several underground and main line railway stations, and within a Baskerville hound's bark of Holmes's 'residence' at 221B Baker Street, this chic, modern boutique hotel used to be a pair of 18th-century townhouses. Its beautifully decorated air-conditioned bedrooms and suites are equipped with the latest technology, including high-speed internet access and international power sockets, while sliding frosted glass doors maximise bathroom space. Public rooms include a popular bar and Sherlock's Grill, which has smart leather seating, white linen tablecloths and open-plan dining. Awarded an AA Rosette, the Grill serves modern European cuisine, most cooking being done over a charcoal grill or in a mesquite-wood-burning oven. On Sundays, when the restaurant is closed, a full bar menu offers Mediterranean tapas, pizzas, salads and other light meals to eat in the bar itself, the lounge or taken outside to tables on the bustling pavement. On the lower ground floor is a fitness centre with gym, sauna, steam room and beauty treatments. The hotel has teamed up with a company that stages interactive murder mystery and comedy entertainment, which following a taxing corporate team-building exercise in one of the well-equipped function rooms, could be just what today's young execs need.

Recommended in the area

Madame Tussauds; Regents Park; Wallace Collection

Lancaster London

★★★★ 82% ◉◉ HOTEL
Address: Lancaster Terrace, LONDON, W2 2TY
Tel: 020 7262 6737
Fax: 020 7724 3191
Email: book@lancasterlondon.com
Website: www.lancasterlondon.com
Map ref: 3, TQ38
Directions: Adjacent to Lancaster Gate underground station, 5 min walk to Paddington Station
Rooms: 416 (11 fmly) **Facilities:** STV Wi-fi
Parking: 65 **Notes:** ⊗ in bedrooms

There's one thing guests at Lancaster London must surely always agree on – the views are breathtaking. With Hyde Park directly to the south, and vistas east to the City of London, the hotel has arguably the best outlook in the capital. And those stunning views can be enjoyed from on high in the superior bedrooms or from the hotel's restaurants. Of course, you needn't just see the heart of the city from behind glass – from here you can easily venture out and explore, with Marble Arch and the plethora of Oxford Street shops just an easy stroll from the hotel, and Harrods and the rest of Knightsbridge only 10 minutes by taxi. Even Heathrow Airport is a mere 20-minute ride on the Heathrow Express from nearby Paddington Railway Station. Alongside world-class guest service and a strong environmental ethos, the hotel boasts an elegant Lounge Bar, two award-winning restaurants and some of London's largest, most flexible banqueting and event facilities. Designed to be the perfect base for both business and leisure visits to the city, the 416 guest rooms offer every luxury, with beautiful oak furniture, deep-pile carpets and exquisite marble bathrooms. Modern facilities include flat-screen TVs, high-speed Wi-fi access and multi-lingual voicemail.

Recommended in the area

Kensington Gardens and Hyde Park; Marble Arch; Royal Albert Hall

Royal Garden Hotel

★★★★★ ◉◉◉ HOTEL

Address: 2-24 Kensington High Street, LONDON,
W8 4PT

Tel: 020 7937 8000

Fax: 020 7361 1991

Email: sales@royalgardenhotel.co.uk

Website: www.royalgardenhotel.co.uk

Map ref: 3, TQ38

Directions: Next to Kensington Palace

Rooms: 394 **S** £198.58-£245.58

D £233.83-£280.83 **Facilities:** STV Wi-fi Gym Spa **Notes:** ⊗ in bedrooms

In the heart of Kensington, the Royal Garden Hotel is the perfect place to stay whether on business or exploring London. There are 394 beautifully appointed bedrooms to choose from, including 37 suites, plus two restaurants, three bars, a 24-hour business centre and 24-hour room service. The hotel also has a choice of 10 conference and banqueting rooms that can accommodate up to 550 delegates. The Soma centre is the holistic health centre and spa, offering a gym, sauna and steam room, plus a wide range of beauty treatments and classes in yoga, Pilates and kick boxing. Head to the award-winning Min Jiang restaurant on the 10th floor for an authentic Chinese experience in an elegant setting looking out over Kensington Gardens, Hyde Park and the London skyline beyond. Enjoy superb dim sum and be sure not to miss the famous Beijing duck roasted in a special wood-burning oven. Alternatively, the Park Terrace restaurant, lounge and bar on the ground floor is open for breakfast, lunch, afternoon tea, dinner and all-day snacks. Here, the setting is relaxed and informal, the focus is on fresh British produce, and there are large windows through which to enjoy the vista of Kensington Gardens and Palace.

Recommended in the area

Harrods; Hyde Park; Kensington Gardens Serpentine Gallery; Natural History Museum; V&A Museum

Bridge at Richmond-upon-Thames

Bingham

★★★ 81% ◉◉◉ TOWN HOUSE HOTEL

Address: 61-63 Petersham Road,
RICHMOND UPON THAMES, TW10 6UT
Tel: 020 8940 0902
Fax: 020 8948 8737
Email: info@thebingham.co.uk
Website: www.thebingham.co.uk
Map ref: 3, TQ38
Directions: On A307
Rooms: 15 (2 fmly) **S** £130-£170 **D** £130-£285
Facilities: Wi-fi **Parking:** 8 **Notes:** ⊗ in bedrooms

A chic Georgian townhouse, restaurant and bar right on the River Thames, close to the town centre and, for those who like unusual museums, even closer to that belonging to Royal British Legion's poppy factory. In 1821, Lady Anne Bingham, daughter of the 2nd Lord Lucan, added the wonderfully ornate room now known as the Bingham Bar, and poets Katherine Harris Bradley and Edith Emma Cooper, who wrote together as Michael Field, lived here later that century. Refurbished to the max, the lavish interior features statement chandeliers and mirrored walls, and it is plain to see that similar care has been taken in designing the air-conditioned guest rooms, all featuring Art Deco furniture (two with four-posters), digital TVs with DVD players, complimentary Wi-fi and built-in music systems with dedicated music library. River and Super River Rooms not only enjoy the obvious views, but whirlpool baths too. The AA has awarded three Rosettes to the softly lit restaurant, where modern British dishes include squab pigeon; slow-cooked suckling pig; and roast halibut, all extremely imaginatively accompanied. The cocktail bar is a glamorous place for afternoon tea, or something stronger, which you can take out to the terrace overlooking the river.

Recommended in the area

Kew Gardens; Hampton Court; Wimbledon Lawn Tennis

The Liver Building, Liverpool

RiverHill Hotel

★★★ 80% HOTEL

Address: Talbot Road, Prenton,
BIRKENHEAD, CH43 2HJ
Tel: 0151 653 3773
Fax: 0151 653 7162
Email: reception@theriverhill.co.uk
Website: www.theriverhill.co.uk
Map ref: 5, SJ38
Directions: M53 junct 3, A552. Left onto B5151 at
lights, hotel 0.5m on right
Rooms: 15 (1 fmly) **S** £50-£69.75 **D** £70-£89.75 **Facilities:** STV Wi-fi
Parking: 32 **Notes:** ⊗ in bedrooms

The privately-owned RiverHill Hotel stands in its own beautiful grounds in the quiet residential area of Oxton, which is conveniently placed for public transport links to Liverpool and has easy access to the Irish ferry terminal, Cammell Lairds, Chester and the motorway networks. The individually decorated bedrooms offer everything you need for a comfortable and enjoyable stay – a flat-screen TV, direct dial telephone, in-room safe, trousers press, hairdryer and complimentary fresh fruit, water, snacks and hot drinks facilities. There are two bridal suites, each with a four-poster bed and the option of choosing a champagne breakfast perhaps by way of marking a celebration. The elegant Baytree Restaurant offers a carte menu of dishes based on locally sourced ingredients, together with quality wines. The Wirall is an ideal place for spending leisure time, with no less than 14 golf courses including the Royal Liverpool and Wallasey, plus many art galleries, museums and historical landmarks. A warm welcome awaits from the owners and their staff, who are happy to help with any particular guest requirements.

Recommended in the area

Speke Hall (NT); Bidston Observatory; Ness Botanic Gardens

Grove House Hotel

★★★ 80% HOTEL

Address: Grove Road, WALLASEY, CH45 3HF
Tel: 0151 639 3947 & 0151 630 4558
Fax: 0151 639 0028
Email: reception@thegrovehouse.co.uk
Website: www.thegrovehouse.co.uk
Map ref: 7, SJ29
Directions: M53 junct 1, A554 (Wallasey New Brighton), right after church onto Harrison Drive, left after Windsors Garage onto Grove Rd **Rooms:** 14 (7 fmly) **S** £59-£69.75 **D** £70-£89.75 **Facilities:** Wi-fi **Parking:** 28 **Notes:** ⊗ in bedrooms

Located on the Wirral peninsula, Grove House Hotel has miles of coastal walks, water-based activities and first-class golf courses right on its doorstep. It's also a convenient base for exploring the city of Liverpool, with its World Heritage listed waterfront and excellent museums and entertainment venues. The hotel boasts a pretty garden and is peacefully situated in a residential area of the town, yet it's only a short distance from the seafront promenade and the underground station for Liverpool, and just a mile away from the M53. The bedrooms are beautifully furnished and equipped with facilities for making hot drinks, a trouser press and direct-dial telephone, and each has a luxurious bathroom. One of the rooms is large enough to accommodate a family, and there is also a bridal suite with four-poster bed, which can be booked to include a champagne breakfast. The bar-lounge is a great place to relax at the end of the day before enjoying a meal in the oak-panelled restaurant, which overlooks the garden. Here, service is impeccable and the excellent choice of dishes on both the carte and set menus is complemented by a wide-ranging wine list. All in all, this is a friendly place offering high standards and good value.

Recommended in the area

Heritage Centre of Port Sunlight; Williamson Art Gallery & Museum; Ellesmere Port Boat Museum

NORFOLK

Sunset at Burnham Overy Staithe

The Blakeney Hotel

★★★ 82% ● HOTEL

Address: The Quay, BLAKENEY, Holt, NR25 7NE
Tel: 01263 740797
Fax: 01263 740795
Email: reception@blakeney-hotel.co.uk
Website: www.blakeney-hotel.co.uk
Map ref: 4, TG04
Directions: Off A149, 8m W of Sheringham
Rooms: 64 (18 GF) (20 fmly) **S** £78-£127
D £156-£378 (incl. bkfst) **Facilities:** Wi-fi ☜ Gym
Sauna **Parking:** 60

A traditional, privately owned hotel right on the quayside, overlooking the estuary and salt marshes. Many of the rooms, some with balconies, look out over the impressive landscape to Blakeney Point, now part of the North Norfolk Heritage Coast. Terraces lead from others to the south-facing gardens. There are two comfortable lounges, one with an open fire. The restaurant and bar share the same panorama as a backdrop to hearty English breakfasts, light lunches and seasonal cuisine.

Recommended in the area

Seal trips to Blakeney Point; National Trust properties; North Norfolk Railway

Hoste Arms Hotel

★★★ 87% ●● HOTEL

Address: The Green, BURNHAM MARKET,
King's Lynn, PE31 8HD
Tel: 01328 738777
Fax: 01328 730103
Email: reception@hostearms.co.uk
Website: www.hostearms.co.uk
Map ref: 4, TF84 **Directions:** Signed from B1155,
5m W of Wells-next-the-Sea **Rooms:** 35 (7 GF)
S £117-£195 **D** £143-£232 (incl. bkfst)
Facilities: STV Wi-fi **Parking:** 45

This 17th-century former coaching inn, the hub of the community, is close to unspoilt beaches. It prides itself on providing a relaxed atmosphere, but not at the expense of the highest standards. There are doubles, family rooms, four-poster rooms, junior suites and a penthouse, all with pure Egyptian cotton bed linen and plasma TVs. If not staying over then drop in for lunch in the buzzy bar, choose a table in the Moroccan garden, or take afternoon tea in the conservatory. The imaginative menus owe much to locally-sourced produce, especially seafood; an excellent 200-bin wine list complements the dishes.

Recommended in the area

Holkham Hall; Brancaster Beach; Sandringham

The Lawns Wine Bar

★★★★ ⊛ RESTAURANT WITH ROOMS

Address: 26 Station Road, HOLT, NR25 6BS
Tel: 01263 713390
Email: mail@lawnsatholt.co.uk
Website: www.lawnsatholt.co.uk
Map ref: 4, TG03
Directions: A148 (Cromer road). 0.25m from Holt rdbt, turn left, 400yds along Station Rd
Rooms: 8 en suite **S** £85 **D** £95-£110
Notes: Wi-fi **Parking:** 14

The Lawns is a three-minute walk from the centre of the Georgian town of Holt, and close to the big skies and long beaches of the north Norfolk coast. A fully licensed wine bar serving a variety of beers and a large selection of wines, and a popular dining room with a menu that makes use of locally produced, seasonal foods are open to both residents and non-residents. Upstairs there are eight light and airy en suite bedrooms, each with a double bed, TV, DVD player and free W-fi. There is a south-facing garden and a private car park.

Recommended in the area

Norfolk Coast Path; Blickling Hall; North Norfolk Railway

Wells-next-the-Sea

Caley Hall Hotel

★★★ ◉ 83% HOTEL

Address: Old Hunstanton Road, HUNSTANTON, PE36 6HH
Tel: 01485 533486
Fax: 01485 533348
Email: mail@caleyhallhotel.co.uk
Website: www.caleyhallhotel.co.uk
Map ref: 4, TF64
Directions: 1m from Hunstanton, on A149
Rooms: 39 (30 GF) (20 fmly) S £59-£109
D £80-£200 (incl. bkfst) Facilities: STV Wi-fi Parking: 50

Located where the north Norfolk coast curves southwest into The Wash, this is a good base for long walks along wide beaches and exploring unspoilt countryside dotted with sleepy villages. Caley Hall is a lovely 17th-century brick-and-flint house which, from the front, presents a fairly modest farmhouse appearance, but former barns, stables and extensions tucked away at the back have been beautifully converted to provide additional accommodation. Most of the rooms, all with en suite bathrooms, are at ground level, grouped around several sheltered patio areas, and have satellite TV, DVD and CD players, a fridge and tea- and coffee-making facilities. There's individual heating in each room, so guests can adjust the temperature. The deluxe rooms are more spacious, one has a four-poster bed, and there's a suite with a whirlpool bath, plus some rooms for mobility-impaired guests. The restaurant is housed in the old stables, but the decor is chic rather than rustic, with high-back leather chairs and modern light-wood tables. Breakfast, lunch and dinner are served, with an evening menu that might include grilled sea bass, braised local beef, a traditional roast and vegetarian options. There's also a bright, spacious bar, open all day, with lots of cosy, soft leather sofas.

Recommended in the area

Sandringham; Titchwell RSPB Reserve; Holkham Hall

St Giles House Hotel

★★★★ 81% ◉◉ HOTEL

Address: 41-45 St Giles Street, NORWICH, NR2 1JR
Tel: 01603 275180
Fax: 0845 299 1905
Email: reception@stgileshousehotel.com
Website: www.stgileshousehotel.com
Map ref: 4, TG20
Directions: A11 into central Norwich. Left at rdbt (Chapelfield Shopping Centre). 3rd exit at next rdbt. Left onto St Giles St. Hotel on left
Rooms: 24 S £120-£210 D £130-£220 (incl. bkfst)
Facilities: Wi-fi Spa **Parking:** 30 **Notes:** ⊗

In the centre of historic Norwich, a baroque-style, Grade II listed building and an adjacent Georgian building have been stunningly restored and transformed into this luxurious boutique hotel. Exceptionally chic throughout, several features are outstanding, including the spectacular glass dome and crystal chandelier in the main lounge of the Walnut Suite – one of the three function and conference suites – and the delightful Parisian-style terrace. Many original features have been retained throughout the building, including fabulous wood panelling, ornamental plasterwork and marble floors. All of the bedrooms and suites are spacious, luxurious and have been individually designed. They are equipped with flat-screen TVs and DVD players, mini-bars and tea and coffee-making equipment and free Wi-fi access. The stylish, open-plan lounge bar and restaurant offers contemporary dining in a relaxing atmosphere, and the menus focus on local ingredients, with a commitment to providing top quality as well as good value.

Recommended in the area

Norwich Cathedral; Norwich Castle; Theatre Royal

Titchwell Manor

★★★ 86% ◉◉ HOTEL

Address: TITCHWELL, Brancaster, PE31 8BB
Tel: 01485 210221
Fax: 01485 210104
Email: margaret@titchwellmanor.com
Website: www.titchwellmanor.com
Map ref: 4, TF74
Directions: On A149 (coast road) between Brancaster & Thornham
Rooms: 26 (16 GF) (4 fmly) S £65-£190 D £110-£250 (incl. bkfst) **Facilities:** Wi-fi
Parking: 50

Golfers come for the two championship courses nearby; nature lovers come for the rich birdlife of the marshes; foodies come for the cuisine of head chef Eric Snaith, and others come just for the relaxing atmosphere and stylish accommodation. Situated near Brancaster and Burnham Market, this elegant property commands stunning views towards the coast and RSPB reserve; it is a common sight to see Marsh Harriers circling overhead. The guest rooms are in an converted barn, in a cottage, around a herb-filled courtyard and in the main building - a brick-and-flint Victorian former farmhouse. All boast chic, contemporary furnishings and some have sea views. There are family rooms and even dog-friendly rooms complete with bowls and biscuits. The fine dining Conservatory Restaurant offers a selection of innovative, beautifully presented, daily-changing dishes either from a set menu or a tasting menu, while the newly created Eating Rooms, that leads onto a sea-view terrace, is the perfect place for more informal eating or for just relaxing with a drink. The gardens are a real delight and a favourite spot with guests is the summerhouse where total peace and tranquillity can be enjoyed.

Recommended in the area

RSPB Titchwell Marsh Reserve; Peddars Way and Norfolk Coast Path; Norfolk Lavender

Broad House Hotel

★★★ 87% ◉ COUNTRY HOUSE HOTEL

Address: The Avenue, WROXHAM, NR12 8TS
Tel: 01603 783567
Fax: 01494 400333
Email: info@broadhousehotel.co.uk
Website: www.broadhousehotel.co.uk
Map ref: 4, TG31
Rooms: 9 (1 fmly) D £160-£259 (incl. bkfst)
Facilities: Wi-fi ☜ Gym **Parking:** 60
Notes: ⊗ in bedrooms

In the heart of the Norfolk Broads stands this delightful Queen Anne country house hotel in 24 acres of secluded parkland, incorporating an eight-acre meadow and small woodland. Awaiting overnight guests is a range of beautifully decorated and individually furnished bedrooms and suites with sumptuous beds and opulent bathrooms. Meet friends in Edward's Bar or the Library before dining in the rich-red Trafford's Restaurant, from whose menu might come Norfolk-sourced pan-fried monkfish; rump of Swannington beef; and double-baked goats' cheese soufflé with pan haggerty. Enjoy a mid-morning coffee or light lunch under a shady umbrella on the terrace.

Recommended in the area

Norfolk Broads; Blickling Hall (NT); City of Norwich

Norwich Cathedral

The Rushton Triangular Lodge

Rushton Hall Hotel and Spa

★★★★ 84% ◉◉ COUNTRY HOUSE HOTEL
Address: KETTERING, NN14 1RR
Tel: 01536 713001
Fax: 01536 713010
Email: enquiries@rushtonhall.com
Website: www.rushtonhall.com
Map ref: 3, SP87
Directions: A14 junct 7. A43 to Corby then A6003 to Rushton turn after bridge
Facilities: Wi-fi ⓦ Gym Spa Sauna **Parking:** 140
Notes: ⊗ in bedrooms

Rushton Hall is a magnificent Grade I listed Elizabethan country house, surrounded by beautiful, tranquil countryside where a wide range of activities and country pursuits are available. The east Midlands road network makes it easy to get to, so it is a popular conference and wedding venue. The grandeur of the building is balanced by an ambience of comfort, where guests can relax by one of the big open fireplaces and enjoy the attentive hospitality. Bedrooms are richly decorated in individual style, from elegant superior rooms to wood-panelled rooms with magnificent four-poster beds. All have Wi-fi and flat-screen TVs, and some of the en suite bathrooms have a large bath and separate shower. The restaurant occupies the grand oak-panelled dining room and as much attention is paid to the sourcing of ingredients as to the creation of the menus. There is also a brasserie, and afternoon tea is served in the Great Hall or in the courtyard when the weather is good. Guests have the use of a fitness suite, outdoor tennis court, billiard table, swimming pool, indoor and outdoor spa, steam room, sauna and sun shower. Beauty treatments are also available.

Recommended in the area
Triangular Lodge; Boughton House; Rockingham Speedway; Rockingham Castle; Rutland Water

NORTHUMBERLAND

Hadrian's Wall, Northumberland National Park

Waren House Hotel

★★★ 82% ● COUNTRY HOUSE HOTEL

Address: Waren Mill, BAMBURGH, NE70 7EE
Tel: 01668 214581   **Fax:** 01668 214484
Email: enquiries@warenhousehotel.co.uk
Website: www.warenhousehotel.co.uk
Map ref: 10, NU13 **Directions:** B1342 to Waren
Mill, at T-junct right, hotel 100yds on right
Rooms: 15 (3 GF) **S** £125-£155 **D** £140-£190 (incl.
bkfst) **Facilities:** Wi-fi **Parking:** 20
Notes: ⊗ in bedrooms ⊁ 14yrs

On Northumberland's impressive coast, this charming Georgian mansion stands in six acres of woodland and landscaped grounds. Some of the individually themed bedrooms have walk-in showers, others have baths; there are suites too. Grays restaurant, with antique tables and walls hung with prints and paintings, and holder of an AA Rosette, is a textbook example of classic country house style. Typical of the good, home-cooked food are monkfish loin wrapped in mousse and Craster-smoked salmon; and ballottine of maize-fed chicken breast and leg confit. Relax in the gardens, lounge or library, or walk seemingly for ever along the sandy shore.

Recommended in the area

Alnwick Castle & Gardens; Holy Island; Farne Islands

Bamburgh Castle

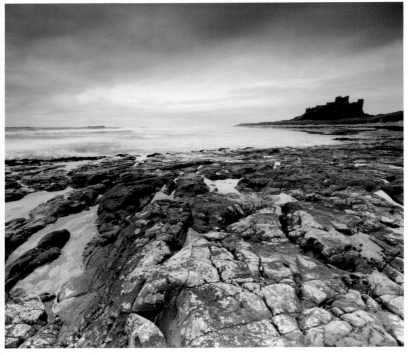

Langley Castle Hotel

★★★★ 82% ◉◉ HOTEL

Address: Langley, HEXHAM, NE47 5LU
Tel: 01434 688888
Fax: 01434 684019
Email: manager@langleycastle.com
Website: www.langleycastle.com
Map ref: 6, NY96
Directions: A69, S A686 for 2m. Hotel on right
Rooms: 27 (9 GF) (8 fmly) S £120-£209.50
D £150-£285 (incl. bkfst) **Facilities:** STV Wi-fi
Parking: 70 **Notes:** ⊗ in bedrooms

A genuine 14th-century castle, restored and transformed into a magnificent and comfortable hotel, set in its own 12-acre woodland estate. The guest bedchambers have private facilities, and some boast window seats set into 7ft-thick walls, four-poster beds, and even a sauna and spa bath. CastleView and CastleView Lodge, converted Grade I listed buildings within the grounds, offer additional guest rooms. All the bedrooms have draped canopies over the beds, satellite TV and stunning views up to the main castle. The splendid drawing room, with blazing log fire, traceries and stained glass, together with the oak-panelled cocktail bar, complement the intimate atmosphere of the Josephine Restaurant. The food served here is of the high order, making the most of fresh, local produce, with fish and game a speciality. The exclusive nature of the castle makes Langley the perfect destination to be pampered in unique surroundings, and it's ideally located for discovering the delights of Hadrian's Wall, Bamburgh Castle, Holy Island and the Scottish Borders. The Castle is only 30 minutes from Newcastle city centre and 40 minutes from Newcastle Airport.

Recommended in the area

Hadrian's Wall; Bamburgh Castle; Hexham Abbey

NOTTINGHAMSHIRE

Robin Hood statue, Nottingham Castle

The Grange Hotel

★★★ 82% ◉ HOTEL

Address: 73 London Road, NEWARK, NG24 1RZ
Tel: 01636 703399
Fax: 01636 702328
Email: info@grangenewark.co.uk
Website: www.grangenewark.co.uk
Map ref: 8, SK75
Directions: From A1 follow signs to Balderton, hotel opposite Polish War Graves
Rooms: 19 (1 fmly) **S** £85-£120 **D** £120-£165 (incl. bkfst) **Facilities:** Wi-fi **Parking:** 17 **Notes:** ⊗ in bedrooms

A family-run, Victorian-era hotel in a conservation area, just a short walk from the town centre. Skilfully renovated, Newark Civic Trust gave it an award for the way original features, such as a beautiful tiled floor in one of the entrance areas, have been retained. Public rooms include a bar called Potters, with framed illustrations of old crockery, and a residents' lounge. Beyond Potters is a stone-flagged patio shaded by tall yews and the immaculate landscaped garden, winner of a 'Newark in Bloom' award. The bedrooms, some with four-posters, all feature excellent bathrooms with bath and shower, co-ordinated soft furnishings, desk space with phone and computer access point, TV, radio alarm, beverage-making and ironing facilities, hairdryer, trouser press and, last but not least, a rubber duck for the very young. High-ceilinged Cutlers restaurant, named after the antique cutlery on display, offers a frequently changing carte menu, with main courses such as braised blade of beef; baked herb-crusted sea bass; and broccoli, cheese and potato bake. That it attracts non-residents as well as hotel guests says much about the restaurant's local reputation. Weddings and business functions are expertly catered for.

Recommended in the area

Newark Castle & Gardens; Newark International Antiques Fair; Newark Air Museum

Hart's Hotel

★★★★ 82% ◉◉ HOTEL

Address: Standard Hill, Park Row, NOTTINGHAM,
NG1 6GN

Tel: 0115 988 1900

Fax: 0115 947 7600

Email: reception@hartshotel.co.uk

Website: www.hartsnottingham.co.uk

Map ref: 6, SK53

Directions: At junct of Park Row & Ropewalk, close
to city centre **Rooms:** 32 (7 GF) (1 fmly) **D** £120–
£260 **Facilities:** STV with Blu-ray & DVD player Wi-fi Gym **Parking:** 16

A privately owned boutique hotel built to an award-winning design on the former ramparts of Nottingham's medieval castle, close to the bustling city centre. Light, contemporary rooms feature top quality beds with goose-down pillows and duvets, and Egyptian cotton bed linen. Mini-bars are stocked with wines, beers and fresh milk for your cafetière coffee, while other standard features include CD, radio, flat-screen digital TV with Blu-ray and DVD player, satellite channels, internet access, DDI lines and voicemail. Some rooms have French doors leading out into the pretty garden – a perfect spot for a relaxing gin and tonic before dinner in Hart's Restaurant. Dine on modern British cooking in one of the intimate booths and choose from owner Tim Hart's wine list, which has a generous selection from smaller producers. An alternative to the restaurant is the more casual Park Bar, with original artwork on display, high-backed sofas, red leather armchairs, and courtyard seating. Hart's Upstairs is a popular venue for private parties, weddings and business meetings. From the hotel's garden there are extensive views across the city and beyond. A nightly charge is made for the secure, barrier-controlled car park.

Recommended in the area

City of Caves; Nottingham Royal Centre; Nottingham Playhouse

Park Plaza Nottingham

★★★★ 73% HOTEL

Address: 41 Maid Marian Way, NOTTINGHAM,
NG1 6GD
Tel: 0115 947 7200
Fax: 0115 947 7300
Email: ppnsales@pphe.com
Website: www.parkplaza.com/nottinghamuk
Map ref: 8, SK53 **Directions:** A6200 onto Wollaton
St. 2nd exit onto Maid Marian Way. Hotel on left
Rooms: 178 (10 fmly) **Facilities:** STV Wi-fi Gym

An ultra-modern hotel in the city centre, with everything worth seeing and doing on the doorstep, including Ye Olde Trip to Jerusalem, which purports to be England's oldest pub, and the historic Lace Market district. Bedrooms are spacious and comfortable, with many extras, including wired and Wi-fi internet access, laptop safes, high-speed phone lines and air conditioning. The award-winning Chino Latino Restaurant is where you can eat expertly prepared Pan-Asian cuisine from carte, set, tasting and bento menus, the latter a compendium of boxed fish, meat and rice-based meals – how very Japanese. Dim sum, tempura, sushi and sashimi are served to share and are brought at intervals to the table, while main course dishes include pork ribs in black bean and oyster sauce; and Chilean sea bass cooked in Shaoxing rice wine. The bar serves signature cocktails, bottled beers and bar platters in a distinctively Latin atmosphere. For added convenience, the hotel also offers casual dining at the bar in the lobby. The 11th-floor Fitness Suite features not just bikes, rowing machines, weights and treadmills, but good views of the city. Local businesses make full use of the 12 well-equipped meeting rooms.

Recommended in the area

Museum of Nottingham Lace; The Galleries of Justice; Nottingham Castle Museum & Art Gallery

Best Western Lion Hotel

★★★ 80% HOTEL

Address: 112 Bridge Street, WORKSOP, S80 1HT
Tel: 01909 477925
Fax: 01909 479038
Email: reception@thelionworksop.co.uk
Website: www.thelionworksop.co.uk
Map ref: 8, SK57
Directions: A57 to town centre, right at Sainsburys,
to Norfolk Arms, turn left Rooms: 46 (7 GF) (3 fmly)
Facilities: STV Wi-fi Parking: 50

Its appearance is late 18th century, but an old inventory indicates a change of ownership in 1601, and one doesn't have to be a historian to deduce that this privately owned hotel is older than it looks. Assuming at least four centuries of existence, it's perhaps not surprising that it's had its ups and downs, but under the ownership today of Cooplands, a Doncaster-based family baking company, it is decidedly in up mode as a well-renowned hotel with excellent modern amenities. It still retains plenty of its historic charm and character though, and somewhere within its walls is the ghost of Alice, a spurned serving wench who rather likes haunting a specific bedroom. Standard rooms, and the more spacious executives, all have a double bed, en suite bathroom, tea and coffee facilities, desk or dressing table, flat-screen TV, and all the usual appliances. Features in some are different: one, for example, has a brass bed, another a queen-size mud bed. Grill@114 will rustle up pasta, risotto, fish and chips, and homemade burgers, while the newer 108 restaurant offers a good range of the more sophisticated confit belly pork; Cajun breast of chicken; and pan-fried sea bass.

Recommended in the area

Chatsworth House & Gardens; Newstead Abbey; Newark Air Museum

OXFORDSHIRE

Goring Lock on the River Thames

The Lamb Inn

★★★ 83% ◉◉ SMALL HOTEL
Address: Sheep Street, BURFORD, OX18 4LR
Tel: 01993 823155
Fax: 01993 822228
Email: info@lambinn-burford.co.uk
Website: www.cotswold-inns-hotels.co.uk/lamb
Map ref: 3, SP21
Directions: A40 into Burford, downhill, 1st left into Sheep St, hotel last on right
Rooms: 17 (4 GF) (1 fmly) D £150-£175 (incl. bkfst)
Facilities: Wi-fi

To quote the owners, "The phrase 'charming old inn' is used much too freely, but the Lamb has a genuine right to it", with stone-flagged floors, log fires and many other time-worn features. The cosy lounges, with deep armchairs, are tranquillity itself. The en suite bedrooms contain fine furniture, much of it antique, in addition to the usual amenities, including home-made cookies. All overlook leafy side streets, or the hotel courtyard. The airy restaurant serves traditional English food with a modern twist.
Recommended in the area
Cotswold Wildlife Park; Blenheim Palace; City of Oxford

The Bay Tree Hotel

★★★ 81% ◉ HOTEL
Address: Sheep Street, BURFORD, OX18 4LW
Tel: 01993 822791
Fax: 01993 823008
Email: info@baytreehotel.info
Website: www.cotswold-inns-hotels.co.uk/bay-tree
Map ref: 3, SP21
Directions: A40 or A361 to Burford. From High St turn into Sheep St, next to old market square. Hotel on right
Rooms: 21 (2 fmly) D £165-£175 (incl. bkfst) **Facilities:** Wi-fi **Parking:** 50

Much of this delightful old inn's character comes from the flagstone floors, tapestries, high-raftered hall, galleried stairs and tastefully furnished oak-panelled bedrooms, some with four-poster or half-tester beds. Public areas consist of the country-style Woolsack Bar, a sophisticated airy restaurant with original leaded windows, a selection of meeting rooms and an attractive walled garden. An alternative to the restaurant's candle-lit atmosphere is the Woolsack's extensive menu of lighter meals.
Recommended in the area
Cotswold Wildlife Park; Blenheim Palace; City of Oxford

The Miller of Mansfield

★★★★★ ⑳ RESTAURANT WITH ROOMS
Address: High St, GORING, RG8 9AW
Tel: 01491 872829
Fax: 01491 873100
Email: reservations@millerofmansfield.com
Website: www.millerofmansfield.com
Map ref: 3, SU67
Directions: M40 junct 7, S on A329 towards
Benson, A4074 towards Reading, B4009 towards
Goring. Or M4 junct 12, S on A4 towards Newbury.

3rd rdbt onto A340 to Pangbourne. A329 to Streatley, right at lights onto B4009 into Goring
Rooms: 13 en suite (2 fmly rooms) **Notes:** Wi-fi **Parking:** 2

The Miller of Mansfield is a haven of laid back calm in a quiet village setting in Goring-on-Thames, overlooking the beautiful Chiltern Hills. The eclectically designed guest rooms and suites offer all the comforts one would expect, including flat-screen digital TVs, marble bathrooms with stone resin freestanding baths and/or luxury rain showers, and amazing organic latex mattresses. Further pampering comes in the form of natural REN toiletries, Egyptian cotton linens and thick bathrobes. Culinary treats of the modern British kind await in the acclaimed restaurant and bar. Menus change regularly to reflect the seasons and the kitchen uses the best of local and British produce; you're bound to find something to excite on the wine list and there's also a fine selection of local real ales. The Miller is the perfect destination for a relaxing break away, either over the weekend or for a quiet midweek escape. For business users, free hi-speed Wi-fi access, great meeting facilities and exemplary levels of service and hospitality make the Miller the ideal home-away-from-home when you need to stay in the Thames Valley.

Recommended in the area

Basildon Park (NT); Beale Park Wildlife Park & Gardens; Henley-on-Thames

The Feathers Hotel

★★★★ 78% ◉◉ TOWN HOUSE HOTEL
Address: Market Street, WOODSTOCK, OX20 1SX
Tel: 01993 812291
Fax: 01993 813158
Email: enquiries@feathers.co.uk
Website: www.feathers.co.uk
Map ref: 4, SP41
Directions: A44 (Oxford to Woodstock), 1st left after lights. Hotel on left **Rooms:** 21 (2 GF) (4 fmly)
D £195-£315 (incl. bkfst) **Facilities:** Wi-fi

It was a former hotelier's love of stuffed birds that turned the 17th-century Dorchester Inn into The Feathers, which, with its ivy-covered façade, oak beams and open fireplaces, time might appear to have passed by. Indeed, proof might be assumed from the hands on its grandfather clock being forever stuck at ten to eight, but in this pretty Cotswolds market town even hoteliers like to keep up. That's why you'll get bold designer fabrics, eye-catching colours, a Wi-fi in the study and a smart bathroom in the ultra-chic bedrooms. Public spaces include a bar and an attractive restaurant with two AA Rosettes.

Recommended in the area

Blenheim Palace; City of Oxford; Bicester Shopping Village

Blenheim Palace, Woodstock

RUTLAND

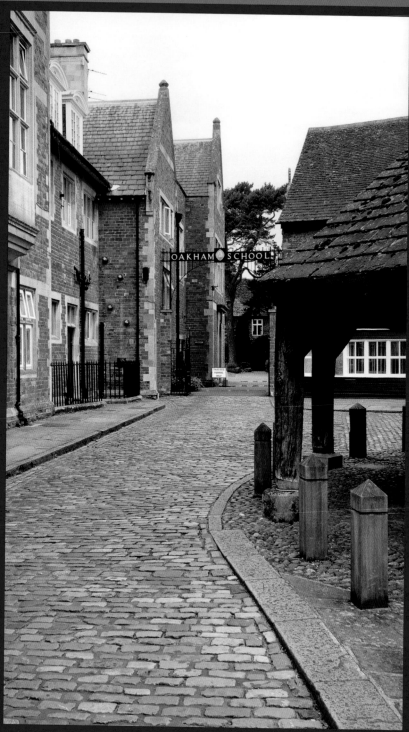

Oakham School, Oakham

Hambleton Hall

★★★★ ◎◎◎◎ COUNTRY HOUSE HOTEL
Address: Hambleton, OAKHAM, LE15 8TH
Tel: 01572 756991
Fax: 01572 724721
Email: hotel@hambletonhall.com
Website: www.hambletonhall.com
Map ref: 3, SK80
Directions: 3m E off A606
Rooms: 17 S £195-£215 D £235-£400 (incl. bkfst)
Facilities: STV ⃗ Private access to lake
Parking: 40

This family-run hotel is a magnificent Victorian house, standing in its own beautiful gardens and enjoying fine views over Rutland Water, the largest man-made lake in western Europe. The bedrooms are highly individual in character, furnished with fine fabrics and sumptuous furniture; ranging from the largest master rooms, many with wonderful views of the lake, to smaller standard rooms that overlook the manicured lawns and handsome cedar trees. The most luxurious accommodation is in the Croquet Pavilion, a two-bedroom folly just 50 yards from the main building. The cuisine here is outstanding. On frequently changing menus the kitchen bases the dishes on fresh, seasonal and locally sourced produce. The hotel won the AA Wine Award for England and was also the Overall Winner for 2011; each month there is a wine dinner. In the public areas there are open fireplaces in the cosy bar and an elegant drawing room. The hotel is popular for prestigious private functions of all kinds, including wedding receptions. For corporate guests there is full business support, including secretarial and translation services.

Recommended in the area

Burghley House; Rutland Water; Grimsthorpe Castle; Kelmarsh Hall Gardens

Barnsdale Lodge Hotel

★★★ 75% ◉ HOTEL

Address: The Avenue, Rutland Water, North Shore,
OAKHAM, LE15 8AH
Tel: 01572 724678
Fax: 01572 724961
Email: enquiries@barnsdalelodge.co.uk
Website: www.barnsdalelodge.co.uk
Map ref: 3, SK80 **Directions:** Off A1 onto A606.
Hotel 5m on right, 2m E of Oakham **Rooms:** 44 (15
GF) (2 fmly) **S** £71.50-£92 **D** £87-£148 (incl. bkfst)
Facilities: Spa **Parking:** 200

This hotel has been in Thomas Noel's family since 1760 and formed part of the adjoining Exton Park, seat of the Earls of Gainsborough. Originally a farmhouse, the building was converted into a hotel over twenty years ago. It occupies a delightful location on the north shore of Rutland Water in the heart of the beautiful, unspoilt, county of Rutland, just a few minutes from the historic towns of Oakham and Stamford. Bedrooms all have views of either the surrounding countryside or the pretty courtyard.

Recommended in the area

Rutland Water; Barnsdale Gardens; Burghley House

Sailing on Rutland Water

Nick's Restaurant at Lord Nelson's House

★★★★ ◎◎ 🛏 RESTAURANT WITH ROOMS

Address: 11 Market Place, OAKHAM, LE15 6HR
Tel: 01572 723199
Email: simon@nicksrestaurant.co.uk
Website: www.nicksrestaurant.co.uk
Map ref: 3, SK80
Directions: A1(M), A606, after 2nd rdbt, Market Place on right
Rooms: 4 en suite Notes: Wi-fi ⊗ in bedrooms Parking: 3

Nestled in the corner of the square in the charming market town of Oakham, this restaurant with rooms makes the perfect weekend retreat. The quaint and cosy period dining room is a welcoming setting for some fine modern European cooking based around seasonal, high quality local produce. Dinner might begin with red mullet and roast pepper tart au fin with aubergine caviar and tempura of tiger prawn, followed by roast pork belly with champ potato cake, black pudding and red onion souffle, crackling, braised Savoy cabbage and a cider jus. Dessert could be blueberry creme brûlée with blueberry compote and sorbet, or you could go for a selection of local cheeses with fig and walnut bread and damson chutney. The small but carefully chosen wine list offers a good selection by the glass. The four en suite guest bedrooms are individually designed, with plenty of period features and antiques along with modern comforts like flat-screen TVs, mini-bars and free Wi-fi. Take your pick from the nautical themed Lord Horatio Nelson Room, the romantic Lady Emma Hamilton Room, the contemporary Lady Fanny Nelson Room, or the colonial style Sir Thomas Hardy Room.

Recommended in the area

Oakham Castle; Rutland Water; Rutland Railway Museum

Offa's Dyke footpath, Knighton

Rowton Castle Hotel

★★★ 88% ☻ HOTEL

Address: Halfway House, SHREWSBURY, SY5 9EP
Tel:　　01743 884044
Fax:　　01743 884949
Email:　post@rowtoncastle.com
Website: www.rowtoncastle.com
Map ref: 2, SJ41
Directions: From A5 near Shrewsbury take A458 to Welshpool. Hotel 4m on right
Rooms: 19 (3 fmly)
Facilities: Wi-fi **Parking:** 100 **Notes:** ⊗ in bedrooms

A castle has stood in the grounds at Rowton for nearly 800 years. The building has seen many changes and alterations over the centuries but has remained primarily a family home. It has now been transformed into a luxury country hotel, retaining the spendour of yesteryear whilst providing the facilities anticipated by the most discerning of guests. Rowton Castle is a beautiful 17th-century, Grade II listed building, set in 17 acres of tranquil grounds, six miles west of the historic town of Shrewsbury. The castle boasts 19 charming, individually designed bedrooms, seven with period four-poster beds. Each beautifully appointed room has a fully equipped bathroom, TV, direct-dial telephone, Wi-fi and excellent beverage-making facilities. Personal service and attention to detail are hallmarks of Rowton Castle's excellent reputation and this is ably demonstrated in the hotel's award-winning Cedar Restaurant. Oak panelling with 17th-century carving, velvet armchairs and intimate lighting are a perfect backdrop to this fine-dining experience. An extensive fixed price menu offers a mouthwatering selection for all tastes, complemented by an interesting choice of wines from around the world. Rowton Castle is a fairytale venue for weddings and has excellent conference facilities.

Recommended in the area

The Long Mynd; Welshpool and Llanfair Light Railway; Offa's Dyke Path

SOMERSET

Fan vaulted ceiling, Bath Abbey

The Queensberry Hotel

★★★ ◉◉◉ HOTEL

Address: Russel Street, BATH, BA1 2QF
Tel: 01225 447928
Fax: 01225 446065
Email: reservations@thequeensberry.co.uk
Website: www.thequeensberry.co.uk
Map ref: 2, ST76
Directions: 100mtrs from the Assembly Rooms
Rooms: 29 (2 GF) (2 fmly) **S** £120-£180
D £125-£435 **Facilities:** Wi-fi **Parking:** 6
Notes: ⊗ in bedrooms

Four Georgian town houses form this charming hotel, located in a quiet residential street close to the city centre. The hotel is run with a passion by Laurence and Helen Beere who, together with their staff, maintain a refreshingly old-fashioned attitude to guest service, making a stay here a memorable one. The spacious bedrooms are individually designed, combining up-to-date comfort and sophistication with the buildings' original features. Expect marble bathrooms, flat-screen TVs and White Company toiletries. There is a choice of sumptuously furnished drawing rooms, an inviting bar and secluded terraced gardens. The stylish Olive Tree restaurant offers innovative menus of modern British dishes with Mediterranean influences; in the main, local and trusted suppliers are relied upon to provide the seasonal ingredients that create the award-winning cuisine. The popular 'quintessentially British' Old Q Bar is a great place to relax and enjoy a drink and choose a snack or light meal from the bar menu. All the attractions of historic Bath are just a few minutes' walk away, and if arriving by car, the hotel offers a valet service.

Recommended in the area

Thermae Bath Spa; Beckford's Tower; Claverton Pumping Station

Dukes Hotel

★★★ 82% ◉◉ SMALL HOTEL

Address: Great Pulteney Street, BATH, BA2 4DN

Tel: 01225 787960

Fax: 01225 787961

Email: info@dukesbath.co.uk

Website: www.dukesbath.co.uk

Map ref: 2, ST76

Directions: A46 to Bath, at rdbt right on A4. 4th set of lights turn left (A36), then right onto Great Pulteney St. Hotel on left

Rooms: 17 (2 GF) (5 fmly) S £99-£140 D £139-£179 (incl. bkfst) **Facilities:** Wi-fi

An expertly restored, bow-fronted, Grade I listed Georgian townhouse where the rooms are decorated with period furniture, fine fabrics, prints and portraits. Surviving original plasterwork includes delicate features such as Adams-style urns and floral swags. In winter a blazing log fire in the lounge gives a warm welcome, while in summer the peaceful courtyard terrace, with a sparkling fountain, is perfect for a relaxing meal or drink. The en suite bedrooms and six suites (two with four-posters) have been restored to their original spacious dimensions. Many have enormous sash windows and splendid views over Great Pulteney Street, the Bath skyline or the surrounding countryside. Each differs in size and design, some Georgian themed, others more contemporary. All have bath and/or power shower, large fluffy towels and bathrobes, digital TV, Wi-fi access and hairdryer. The Cavendish Restaurant and Bar offers modern British seasonal cooking, using carefully sourced, locally grown and reared organic and free-range produce. A fixed-price lunch menu offers two or three courses and the dinner menu is à la carte. There are two smaller, more intimate, dining rooms which can be reserved for private receptions.

Recommended in the area

Thermae Bath Spa; Roman Baths; Royal Crescent and Circus

Best Western The Cliffe Hotel

★★★ 83% ◉ HOTEL

Address: Cliffe Drive, Crowe Hill, Limpley Stoke,
BATH, BA2 7FY
Tel: 01225 723226
Fax: 01225 723871
Email: cliffe@bestwestern.co.uk
Website: www.bw-cliffehotel.co.uk
Map ref: 2, ST76
Directions: A36 S from Bath onto B3108 at lights
left towards Bradford-on-Avon, 0.5m. Right before
bridge through village, 2nd hotel on right
Rooms: 11 (4 GF) (2 fmly) **S** £111-£150 **D** £137-£200 (incl. bkfst) **Facilities:** Wi-fi ⚡ **Parking:** 20
The peace and tranquillity here is not surprising, given its setting in over three acres of woodland, with
spectacular views over the Avon Valley. Individually styled bedrooms include two with four-posters and
one with whirlpool bath, and after a fine meal in the restaurant, you can relax in the comfortable lounge.
A small meeting room is available. A heated outdoor pool is open from June to September, weather
permitting, and canal day boats and bikes can be hired locally.
Recommended in the area
World Heritage City of Bath; Lacock Abbey and Village (NT); Westwood Manor (NT)

The Oaks Hotel

★★★ ◉ HOTEL

Address: PORLOCK, TA24 8ES
Tel: 01643 862265
Fax: 01643 863131
Email: nfo@oakshotel.co.uk
Website: www.oakshotel.co.uk
Map ref: 2, SS84
Directions: From E of A39, enter village then follow
hotel sign. From W: down Porlock Hill, through
village. **Rooms:** 8 **S** from £135 **D** from £200
(incl. dinner) **Facilities:** Wi-fi **Parking:** 12 **Notes:** ⊗ in bedrooms ⚡ 8yrs
Tim and Anne Riley have excelled in restoring this Edwardian country house set among the majestic
trees that gave it its name. From its lofty location, it has wonderful views of Exmoor and the Bristol
Channel from bedrooms and the dining room. The lounge, with log fires in winter, is the place for
afternoon tea and after-dinner coffee, or just to relax after a walk. Bedrooms have en suite baths and
showers, fresh flowers, Egyptian cotton linen, TV and tea-making facilities. The dining room has a
four-course, largely traditional menu, on which everything, from marmalade to after-dinner chocolates,
is home made.
Recommended in the area South West Coast Path; Watersmeet House (NT); Exmoor Bird Gardens

Holbrook House

★★★ 79% ◉◉ COUNTRY HOUSE HOTEL

Address: Holbrook, WINCANTON, BA9 8BS
Tel: 01963 824466 & 828844
Fax: 01963 32681
Email: enquiries@holbrookhouse.co.uk
Website: www.holbrookhouse.co.uk
Map ref: 2, ST72
Directions: From A303 at Wincanton left onto A371 towards Castle Cary & Shepton Mallet
Rooms: 21 (5 GF) (2 fmly) S £105-£155 D £150-£250 (incl. bkfst) **Facilities:** Wi-fi ⊗ Tennis Gym Spa Sauna **Parking:** 100

This privately owned Georgian country-house hotel is surrounded by 20 acres of unspoiled woodland and rolling pastures. There are 21 luxurious, characterful bedrooms, split between the main house and the walled garden. The Cedar Restaurant is an elegant setting for some superb Anglo-French cuisine, while more informal dining can be enjoyed in the Stables Bar, part of the health club and spa. A third dining option is the Morning Room, serving afternoon tea, lighter dishes and Sunday roast lunches.

Recommended in the area

Fleet Air Museum; Montacute House (NT); Wells Cathedral

Wells Cathedral

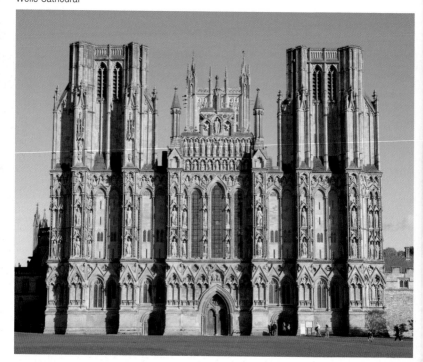

STAFFORDSHIRE

Lichfield

Three Queens Hotel

★★★ 81% ◉ HOTEL

Address: One Bridge Street, BURTON UPON TRENT,
DE14 1SY

Tel: 01283 523800 & 0845 230 1332

Fax: 01283 523823

Email: hotel@threequeenshotel.co.uk

Website: www.threequeenshotel.co.uk

Map ref: 6, SK22

Directions: On A511 in Burton upon Trent at junct of Bridge
St & High St. Town side of Old River Bridge **Rooms:** 38

Facilities: STV Wi-fi **Parking:** 40 **Notes:** ⊗

The privately owned Three Queens Hotel is a special venue for both business and pleasure, set in the heart of the brewery town of Burton upon Trent, minutes away from scenic walks, cultural sights and family attractions. The hotel's abiding philosophy is, 'find the things that the group hotels can't do – and do it!', thus you can expect excellent service from the moment you arrive. Forget the usual laborious registration procedure - here it's a simple question of whether you'd like breakfast and a complimentary newspaper, then a helping hand with your luggage, assistance to ensure the key card works, and a car wash if you stay midweek. The en suite bedrooms are equipped with the latest Genesis flat-screen in-room entertainment system, with high-speed internet access either on-screen or through your own laptop. A selection of function rooms provides perfect spaces for intimate meetings or larger conferences, while the dining facilities cater for all business and social occasions. Snacks are served in the Princes Bar, and breakfast in the Kings Room is the ideal way to start the day. In the evening treat yourself to a three-course dinner in the Rosette-awarded Grill Room. Wine tastings, gourmet evenings and champagne breakfasts are held throughout the year.

Recommended in the area

Alton Towers; Donnington Park; Calke Abbey (NT)

Swinfen Hall Hotel

★★★★ ◉◉ HOTEL
Address: Swinfen, LICHFIELD, WS14 9RE
Tel: 01543 481494
Fax: 01543 480341
Email: info@swinfenhallhotel.co.uk
Website: www.swinfenhallhotel.co.uk
Map ref: 3, SK10
Directions: Set back from A38, 2.5m outside Lichfield, towards Birmingham
Rooms: 17 (5 fmly) S £135-£290 D £165-£315 (incl. bkfst) **Facilities:** STV Wi-fi **Parking:** 80 **Notes:** ⊗ in bedrooms

Standing grandly at the end of a long driveway, this lavishly decorated Georgian mansion is surrounded by 100 acres of deer park, formal gardens, meadows and woodland. Painstakingly restored by the present owners, the public rooms are particularly stylish, with intricately carved ceilings and impressive oil portraits. The first-floor guest rooms retain their tall sash windows and other period features, while those on the second floor (the former servants' quarters) are smaller and more contemporary. All provide goose-down duvets, Egyptian cotton sheets, large white fluffy towels and free Wi-fi, satellite TV, DVD and well-stocked hospitality tray. The oak-panelled Four Seasons Restaurant has a reputation for fine dining, while lighter meals may be eaten in the bar or on the cocktail terrace. Venison from the estate features high on the menus alongside an abundance of fruit, vegetables and herbs from the Victorian walled garden. The food is complemented by frequently changing wines bought directly from vineyards, through specialist merchants and at auction. With only 17 bedrooms and suites guests will be assured of personal service combined with a friendly, relaxed atmosphere.

Recommended in the area

Lichfield Cathedral; Shugborough Hall; The Potteries

The Moat House

★★★★ 84% ◎◎ HOTEL

Address: Lower Penkridge Road, Acton Trussell,
STAFFORD, ST17 0RJ
Tel: 01785 712217 **Fax:** 01785 715344
Email: info@moathouse.co.uk
Website: www.moathouse.co.uk
Map ref: 7, SJ92 **Directions:** M6 junct 13, A449
through Acton Trussell. Hotel on right on exiting
village **Rooms:** 41 (15 GF) (4 fmly) **Facilities:** Wi-fi
Parking: 200

Narrowboats on the Staffordshire & Worcestershire Canal chug gently past this 14th-century, moated manor house standing atop a mound sufficiently historic to be deemed a Scheduled Ancient Monument. The east-facing wing of the house has been expertly restored to near-medieval condition, with the original timber frame on show in the bar and upper function room. Without losing any of its unique charm or personality it has, over its 56 years in the hands of the Lewis family, become an award-winning hotel and fine-dining restaurant, with excellently appointed bedrooms, a bar, and conference and banqueting facilities for up to 200 people.

Recommended in the area

Shugborough Estate (NT); Alton Towers; The Potteries

Shugborough Hall

SUFFOLK

Beach huts at Southwold

Wentworth Hotel

★★★ 88% ◉◉ HOTEL

Address: Wentworth Road, ALDEBURGH, IP15 5BD
Tel: 01728 452312
Fax: 01728 454343
Email: stay@wentworth-aldeburgh.co.uk
Website: www.wentworth-aldeburgh.com
Map ref: 4, TM45
Directions: Off A12 onto A1094, 6m to Aldeburgh,
with church on left, left at bottom of hill
Rooms: 35 (5 GF) **S** £60.50-£115 **D** £112-£248
(incl. bkfst) **Facilities:** Wi-fi **Parking:** 30

This triple-gabled hotel has been managed by the Pritt family since 1920, and this continuous thread is responsible for the fact that the Wentworth is everything a seaside hotel should be. The attractive and well-maintained public rooms include three lounges furnished with comfortable chairs and sofas, which are sunny spots in summer and cosy places to relax by an open fire in winter. Outside are two sea-facing gardens in which to soak up the sun with a morning coffee, light lunch or cream tea. Many of the regularly refurbished en suite bedrooms have good views of the North Sea, for which the hotel thoughtfully provides binoculars. Seven rooms in Darfield House, just opposite the main building, are particularly spacious and well appointed. For those who find stairs difficult (there's no lift) there are five ground-floor rooms. Room sizes and outlook do vary, and these differences are reflected in the tariff. You can start the day here with a locally smoked kipper, as part of your 'full-house' cooked breakfast. At lunchtime, the terrace bar menu offers a wide choice, from a fresh crab sandwich to traditional cod and chips, and the elegant candlelit restaurant has a daily changing dinner menu based on fresh local produce.

Recommended in the area

Minsmere (RSPB) Reserve; Snape Maltings (Aldeburgh Festival); Suffolk Heritage Coast

The Bildeston Crown

★★★ ◉◉◉ HOTEL

Address: 104 High Street, BILDESTON, Ipswich, IP7 7EB

Tel: 01449 740510

Fax: 01449 741843

Email: hayley@thebildestoncrown.com

Website: www.thebildestoncrown.com

Map ref: 4, TL94

Directions: A12 junct 31, turn right onto B1070 & follow signs to Hadleigh. At T-junct turn left onto A1141, then immediately right onto B1115. Hotel 0.5m

Rooms: 13 S £90-£150 D £150-£250 (incl. bkfst) **Facilities:** STV Wi-fi **Parking:** 30

In a village deep in picturesque countryside, stands this 15th-century, heavily timbered coaching inn. Original features, including log fires, oak beams and period furniture ensure that you'll remain conscious of its ancestry. Much thought has gone into the bedrooms, each of which includes flat-screen TV, an extensive library of music available via an in-wall control panel, concealed speakers in the en suite bathroom and shower area, and internet access. The luxurious Black Fuschia room, with dramatic black decor and a super king-sized bed, is apparently 'not for the faint-hearted'. At the centre of the Crown lies the restaurant, where paintings line the walls and locally sourced seasonal cuisine ranges from the classic to interpretations of the traditional. A typical dinner might be pan-seared fillet of mackerel with leek tart, followed by breast of Suffolk chicken with confit leg and poached lobster, and set-milk cream with balsamic figs to finish. Red Poll beef from the hotel's own herd is always a possibility, and there's also an eight-course tasting menu. On a fine day, eat or drink in the central courtyard, or try one of the two bars where the full restaurant menu is also available.

Recommended in the area

Lavenham; Colne Valley Railway; Constable Country

Suffolk

Hintlesham Hall Hotel

★★★★ ◎◎ HOTEL

Address: George Street, HINTLESHAM, Ipswich,
IP8 3NS
Tel: 01473 652334
Fax: 01473 652463
Email: reservations@hintleshamhall.com
Website: www.hintleshamhall.com
Map ref: 4, TM04
Directions: 4m W of Ipswich on A1071 to Hadleigh
& Sudbury **Rooms:** 33 (10 GF) **S** £99-£120
D £120-£160 (incl. bkfst) **Facilities:** Wi-fi ⚡ Tennis Gym **Parking:** 60

Hospitality and service are absolute priorities at this imposing 16th-century, Grade I listed country house hotel in 175 acres of landscaped gardens and grounds. The building is distinguished by its Georgian additions, most notably the façade, as well as by earlier Stuart interior embellishments. Works of art and antiques abound throughout, particularly in the spacious public rooms and restaurants. Individually decorated bedrooms and suites come in varying shapes, sizes and styles, but consistently applied are their high degree of comfort, tasteful furnishings and thoughtful extras. Wander around the grounds before heading for the grand Salon, largest of the three dining rooms, and Head Chef Alan Ford's well-balanced carte, from which examples include grilled fillet of haddock served in a mussel and clam chowder, and tournedos of beef with braised oxtail and horseradish. Many of the dishes encompass fresh herbs from the famous garden, designed by the late Robert Carrier, who bought the then derelict Hall in 1972. The award-winning 350-bin wine list includes a generous selection of half bottles. Health and beauty and specialist treatments, and a gym with instructors, complement the seasonal pool. A championship PGA golf course is adjacent to the Hall.

Recommended in the area

Constable Country; Aldeburgh; Newmarket Racecourse

Salthouse Harbour Hotel

★★★★ ◉◉ TOWN HOUSE HOTEL
Address: No 1 Neptune Quay, IPSWICH, IP4 1AX
Tel: 01473 226789
Fax: 01473 226927
Email: staying@salthouseharbour.co.uk
Website: www.salthouseharbour.co.uk
Map ref: 4, TM14 **Directions:** A14 junct 56 follow
town centre & Salthouse signs **Rooms:** 70 (6 fmly)
S from £110 D from £125 (incl. bkfst)
Facilities: Freeview TV Wi-fi **Parking:** 30

Just a short walk from the town centre, this waterfront warehouse has been converted into a striking contemporary hotel full of local urban art and curios, a good example being the sculpture of a scorpion acquired by chance in the East End of London. Providing luxurious comfort are the spacious bedrooms, some with feature bathrooms, some with balconies; then there are the two air-conditioned penthouse suites, both with telescopes to fully appreciate the striking views of the marina and beyond. Award-winning, modern food, such as fillet of Dedham Vale beef with potato rösti, is served in the busy, ground-floor eaterie.

Recommended in the area

Flatford Mill & Lock; Snape Maltings; Lavenham village

milsoms Kesgrave Hall

★★★ 86% ◉ HOTEL
Address: Hall Road, Kesgrave, IPSWICH IP5 2PU
Tel: 01473 333741
Fax: 01473 617614
Email: reception@kesgravehall.com
Website: www.milsomhotels.com
Map ref: 4, TM46
Directions: A12 N of Ipswich, left at Ipswich/
Woodbridge rdbt onto B1214. Right after 0.5m into
Hall Rd. Hotel 200yds on left

Rooms: 23 (8 GF) (4 fmly) D £120-£245 (room only) **Facilities:** STV Wi-fi **Parking:** 100

A Grade II listed mansion transformed into a contemporary brasserie with private dining, meeting spaces and bedrooms, situated in over 38 acres of park and woodland. The bedrooms are all different in style and range from standard to super deluxe with huge walk-in showers. In the open-plan restaurant, head chef Stuart Oliver champions all that is great about Suffolk produce, with food served all day and dining on the terrace under a huge architectural sail.

Recommended in the area

Suffolk Heritage Coast; Aldeburgh & Snape; Sutton Hoo (NT)

The Swan

★★★★ 83% ◉◉ HOTEL

Address: High Street, LAVENHAM, CO10 9QA
Tel: 01787 247477
Fax: 01787 248286
Email: info@theswanatlavenham.co.uk
Website: www.theswanatlavenham.co.uk
Map ref: 4, TL94
Directions: From Bury St Edmunds take A134 (S), then A1141 to Lavenham
Rooms: 45 (13 GF) (11 fmly) S £95-£105
D £180-£300 (incl. bkfst) **Facilities:** STV Wi-fi **Parking:** 62

This iconic hotel dates back to the 15th century and is located in a village famous for the similarly ancient buildings that line its streets. Many people visit Lavenham just to marvel at its historic charms, but a stay at The Swan truly completes the experience. Ancient oak beams, inglenook fireplaces and original medieval wall paintings, together with a beautiful decor of rich fabrics, provide a perfect ambience. History oozes from every fibre of the building. The Old Bar is particularly interesting for its World War II memorabilia and a wall signed by British and American airmen who were stationed at Lavenham Airfield. The bedrooms are equally historic, but with contemporary furnishings sympathetically incorporated. Expect modern bathrooms, plasma-screen TVs and facilities for making tea and coffee. As well as standard double rooms there are mezzanine suites, and some have four-poster beds. The Swan offers several dining options, including the informal Garden Lounge, the Old Bar, outdoors in the garden in summer, or the elegant Gallery Restaurant. The Swan's modern British cuisine has won the hotel an enviable reputation for fine dining including the award of two AA Rosettes. The sumptuous traditional afternoon teas are as good as they get.

Recommended in the area

Lavenham Guildhall; Kentwell Hall; Ickworth House

The Angel

★★★★ ◎ RESTAURANT WITH ROOMS
Address: Market Place, LAVENHAM, CO10 9QZ
Tel: 01787 247388
Fax: 01787 248344
Email: angel@maypolehotels.com
Website: www.maypolehotels.com
Map ref: 4, TL94
Directions: From A14 take Bury E & Sudbury turn onto A143. After 4m take A1141 to Lavenham. Off High Street **Rooms:** 8 en suite (1 fmly rooms) (1 GF)
S £85-£95 **D** £105-£120 **Notes:** Wi-fi **Parking:** 5

The Angel was first licensed in 1420 and is believed to be the oldest inn in the medieval town of Lavenham. Although much altered over the centuries, the building retains plenty of old-world character, including exposed beams and a large inglenook fireplace. There are eight smart, comfortable bedrooms with TV, telephone, tea- and coffee-making facilities and hairdryer. The Angel has held an AA Rosette consistently since 1995 and everything is prepared on the premises from mostly local ingredients. The same menu is served in the restaurant, bar, snug or out on the terrace or in the garden.

Recommended in the area

Lavenham town; Bury St Edmunds; Orford

14th-century Little Hall, Lavenham

The Olde Bull Inn

★★★ 83% ◉ HOTEL

Address: The Street, Barton Mills, MILDENHALL,
Bury St Edmunds, IP28 6AA
Tel: 01638 711001
Fax: 01638 712003
Email: bookings@bullinn-bartonmills.com
Website: www.bullinn-bartonmills.com
Map ref: 4, TL77 **Directions:** Off A11 between Newmarket &
Mildenhall, signed Barton Mills. Hotel by Five Ways rdbt
Rooms: 14 (2 GF) (2 fmly) S £75-£95 D £85-£125 (incl. bkfst)
Facilities: STV Wi-fi **Parking:** 60 **Notes:** ⊗ in bedrooms

This 16th-century coaching inn in the lovely village of Barton Mills was rescued from dereliction and reopened as a hotel over ten years ago. More recently the current owners transformed the bedrooms into charming boutique accommodation with a mixture of period details, designer fabrics and wallpapers and contemporary furniture. Every bedroom is individually designed and has an en suite bathroom along with flat-screen TV with Freeview, direct-dial telephone, beverage tray and hairdryer. Food is one of the biggest draws at The Olde Bull Inn, with everything made in-house using the best, freshest ingredients from local suppliers. The charming Oak Room Restaurant has an AA Rosette and serves modern British food, including the signature 'fillet steak tower' – best local beef covered in a creamy pepper sauce, layered with onions and resting on a parsnip and potato rösti. The daily specials board always offers something seasonal to supplement the main menu, such as Brancaster mussels or Thornham oysters. Less formal meals and snacks – along with local real ales – are served in the cosy bar with its log fire, and in the summer you can dine alfresco in the courtyard.

Recommended in the area

Shopping & punting in Cambridge; Center Parcs spa at Elveden Forest; Go Ape! at Thetford Forest

The Crown & Castle

★★★ 86% ◎◎ HOTEL

Address: ORFORD, IP12 2LJ
Tel: 01394 450205
Email: info@crownandcastle.co.uk
Website: www.crownandcastle.co.uk
Map ref: 4, TM45
Directions: Turn right from B1084 on entering village, towards castle
Rooms: 19 (11 GF) (1 fmly) **Facilities:** Wi-fi
Parking: 20 **Notes:** ✱ 4yrs

Ruth and David Watson have created a delightful inn that brings together good food, a genial atmosphere, and stylishly simple, well designed accommodation. The location, next to Orford's old castle keep, is peaceful and perfect for exploring the Suffolk Heritage Coast. Bedrooms are bright and airy, with contemporary decor and furnishings. Garden rooms are the most spacious, and have a semi-private terrace overlooking the castle. Food is a highlight – hardly surprising, since Ruth is an award-winning food writer – with interesting dishes featuring the finest locally sourced ingredients.

Recommended in the area

Snape Maltings; Orford Ness (NT); Sutton Hoo

Orford Castle

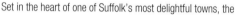

Swan Hotel

★★★★ 78% ◉◉ HOTEL

Address: Market Place, SOUTHWOLD, IP18 6EG

Tel: 01502 722186

Fax: 01502 724800

Email: swan.hotel@adnams.co.uk

Website: www.adnams.co.uk

Map ref: 4, TM57

Directions: A1095 to Southwold. Hotel in town centre. Parking via archway to left of building

Rooms: 42 (17 GF) **Facilities:** STV **Parking:** 42

Set in the heart of one of Suffolk's most delightful towns, the Swan dates back to the 14th century, though today it represents a mixture of 18th-century ambience in its public areas and 21st-century comforts in the bedrooms. Stay in the main hotel itself or in the Lighthouse Rooms in the peaceful garden from where you can see Southwold's Victorian lighthouse. All the bedrooms and suites are beautifully and individually furnished – the 16 Lighthouse Rooms even have their own private patios. In the main building, the drawing room facing the Market Square is the perfect place to chat, read and relax or treat yourself to afternoon tea. The famous Adnams beer is brewed at the back of The Swan, and you can enjoy it in the hotel bar while catching up on the local gossip, as well as on a tour of the brewery. Contemporary British cooking, based on top-notch local produce, is the name of the game in the award-winning restaurant, where a meal might take in seared scallops with chorizo, fennel and lemon oil, followed by pork fillet and belly with cabbage and bacon and rosemary mash. Entertainment at The Swan ranges from literary lunches to wine weekends. Dogs are welcome to stay in selected rooms by prior arrangement.

Recommended in the area

Adnams Brewery; Southwold; RSPB Minsmere reserve

The Crown

★★ 85% ◉ HOTEL

Address: 90 High Street, SOUTHWOLD, IP18 6DP
Tel: 01502 722275
Fax: 01502 727263
Email: crown.hotel@adnams.co.uk
Website: www.adnams.co.uk
Map ref: 4, TM57
Directions: A12 onto A1095 to Southwold. Hotel on left in High
Street **Rooms:** 14 (2 fmly) **Parking:** 15 **Notes:** ⊗ in bedrooms

Situated right in the heart of the unspoilt town of Southwold,
The Crown is an intimate combination of a small hotel, a wine bar
and a restaurant. It is renowned for its gastro-pub style cuisine that uses high quality, locally-sourced
food which is complemented by an eclectic and celebrated selection of wines. The individually designed
bedrooms are reached through twisting corridors, and include beamed attic rooms, premier rooms and
a spacious suite ideal for families. You can't reserve a table but booking a room early is advisable.

Recommended in the area

Suffolk Heritage Coast; RSPB Minsmere reserve; Snape Maltings

Sutherland House Hotel

★★★★★ ◉◉ RESTAURANT WITH ROOMS

Address: 56 High Street, SOUTHWOLD, IP18 6DN
Tel: 1502 724544
E-mail: enquiries@sutherlandhouse.co.uk
Web: www.sutherlandhouse.co.uk
Map ref: 4, TM57 **Directions:** A1095 into Southwold, on High
St on left after Victoria St **Rooms:** 4 (1 fmly) **S** £140-£200 **D**
£140-£250 **Facilities:** Wi-fi **Parking:** 1 **Notes:** ⊗

Dating from 1455, this elegant, pink-washed townhouse has
the distinction of being one of Southwold's most historically
important buildings. When James II stayed here he doubtless
warmed his hands in front of one of the huge fireplaces, but how
much he admired the impressive pargetted plasterwork ceilings
and ancient beams goes unrecorded. Tastefully decorated bedrooms respect the building's generous
medieval proportions and retain many features from those times. The AA has awarded the restaurant
two Rosettes for its high standards, with dishes including fresh, locally caught fish; home-made black
pudding sausages and mash; and roasted winter vegetable salad with chilli.

Recommended in the area

Suffolk Heritage Coast; Minsmere Nature Reserve; Snape Maltings

The Westleton Crown

★★★ 79% ◉◉ HOTEL

Address: The Street, WESTLETON, Nr Southwold,
IP17 3AD
Tel: 01728 648777
Fax: 01728 648239
Email: info@westletoncrown.co.uk
Website: www.westletoncrown.co.uk
Map ref: 4, TM46
Directions: A12 N, right for Westleton just after
Yoxford. Hotel opposite on entering Westleton

Rooms: 34 (12 GF) (7 fmly) **S** £80-£100 **D** £90-£215 (incl. bkfst) **Facilities:** Wi-fi **Parking:** 45

Whether you want to get away from it all on a short break or simply need somewhere to stay on the Suffolk coast, the Westleton Crown has it all. Dating back to the 12th century, this traditional coaching inn retains the character and rustic charm of its heritage, but with all the comforts the 21st-century traveller could hope for. The bar has the feel of a genuine local, with a warm welcome and plenty of Suffolk ales to enjoy. Meals may be taken in the bar, elegant dining room or stylish Garden Room, as well as in the charming terraced gardens during warmer weather. Food is taken extremely seriously at the Westleton Crown, with everything – from bread to soups, pates and ice cream – made in-house from the finest, freshest ingredients. Menus are imaginative and varied and complemented by an extensive wine list. The bedrooms are individually designed and exceptionally comfortable. Those in the main inn are more traditional in style, while more contemporary rooms can be found in the converted stables and cottages. Whichever you choose, expect flat-screen TVs, tea and coffee-making facilities, beautiful bathrooms and luxuriously large beds with fully sprung mattresses, goose down duvets and crisp white Egyptian cotton linen.

Recommended in the area

RSPB Minsmere reserve; Dunwich; Snape Maltings

Satis House

★★★ 88% ◎◎ COUNTRY HOUSE HOTEL

Address: YOXFORD, IP17 3EX
Tel: 01728 668418
Fax: 01728 668640
Email: enquiries@satishouse.co.uk
Website: www.satishouse.co.uk
Map ref: 4, TM36
Directions: Off A12 between Ipswich & Lowestoft.
9m E Aldeburgh & Snape
Rooms: 10 (2 GF) (1 fmly)
Facilities: STV Wi-fi **Parking:** 30 **Notes:** ⊗ in bedrooms

This hotel is a Grade II listed country house built in 1769 that sits in three acres of wooded grounds. Charles Dickens is said to have written *Great Expectations* while staying at this residence as a friend of the owners, and he chose the name Satis House as Miss Havisham's residence in the novel. Today it remains the same elegant house it was during Dickens' visit in 1860, but it's been completely refurbished in recent years and offers a variety of en suite rooms ranging from antique chic to contemporary, some with feature beds and one with a large balcony. Each room is individually designed but all have Egyptian cotton sheets, tea- and coffee-making facilities, flat-screen TV and DVD player. The restaurant serves award-winning modern British cuisine based around the best seasonal and local ingredients, and the kitchen always likes to know the history of how and where the animals were reared. Afternoon tea is served on the lawns when the weather permits. The hotel makes an ideal setting for a wedding venue.

Recommended in the area

Southwold; Aldeburgh; Framlingham Castle

SURREY

Statue at Hampton Court

the runnymede-on-thames

★★★★ 79% HOTEL

Address: Windsor Road, EGHAM, TW20 0AG
Tel: 01784 220600
Fax: 01784 436340
Email: info@therunnymede.co.uk
Website: www.therunnymede.co.uk
Map ref: 3, TQ07
Directions: M25 junct 13, onto A308 towards Windsor
Rooms: 180 (19 fmly) **Facilities:** STV Wi-fi ⊗ ⊀ Gym Spa **Parking:** 280 **Notes:** ⊗ in bedrooms

From its peaceful location beside the River Thames, this large modern hotel offers an excellent range of leisure and corporate facilities. Guest rooms, with either river or courtyard views, are stylishly furnished and offer many delights, from cosy duvets to fast broadband access. In the Leftbank Restaurant, produce is carefully sourced and the result is 'an eclectic fusion' of Mediterranean and British food; an extensive wine list includes some imaginative bins. The Lock, beside the Bell Lock Weir, is the hotel's brand new eatery where guests can dine alfresco when the weather permits. With a bistro-style atmosphere it provides a menu of 'simple and bold' dishes. With its riverside terrace and gardens, the lounge is the place for afternoon tea or even a cocktail or two. Guests here can choose to do a little or as much as they like for this is an excellent place to relax. Perhaps swim in the 18-metre pool, relax in the whirlpool bath, enjoy a sauna or the eucalyptus steam room, or work up a sweat in the dance studio, gym or on the tennis courts. Just nearby are Royal Windsor and Heathrow, and central London is only 40 minutes down the road.

Recommended in the area

Windsor Castle; Legoland; Magna Carta Memorial

Lythe Hill Hotel and Spa

★★★★ 74% <img_2> HOTEL
Address: Petworth Road, HASLEMERE, GU27 3BQ
Tel: 01428 651251
Fax: 01428 644131
Email: lythe@lythehill.co.uk
Website: www.lythehill.co.uk
Map ref: 3, SU93
Directions: From High St onto B2131. Hotel 1.25m on right
Rooms: 41 (18 GF) (8 fmly)
Facilities: Wi-fi ⊠ Gym Spa **Parking:** 200

A haven of comfort and elegance in the heart of the English countryside and set in 22 acres of tranquil Surrey countryside, the small, luxury Lythe Hill Hotel & Spa offers the perfect retreat for the discerning guest. From luxury suites and antique four-poster beds to double rooms and garden suites, each of the 41 bedrooms is individually designed to reflect its unique character. The bedrooms in the historic listed buildings are gracious and stately, while those in the newer buildings are modern and stylish. For an unforgettable dining experience, choose The Restaurant and sit in the oak-panelled dining room or the New Room overlooking the lake and parkland. Amarna Spa is inspired by the life of Queen Nefertiti, whose name means 'the beautiful one has arrived'. Aptly set in the Surrey Hills Area of Outstanding Natural Beauty, Amarna Spa has been designed to reflect Nefertiti's desire for tranquillity underpinned by her passion for pampering.

Recommended in the area

Haslemere; Petworth House (NT); Goodwood horse & motor racing; Lurgashall Winery

EAST SUSSEX

Brighton beach from the pier

The Cooden Beach Hotel

★★★ 80% HOTEL
Address: Cooden Beach, BEXHILL, TN39 4TT
Tel: 01424 842281
Fax: 01424 846142
Email: rooms@thecoodenbeachhotel.co.uk
Website: www.thecoodenbeachhotel.co.uk
Map ref: 4, TQ70
Directions: A259 towards Cooden. Signed at rdbt in
Little Common **Rooms:** 41 (4 GF) (10 fmly) S £60
D £120 (incl. bkfst) **Facilities:** Wi-fi ⊗ Gym Spa
Sauna **Parking:** 60 **Notes:** ⊗ in bedrooms

To the west, Beachy Head plunges dramatically seawards, while from many of the bedrooms in this privately owned, beach-fronting hotel, half the English Channel seems to be on view. All of them have newly installed en suite facilities and most benefit from luxurious king-size beds. Take in more maritime views from the Oceana Restaurant, whose traditional English menu features 'posh' fish and chips with mushy peas. Bar food and daily blackboard specials are also available in the Cooden Tavern, while the Club Bar & Terrace focuses on drinks. Leisure facilities include heated swimming pool, gym and sauna.
Recommended in the area
Bodiam Castle (NT); Rye; Drusillas Zoo Park

Devonshire Park Hotel

★★★ 79% HOTEL
Address: 27-29 Carlisle Road, EASTBOURNE,
BN21 4JR
Tel: 01323 728144
Fax: 01323 419734
Email: info@devonshire-park-hotel.co.uk
Website: www.devonshire-park-hotel.co.uk
Map ref: 4, TV69
Directions: Follow signs to seafront, exit at Wish
Tower. Hotel opposite Congress Theatre
Rooms: 35 (8 GF) S £40-£75 D £80-£150 (incl. bkfst)
Facilities: STV Wi-fi **Parking:** 25 **Notes:** ⊗ in bedrooms 🧒 12yrs

This elegant Victorian hotel boasts one of the finest locations in Eastbourne, opposite Devonshire Park and The Congress Theatre. It's just a short stroll to the shops from here too, and only 150 metres to the main promenade. The rooms are spacious, comfortable and contemporary in style, and all enjoy good views. Two suites have private patios and one has its own sun terrace. The restaurant offers a traditional English menu, while light lunches are served in the bar.
Recommended in the area
Devonshire Park International Tennis Centre; Eastbourne promenade; South Downs National Park

The Grand Hotel

★★★★★ 84% ◉◉ HOTEL

Address: King Edward's Parade, EASTBOURNE,
BN21 4EQ
Tel: 01323 412345
Fax: 01323 412233
Email: reservations@grandeastbourne.com
Website: www.grandeastbourne.com
Map ref: 4, TV69
Directions: On seafront W of Eastbourne, 1m from
railway station **Rooms:** 152 (4 GF) (20 fmly)
D £199-£555 (incl. bkfst) **Facilities:** STV ⊗ ⚲ Gym Spa **Parking:** 80

Standing majestically along the Eastbourne seafront and affectionately known as 'The White Palace', the 19th-century Grand Hotel is a truly impressive venue. The view of the great hall on arrival leaves you in no doubt of this, an impression that continues throughout the hotel, which has played host in the past to such renowned figures as Winston Churchill and Charlie Chaplin. Each of the bedrooms and suites is individually decorated and beautifully presented. Many of the rooms enjoy panoramic views over the English Channel and have their own private balcony. The hotel has 12 private function rooms available for intimate private meetings, large wedding ceremonies and receptions and lavish events. Children are well catered for, with a playroom supervised by qualified carers and a welcome pack on arrival. There is a choice of fine dining in the Mirabelle Restaurant or the equally superb Garden Restaurant. For something lighter, perhaps after a bracing walk along the seafront on the hotel's doorstep, the Grand's afternoon teas, served in the great hall, are not to be missed. Leisure facilities include indoor and outdoor heated pools, a gym and a range of spa treatments.

Recommended in the area

Beachy Head; Glyndebourne Opera House; Drusillas Zoo; Sovereign Harbour

Ashdown Park Hotel & Country Club

★★★★ ◎◎ HOTEL

Address: Wych Cross, FOREST ROW, RH18 5JR
Tel: 01342 824988
Fax: 01342 826206
Email: reservations@ashdownpark.com
Website: www.ashdownpark.com
Map ref: 3, TQ43
Directions: A264 to East Grinstead, A22 to Eastbourne. 2m S of Forest Row at Wych Cross lights. Left to Hartfield, hotel on right 0.75m
Rooms: 106 (16 GF) **D** £199–£465 (incl. bkfst) **Facilities:** STV Wi-fi ⊗ Gym Spa **Parking:** 200

Set within 186 acres of lakes, secret gardens, manicured lawns, woodland trails and unspoilt countryside, Ashdown Park sits proudly at the heart of Ashdown Forest. Evolving from a 19th-century listed mansion house, the hotel provides today's guests with the perfect setting to relax, unwind and indulge. The sense of grandeur carries through to the lavishly decorated bedrooms, which overlook the beautiful grounds. All differ in shape, style and decor, and come with thoughtful extras such as bathrobes, mineral water and Molton Brown toiletries. Facilities include palatial lounges, the Richard Towneley Suite (a sympathetically restored former chapel ideal for exclusive meetings and wedding parties) and the award-winning, fine-dining Anderida Restaurant. Lighter lunches are served in the drawing rooms and Fairways Brasserie located in the Country Club. The extensive indoor and outdoor leisure facilities include an indoor pool, gym, tennis courts, 18-hole golf course and spa with a range of treatments available.

Recommended in the area

Bluebell Railway; Sheffield Park Gardens; Royal Tunbridge Wells

Newick Park Hotel & Country Estate

★★★ ◉◉ HOTEL

Address: NEWICK, BN8 4SB
Tel: 01825 723633
Fax: 01825 723969
Email: bookings@newickpark.co.uk
Website: www.newickpark.co.uk
Map ref: 3, TQ42 **Directions:** Exit A272 at Newick
Green, 1m, pass church & pub. Left, hotel 0.25m
Rooms: 16 (1 GF) (5 fmly) **S** £125-£245 **D** £165-£285 (incl. bkfst) **Facilities:** Wi-fi ⚲ **Parking:** 50
This is a beautiful Grade II listed Georgian country-house set in over 200 acres of landscaped grounds
with stunning views, where guests enjoy an outstanding level of award-winning service along with
complete peace and privacy. The spacious bedrooms are beautifully furnished, with wonderfully
comfortable beds and fine antique furniture. The restaurant makes fine use of fruit and vegetables from
the walled garden, and game from the estate. For the more adventurous there is an extensive choice of
activities.

Recommended in the area

Glyndebourne Opera; Sheffield Park Gardens; Brighton's Lanes

The Lanes, Brighton

Dale Hill Hotel & Golf Club

★★★★ 81% ⊛ HOTEL

Address: TICEHURST, TN5 7DQ
Tel: 01580 200112
Fax: 01580 201249
Email: info@dalehill.co.uk
Website: www.dalehill.co.uk
Map ref: 4, TQ63
Directions: M25 junct 5/A21. 5m after Lamberhurst right onto B2087 to Flimwell. Hotel 1m on left
Rooms: 35 (23 GF) (8 fmly) S £80–£110 D £100–£210 (incl. bkfst) **Facilities:** STV Wi-fi ⟲ Gym **Parking:** 220 **Notes:** ⊗

Set in magnificent countryside, with views across the High Weald, this modern hotel is only a short drive from the village. Extensive public rooms include a lounge bar, conservatory brasserie, formal restaurant and the lively Spike Bar, which is where golfers, fresh from playing one of the two 18-hole courses, like to congregate (and commiserate). Dale Hill also has an indoor heated swimming pool and gym. Spacious en suite bedrooms feature radio, TV, direct-dial phones, modem access, hairdryer, tea and coffee facilities, safe and trouser press. Those on the south side of the hotel overlook the golf course, the executive rooms having the extra advantage of balconies. The modern European menu in the elegant AA Rosette-winning Wealden View Restaurant is complemented by an international wine list. For simpler dishes, head for The Eighteenth Restaurant, to the Lounge for a traditional Sussex afternoon tea, or the Club House Bar to catch up on the latest sports scores. The conference and banqueting suite can accommodate up to 200 delegates. Ian Woosnam, the 1991 Masters winner, designed the championship standard, 6,500-yard golf course; the Old Course attracts the high handicappers.

Recommended in the area

Groombridge Place; Bodiam Castle; Kent & East Sussex Railway

WEST SUSSEX

Arundel Castle

Bailiffscourt Hotel & Spa

★★★ ◎◎ HOTEL

Address: Climping Street, CLIMPING, BN17 5RW
Tel: 01903 723511
Fax: 01903 723107
Email: bailiffscourt@hshotels.co.uk
Website: www.hshotels.co.uk
Map ref: 3, SU90
Directions: A259, follow Climping Beach signs. Hotel 0.5m on right **Rooms:** 39 (16 GF) (25 fmly) **S** £215-£530 **D** £235-£695 (incl. bkfst) **Facilities:** STV Wi-fi ⊗ ⅃ Gym Spa Sauna **Parking:** 100

Appearances can be deceptive. From the outside, Bailiffscourt is a classic, part-thatched, part-tiled manor house, reached down a quiet lane behind unspoilt Climping beach. But actually, it dates from only the 1920s, when Sir Walter Guinness gathered stone and wood from all over England to create the buildings that are Bailiffscourt as a family retreat. Gothic mullioned windows overlook the rose-clad courtyard, whilst narrow passageways lead through a series of intimate lounges and sitting rooms. Many of the public rooms feature open log fires and fine antiques, tapestries and fresh flowers. Located in the grounds, bedrooms vary from the atmospheric, with log fires, oak beams and four-poster beds, to the spacious and contemporary. Baylies, the master suite, with its huge vaulted ceiling, open fire and vast bathroom with walk-in shower and twin baths is for that special occasion. Classic European cooking is the mainstay of The Tapestry Restaurant, and during the summer lunch and afternoon tea may be enjoyed in the courtyard. The award-winning spa has heated indoor and outdoor pools, sauna, steam room, hot tub, gym and treatment rooms. Take a walk through the 30-acre grounds to the beach, counting peacocks along the way.

Recommended in the area

Walk through hotel grounds to beach; Goodwood; South Downs National Park; Arundel Castle

Ockenden Manor

★★★ ◉◉◉ HOTEL

Address: Ockenden Lane, CUCKFIELD, RH17 5LD
Tel: 01444 416111
Fax: 01444 415549
Email: reservations@ockenden-manor.com
Website: www.hshotels.co.uk
Map ref: 3, TQ32
Directions: A23 towards Brighton. 4.5m left onto B2115 towards Haywards Heath. Cuckfield 3m. Ockenden Lane off High St. Hotel at end
Rooms: 22 (4 GF) (4 fmly) S £110-£205 D £187-£376 (incl. bkfst)
Facilities: STV Wi-fi **Parking:** 60

Tucked away down a little country lane lies this charming Elizabethan manor house. With open views across nine acres of beautifully maintained grounds to the South Downs, the hotel is within easy reach of some of the region's great houses and gardens, as well as raffish Brighton and rather genteel Eastbourne. The public rooms, including an elegant sitting room, retain much of their original character. En suite bedrooms are all individually furnished and provided with satellite TV, direct-dial phone, trouser press, hairdryer and hospitality tray. All are named after members of the two families who have owned the hotel since 1520. Merrick, for example, has its own dining room, while Elizabeth is reached by a private staircase and is apparently home to a 'friendly but sad' ghost. In the dining room with sweeping views across the gardens towards the South Downs National Park, you can expect some seriously good French-oriented food. The seven-course tasting menu is worth starving yourself for. A small dining room is suitable for semi-private dining, while in summer light meals can be taken on the terrace or in the gardens. Ockenden has a huge wine cellar, sourced from all over the world.

Recommended in the area

Wakehurst Place; Hever Castle; Glyndebourne Opera House

Felbridge Hotel & Spa

★★★★86% ◉◉ HOTEL

Address: London Road, EAST GRINSTEAD, RH19 2BH

Tel: 01342 337700

Fax: 01342 337715

Email: sales@felbridgehotel.co.uk

Website: www.felbridgehotel.co.uk

Map ref: 3, TQ33 **Directions:** From W exit M23 junct 10, follow signs to A22. From N, exit M25 junct 6. Hotel on A22 **Rooms:** 120 (53 GF) (16 fmly) **S**

£79-£290 **D** £79-£290 **Facilities:** STV Wi-fi ⊗ Gym Spa Sauna **Parking:** 300 **Notes:** ⊗ in bedrooms Conveniently located on the edge of town, with Gatwick Airport about 15 minutes' away, this hotel offers fashionably designed bedrooms that have ultra-comfortable beds, power showers, flat-screen TVs and Wi-fi; complimentary fresh fruit and a bottle of wine await guests in the luxury studios and junior suites. The two-AA Rosette Anise restaurant serves modern British cuisine using produce sourced from Sussex, Surrey and Kent whenever possible. The less formal Bay Tree Restaurant is open for breakfast, lunch and dinner, while a range of food and drinks is also available in the contemporary QUBE Bar, lounge and library.

Recommended in the area Chartwell; Bluebell Railway; Wakehurst Place

Wakehurst Place (NT), Ardingly

Best Western Gatwick Moat House

★★★ 80% HOTEL

Address: Longbridge Roundabout, HORLEY, RH6 0AB

Tel: 0870 443 1671 & 01293 899988

Fax: 01293 899904

Email: gatwick@qmh-hotels.com

Website: www.bestwestern.co.uk

Map ref: 3, TQ24 **Directions:** M23 junct 9, follow North Terminal signs, 4th exit at rdbt signed A23/Redhill. At rdbt take 1st exit then 1st left

Rooms: 125 (20 fmly) **Facilities:** Wi-fi **Parking:** 8

Leave your car securely in the hotel's on-site parking facility and take the shuttle service to catch your flight. Buses run 24 hours a day to the North and South Terminals, both merely minutes away. Given the hotel's location you can expect everything to be geared towards the air traveller, so rooms, including the family ones that sleep up to seven, are comfortably functional with en suite bathrooms, tea and coffee-making facilities and Wi-fi access. They are obviously well sound-proofed, and in any case the airport runway is aligned east-west to the south of the hotel, so that the near-midnight arrival from Istanbul is unlikely to disturb your sleep. Informal Harriet's Restaurant serves a selection of retro classics, traditional grills and dishes such as risotto, sautéed chicken tagliatelle, and grilled sea bass. A children's menu and special entertainment packs will keep them occupied before their flight. If you choose to dine in the Lounge Bar you'll find burgers, scampi and chips, jacket potatoes, pizzas and other quick bites and light snacks. Eight meeting rooms are served by a dedicated café providing unlimited all-day tea and coffee. Best Western's hotel park-and-fly packages include accommodation for one night on a room-only basis.

Recommended in the area

Wakehurst Place (NT); Leonardslee Lakes & Gardens; Leith Hill

Arundel Cathedral

Spread Eagle Hotel and Spa

★★★ 81% ◉◉ HOTEL

Address: South Street, MIDHURST, GU29 9NH
Tel: 01730 816911
Fax: 01730 815668
Email: spreadeagle@hshotels.co.uk
Website: www.hshotels.co.uk/spread/
spreadeagle-main.htm
Map ref: 3, SU82
Directions: M25 junct 10, A3 to Milford, A286 to Midhurst. Hotel adjacent to market square
Rooms: 38 (8 GF) **S** £80-£380 **D** £90-£380 (incl. bkfst) **Facilities:** STV Wi-fi ⊗ Gym Spa Sauna
Parking: 75

This ancient coaching inn has been offering accommodation to travellers since 1430, and was described by Hilaire Belloc as, 'that oldest and most revered of all the prime inns of this world'. The building is brimful of original features, including sloping floors, huge inglenook fireplaces and Tudor bread ovens, while the individually styled bedrooms, oak-panelled in the main house, provide up-to-the-minute comforts. The Tapestry Restaurant serves modern British cuisine.

Recommended in the area

Goodwood Estate; Petworth House; Cowdray Park, West Dean Gardens

Polo match at Cowdray Park

TYNE & WEAR

The Millennium and Tyne Bridges, Newcastle upon Tyne

Vermont Hotel

★★★★ 81% ◉ HOTEL

Address: Castle Garth, NEWCASTLE UPON TYNE,
NE1 1RQ
Tel: 0191 233 1010
Fax: 0191 233 1234
Email: info@vermont-hotel.co.uk
Website: www.vermont-hotel.com
Map ref: 7, NZ26
Directions: City centre by high level bridge & castle keep
Rooms: 101 (12 fmly) **S** £100-£190
D £100-£190 **Facilities:** STV Wi-fi Gym **Parking:** 100

Adjacent to the castle and close to the buzzing Quayside area, this imposing, 12-storey, independently owned hotel enjoys fine views of the Tyne and Millennium Bridges. With an exterior style described as '1930s Manhattan tower', its plush interior is both traditional and contemporary. All bedrooms, including the grand suites, are equipped with three telephones, computer modem fax port, work desk, fully stocked mini-bar, satellite TV, and complimentary tea and coffee facilities. The elegant reception lounge encourages relaxation, while the Bridge Restaurant is open for breakfast, lunch and dinner. Through its windows, the Tyne Bridge looks close enough to reach out and pluck the suspension cables. The Blue Room provides the perfect setting for private dining in luxurious surroundings for up to 80 guests. The informal Redwood Bar is an intimate meeting place serving a large selection of wines and light meals until the early hours. Martha's Bar and Courtyard is popular too, particularly with the 20-somethings. Seven meeting and conference rooms cater as effortlessly for 300 people at a cocktail function as they do for a one-to-one meeting. A health and fitness centre is also available.

Recommended in the area

Newcastle Cathedral; Baltic Centre for Contemporary Art; Sage Centre, Gateshead

Canalside Café, Birmingham

Manor Hotel

★★★★ 82% ⊛ HOTEL

Address: Main Road, MERIDEN, Coventry, CV7 7NH
Tel: 01676 522735
Fax: 01676 522186
Email: reservations@manorhotelmeriden.co.uk
Website: www.manorhotelmeriden.co.uk
Map ref: 3, SP28
Directions: M42 junct 6, A45 towards Coventry.
A452 signed Leamington. At rdbt take B4102 signed
Meriden, hotel on left **Rooms:** 110 (20 GF)
S £60-£140 **D** £70-£180 (incl. bkfst) **Facilities:** Wi-fi **Parking:** 200 **Notes:** ⊗ in bedrooms

A plaque on an old cross on Meriden's village green announces that this is the very centre of England, but sadly in 2002 the Ordnance Survey defined the true geographical centre to be a farm 11 miles north in Leicestershire. Never mind, this Georgian-fronted hotel is more interested in being one of a select few in the luxury class to be conveniently located for the National Exhibition Centre and Birmingham International Airport, though not so close that occupants of its spacious, smartly finished and well-equipped bedrooms are disturbed by the roar of jet engines. Decorated with fresh flowers and artworks, the Regency Restaurant offers fine dining from a frequently changing menu, typically mushroom, ratatouille and asparagus cassoulet; chargrilled pork loin cutlet with cabbage, black pudding and Calvados cream jus; and pan-roasted chicken breast with herb mash, forest mushrooms and red wine sauce. Alternatively, throughout the day the bright and vibrant Houston's Bar & Grill offers handmade ground steak burgers; chicken and crayfish jambalaya; and chilli con carne, as well as freshly made ciabattas and salads. There are tables outside on the heated terrace if you prefer. Meeting rooms are available for conferences and corporate events.

Recommended in the area

National Sea Life Centre, Birmingham; National Motorcycle Museum; Historic Coventry

Fairlawns Hotel & Spa

★★★ 85% ◉◉ HOTEL

Address: 178 Little Aston Road, WALSALL,
WS9 0NU
Tel: 01922 455122
Fax: 01922 743148
Email: reception@fairlawns.co.uk
Website: www.fairlawns.co.uk
Map ref: 3, SP09
Directions: Off A452 towards Aldridge at x-roads
with A454. Hotel 600yds on right
Rooms: 58 (1 GF) (8 fmly) **S** £75-£149.50 **D** £95-£175 (incl. bkfst) **Facilities:** STV Wi-fi ⓧ Tennis
Gym Spa **Parking:** 150

Owned and run by the Pette family since 1984, this hotel lies in open countryside yet is close to Walsall, Sutton Coldfield and Lichfield and has good motorway access. Standing in nine acres of landscaped grounds, it also boasts an adult health club and spa, and guests have complimentary use of all the facilities, including a 20-metre indoor pool, two gyms and an impressive hydrotherapy suite. Beauty treatments and special spa days can also be arranged. The comfortable bedrooms, some modern, some more traditional, include family rooms and suites. All have modern facilities such as free high-speed Wi-fi access, digital flat-screen TV with Sky Sports channels, hairdryer, ironing facilities and good-quality toiletries (note that some smoking rooms are available). Quieter rooms and suites are located in a separate wing, away from normal hotel activities. The award-winning Fairlawns Restaurant offers lunch and dinner in comfortable, elegant surroundings, with attentive service and imaginative food, especially seafood, and it is little wonder that this is a popular local dining venue.

Recommended in the area

Walsall Art Gallery; Lichfield Cathedral; Cannock Chase, Area of Outstanding Natural Beauty

ISLE OF WIGHT

The Needles

Priory Bay Hotel

★★★79% ⚛ HOTEL

Address: Priory Drive, SEAVIEW, PO34 5BU
Tel: 01983 613146
Fax: 01983 616539
Email: enquiries@priorybay.co.uk
Website: www.priorybay.co.uk
Map ref: 3, SZ69
Directions: B3330 towards Seaview, through Nettlestone. (NB do not take Seaview turn, continue 0.5m to hotel sign) **Rooms:** 22 (2 GF) (6 fmly) **S** £90-£225 **D** £160-£300 (incl. bkfst) **Facilities:** Wi-fi ₹ **Parking:** 100 **Notes:** ⊗ in bedrooms

Look out for red squirrels in the 70 acres of private grounds and beach surrounding this creeper-clad, 14th-century hotel. Built by monks as a priory, and extended by Tudor farmers and Georgian gentry, it is now also a popular wedding, corporate events and filming venue. Bedrooms, all with impressive en suite bathrooms, display a fascinating mix of styles and original features; families can also stay in the converted tithe barns and cottages. Specialising in seafood, the Priory Oyster Bar & Grill is decorated in warm terracotta, its French windows opening on to a terrace planted with sub-tropical trees. In the fine-dining Island Room, admire the gilded plasterwork, and the murals of the island painted by Frederick Crace, whom the Prince Regent, later George IV, chose to create the chinoiserie interiors of his exotic Brighton Pavilion. In winter the large wood-burning fire warms the dining room wonderfully, while its floor-to-ceiling windows permit grand views of the Solent. Focusing on local seafood and game, the Island Room's seasonal menus include fillet of bream; roasted wood pigeon; and Briddlesford Farm veal; there's a six-course tasting menu too. Leisure facilities include a six-hole golf course, tennis courts, croquet lawn and outdoor swimming pool.

Recommended in the area

Seaview Wildlife Encounter; Osborne House; Isle of Wight Steam Railway

The Royal Hotel

★★★★ 78% ◉◉ HOTEL

Address: Belgrave Road, VENTNOR, PO38 1JJ
Tel: 01983 852186
Fax: 01983 855395
Email: enquiries@royalhoteliow.co.uk
Website: www.royalhoteliow.co.uk
Map ref: 3, SZ57
Directions: A3055 into Ventnor follow one-way system, after lights left into Belgrave Rd. Hotel on right **Rooms:** 54 (8 fmly) S £115-£195 D £190-£290 (incl. bkfst) **Facilities:** Wi-fi ⊀
Parking: 50 **Notes:** ⊗ in bedrooms

The Royal Hotel has been a destination for the discerning traveller for more than 150 years. Grand yet intimate, this beautiful early Victorian hotel has 54 bedrooms and is set in stunning sub-tropical gardens. The tone is English country house with a contemporary twist, using silks, velvets and elegant toile de jouy fabrics. Many of The Royal's principal bedrooms have delightful views over the garden or Ventnor Bay, and all are individually styled and equipped with flat-screen TVs and direct-dial telephones. A visit to the elegant two-Rosette restaurant, with its high ceilings and crystal chandeliers, is an absolute must. Passion, time and culinary invention go into putting together a constantly changing seasonal menu, which makes the most of excellent local produce. To sum up, this hotel offers award-winning dining, warm, attentive service and a fabulous location – quite simply the perfect destination for a family holiday or stylish getaway.

Recommended in the area:

Coastal walks; Ventnor Botanic Garden; Appuldurcombe House

George Hotel

★★★ ◎◎ HOTEL

Address: Quay Street, YARMOUTH, PO41 0PE
Tel: 01983 760331
Fax: 01983 760425
Email: res@thegeorge.co.uk
Website: www.thegeorge.co.uk
Map ref: 3, SZ38
Directions: Between castle & pier **Facilities:** STV
Notes: ⊗ in bedrooms 🐾 10yrs

This delightful 17th-century hotel enjoys a wonderful location at the water's edge, adjacent to the castle and quay. The entrance is large and light, with stone flags and a sweeping staircase. The cosy lounge is traditional – tapestry cushions and velvet curtains. Dining is in the Brasserie, a bright room with wonderful views over the Solent. Menus are seasonal, contemporary style with a European influence, and fish features regularly. Bedrooms are individually furnished with many thoughtful extras – some have balconies with sea views. The George offers an exciting programme of events throughout the year.

Recommended in the area:

Osborne House; Carisbrooke Castle; Ventnor Botanic Gardens

Osborne House

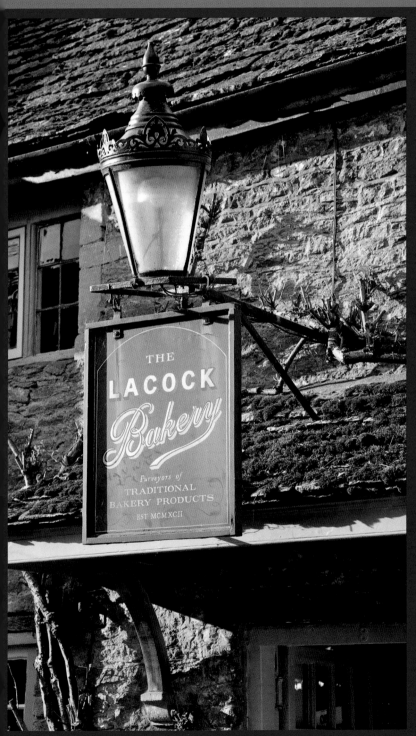

Lacock Bakery, Lacock

Lucknam Park Hotel & Spa

★★★★★ ❀❀❀ COUNTRY HOUSE HOTEL
Address: COLERNE, SN14 8AZ
Tel: 01225 742777
Fax: 01225 743536
Email: reservations@lucknampark.co.uk
Website: www.lucknampark.co.uk
Map ref: 2, ST87
Directions: M4 junct 17, A350 towards
Chippenham. A420 towards Bristol for 3m. At Ford
left to Colerne, 3m, right at x-rds, entrance on right

Rooms: 42 (16 GF) **S** £315-£1065 **D** £315-£1065 **Facilities:** STV Wi-fi ⊗ Tennis Gym Spa
Parking: 70 **Notes:** ⊗ in bedrooms

Lucknam Park Hotel & Spa is a magnificent listed Palladian mansion which sits proudly at the end of a glorious mile-long drive lined with beech and lime trees. The hotel's individually designed bedrooms, including 13 impressive suites, are truly luxurious. For a spot of pampering, head to the stunning spa, with its 20-metre pool, nine state-of-the-art treatment rooms, five thermal cabins, indoor and outdoor hydrotherapy pool, saltwater plunge pool and innovative skin and bodycare experiences. Within the spa, The Brasserie, with its open kitchen and wood-fired oven, offers contemporary and stylish dining, including a healthy option menu. For fine-dining at its best, the elegant three AA-Rosette The Park restaurant, serving accomplished modern British cuisine, is not to be missed. After all that wining and dining, you might feel like a bit of exercise, in which case Lucknam Park has it all: two floodlit tennis courts, a five-a-side football pitch, bicycles, walking and jogging trails, croquet and an extensive equestrian centre are all within the beautiful grounds. AA Hotel of the Year for England 2010-11.

Recommended in the area
Bath; Lacock Village (NT); Wells Cathedral

Whatley Manor

★★★★★ ⧮⧮⧮⧮ HOTEL

Address: Easton Grey, MALMESBURY, SN16 0RB
Tel: 01666 822888
Fax: 01666 826120
Email: reservations@whatleymanor.com
Website: www.whatleymanor.com
Map ref: 2, ST98
Directions: M4 junct 17, follow signs to Malmesbury, continue over 2 rdbts. Follow B4040 & signs for Sherston, hotel 2m on left
Rooms: 23 (4 GF) **S** £295-£855 **D** £295-£855 (incl. bkfst) **Facilities:** STV Wi-fi Gym Spa
Parking: 100 **Notes:** ⛔ 12yrs

This privately-owned hotel sits within 12 acres of pretty Wiltshire countryside. The bedrooms and suites are individually furnished in a sophisticated and contemporary style. With Martin Burge, one the UK's most talented chefs, at the helm, dinner in the elegant Dining Room is not to be missed. Alternatively, Le Mazot is an informal Swiss-style brasserie, open daily for lunch and dinner. The Aquarias spa boasts one of the largest hydrotherapy pools in Britain.

Recommended in the area

Bath; Cheltenham; Westonbirt Aboretum

Westonbirt Arboretum

The Manor

★★★★ RESTAURANT WITH ROOMS
Address: SHREWTON, SP3 4HF
Tel: 01980 620216
Email: info@rollestonemanor.com
Website: www.rollestonemanor.com
Map ref: 3, SU04
Rooms: 7 en suite (3 fmly rooms) (1 GF)
S £45-£115 D £45-£130
Notes: Wi-fi ⊗ in bedrooms
Parking: 40

This Grade II listed manor near Stonehenge has been the home of the Smith family for more than 60 years. When the previous Mrs Smith's children fled the nest she opened The Manor as a traditional B&B, but then the house, still owned by the family, was transformed into a luxury restaurant with rooms. The seven bedrooms come with all the 21st-century comforts you'd expect - such as DVD players, Wi-fi and iPod docks - while retaining much of their period charm and appeal. Each en suite bedroom is named after a past owner of the house and is individually designed, with antiques, beautiful soft furnishings and features such as free-standing roll-top baths and four-poster beds. Some may be used as family rooms and there's a bedroom on the ground floor for those who are unable to manage the stairs. The restaurant at The Manor serves plenty of fine Wiltshire produce from a seasonally changing menu of mainly British and European classics. Steeped in history, The Manor is a charming and peaceful place to stay with a genuinely warm and friendly atmosphere.

Recommended in the area

Stonehenge; Salisbury Cathedral & city; Longleat Safari Park

The Malvern Hills

Cotford Hotel & L'amuse Bouche Restaurant

★★★ 79% ◉ HOTEL

Address: 51 Graham Road, MALVERN, WR14 2HU
Tel: 01684 572427
Fax: 01684 572952
Email: reservations@cotfordhotel.co.uk
Website: www.cotfordhotel.co.uk
Map ref: 2, SO74

Directions: From Worcester A449 to Malvern. Left into Graham Rd signed town centre, hotel on right **Rooms:** 15 (1 GF) (3 fmly) **S** £69.50-£85 **D** £105-£125 (incl. bkfst) **Facilities:** STV Wi-fi **Parking:** 15

This Victorian gothic hotel is set in mature landscaped grounds at the foot of the beautiful Malvern Hills. It was built in 1851 as a summer residence for the Bishop of Worcester, and his private chapel now houses the award-winning L'amuse Bouche Restaurant. It is here that guests will find a taste of French-style cuisine in a quaint English setting. Before or after a meal, relax in front of an open fire in the piano lounge or bar, or perhaps enjoy a drink on the terrace during the summer months. The hotel's landscaped gardens are a joy to explore. The history of this charming property is apparent throughout – from the Bishop's room to the garden room in the coach house, all the rooms are brimming with character. Being only a few minutes' walk from the town centre yet with the feeling that it is miles from anywhere, guests will enjoy the best of both worlds at this hotel. In an Area of Outstanding Natural Beauty, Malvern is rich in heritage, the arts and an amazing range of activities.

Recommended in the area

The Malvern Hills (AONB); Great Malvern Priory; Little Malvern Court

The Cottage in the Wood Hotel

★★★ 85% ◉◉ HOTEL

Address: Holywell Road, Malvern Wells, MALVERN, WR14 4LG
Tel: 01684 588860
Fax: 01684 560662
Email: reception@cottageinthewood.co.uk
Website: www.cottageinthewood.co.uk
Map ref: 3, SO74
Directions: 3m S of Great Malvern off A449, 500yds N of B4209, on opposite side of road
Rooms: 30 (9 GF) S £79-£119 D £99-£195 (incl. bkfst) **Facilities:** Wi-fi **Parking:** 40

A uniquely situated hotel perched high on the Malvern Hills, with a panoramic view of the Severn Plain which fringes the Cotswolds. The 30-mile views are no less than stupendous, but you'll also find a hotel which has been in the same family ownership for 23 years, and is run by a team of enthusiastic people who really enjoy what they do. The comfortable bedrooms, most with large Vi-Spring beds, are spread between three buildings – the main house, which was originally a Georgian dower house, Beech Cottage, which was once a cider house, and The Pinnacles (here you'll find the largest rooms with the most spectacular views). Outlook is the name aptly given to the hotel's acclaimed restaurant, with its floor-to-ceiling windows offering diners a stunning aspect. It would be easy for the food to be upstaged by a vista like that, but the kitchen steps up to the mark, using quality local, seasonal ingredients to produce some ambitious but winning modern British dishes. The extensive wine list offers plenty to excite, too. After a hearty breakfast or an indulgent lunch, you can stroll directly onto the open tracts of the Malvern Hills and gaze from the lofty tops where Elgar gained inspiration for the *Dream of Gerontius* and other famous works.

Recommended in the area

Three Counties Showground; Worcester; Gloucester

NORTH YORKSHIRE

Whitby Harbour

Rudding Park Hotel Spa & Golf

★★★★ ◉◉ HOTEL

Address: Rudding Park, Follifoot, HARROGATE,
        HG3 1JH
Tel: 01423 871350
Fax: 01423 872286
Email: reservations@ruddingpark.com
Website: www.ruddingpark.co.uk
Map ref: 6, SE35
Directions: From A61 at rdbt with A658 take York
exit, follow signs to Rudding Park Rooms: 84 (31 GF)
S £130-£500 D £150-£500 (incl. bkfst) Facilities: STV Wi-fi Gym Spa Parking: 150
Notes: ⊗

Rudding Park is a luxurious retreat sitting in 300 acres of mature parkland just south of the beautiful spa town of Harrogate. The hotel is renowned for its warm welcome. The Clocktower Bar and Restaurant overlooks the gardens and offers modern British cuisine, including a Yorkshire menu. An 18-hole golf course and six-hole short course run through the existing parkland. The new spa opened in February 2011 and has four treatment rooms including a steam room and Hammam.

Recommended in the area

Harewood House; Castle Howard; Jorvik Viking Centre

General Tarleton Inn

★★★★★ ◉◉ RESTAURANT WITH ROOMS

Address: Boroughbridge Rd, Ferrensby,
KNARESBOROUGH, HG5 0PZ
Tel: 01423 340284
Fax: 01423 340288
E-mail: gti@generaltarleton.co.uk
Web: www.generaltarleton.co.uk
Map ref: 8, SE35
Directions: A1(M) junct 48 at Boroughbridge, A6055
to Knaresborough. 4m on right Rooms: 14 (7GF)

S £75-£116 D £129-£150 Facilities: Wi-fi Parking: 40 Notes: ⊗ Closed 24-26 Dec, 1 Jan

A tastefully restored old coaching inn with contemporary features, owned and run for the past 13 years by John and Claire Topham. Conveniently known in the local vernacular as the GT, it is recognised for the comfort of its rooms, all individually decorated and well provided with the usual extras. Menus change daily to reflect the seasons and the pick of the catch or crop. With fresh seafood a speciality, most days fishing boat captains returning to port call the kitchen and within hours the fish is on the plate. Try Little Moneybags signature dish - seafood parcels in lobster sauce.

Recommended in the area

Fountains Abbey (NT); Ripley Castle; Harrogate

Hob Green Hotel

★★★ 82% COUNTRY HOUSE HOTEL
Address: MARKINGTON, HG3 3PJ
Tel: 01423 770031
Fax: 01423 771589
Email: info@hobgreen.com
Website: www.hobgreen.com
Map ref: 6, SE26
Directions: From A61, 4m N of Harrogate, left at Wormald Green, follow hotel signs
Rooms: 12 (1 fmly) S £95-£105 D £120-£140 (incl. bkfst) Facilities: Wi-fi Parking: 40

Hob Green is a late 18th-century property standing in beautiful gardens, surrounded by rolling countryside. The 12 en suite bedrooms are well equipped and individually furnished in a traditional English style. The building retains much of its period character; public rooms are furnished with antiques and offer lovely views over the valley below. A sun room, with an Oriental theme, leads out onto a delightful terrace. The restaurant makes much use of seasonal local produce, including fruit and vegetables from the hotel's own Victorian kitchen garden.

Recommended in the area

Ripon racecourse; Harrogate; Fountains Abbey; Studley Royal Water Garden

Fountains Abbey (NT), Ripon

Three Tuns

★★★★ ⬒ RESTAURANT WITH ROOMS
Address: 9 South End, Osmotherley,
NORTHALLERTON, DL6 3BN
Tel: 01609 883301
Fax: 01609 883988
Email: enquiries@threetunsrestaurant.co.uk
Website: www.threetunsrestaurant.co.uk
Map ref: 8, SE39
Directions: NE of Northallerton. Off A19 into
Osmotherley
Rooms: 7 en suite (1 fmly rooms) (1 GF)

This family-run establishment, situated in the picturesque village of Osmotherley in the North Yorkshire Moors, is full of character. With its friendly, informal atmosphere and great food, it is a popular destination for business travellers, tourists and locals alike. The Charles Rennie Mackintosh-inspired decor sets it apart, and the bedrooms, some situated above the bar, some located in an adjoining annexe, vary in size but are stylishly furnished in pine throughout. All bedrooms are en suite, including one family room and one on the ground floor, and have TV, large beds, fluffy pillows and tea- and coffee-making facilities; some rooms enjoy stunning views of the Cleveland Hills. The homely lounge contains a video and CD player, and there's a film and music collection available for guests to browse through and enjoy. The restaurant offers an imaginative range of wholesome, modern British dishes with the emphasis on fine local produce and with fine wines and traditional cask conditioned ales to wash it all down. A hearty breakfast, lunch, afternoon tea and dinner are all on offer. There is also a beautifully peaceful secret garden to enjoy.

Recommended in the area

The Forbidden Corner; Wensleydale Railway; Mount Grace Priory

Palm Court Hotel

★★★ 79% HOTEL

Address: St Nicholas Cliff, SCARBOROUGH,
YO11 2ES

Tel: 01723 368161

Fax: 01723 371547

Email: info@palmcourt-scarborough.co.uk

Website: www.palmcourtscarborough.co.uk

Map ref: 6, TA08

Directions: Follow signs for town centre & town hall, hotel before town hall on right

Rooms: 40 (7 fmly) **S** £60-£76 **D** £90-£135 (incl. bkfst) **Facilities:** Wi-fi ⊗ **Notes:** ⊗

This elegant small hotel, owned by the same family for some 30 years, boasts one of the best locations in Scarborough. Whether staying on business or purely for pleasure, it makes the perfect base with its free guest parking (a rare find in Scarborough town centre) and close proximity to the beautiful Heritage Coast and North Yorkshire Moors National Park. Accommodation is well appointed and stylish, and a professional and welcoming team is always on hand to help.

Recommended in the area

North Yorkshire Heritage Coast; North Yorkshire Moors National Park; Castle Howard

Castle Howard, Malton

Dunsley Hall

★★★ 81% ® COUNTRY HOUSE HOTEL
Address: Dunsley, WHITBY, YO21 3TL
Tel: 01947 893437
Fax: 01947 893505
Email: reception@dunsleyhall.com
Website: www.dunsleyhall.com
Map ref: 8, NZ81
Directions: 3m N of Whitby, signed off A171
Rooms: 26 (2 GF) (2 fmly) **S** £105-£115
D £145-£175 (incl. bkfst) **Parking:** 30
Notes: ⊗

A Victorian shipping magnate built this mellow-stone hideaway in four acres of landscaped gardens, full today (and who knows, maybe then too) of beautiful rhododendrons. Dunsley Hall is now a family-run country-house hotel, with oak-panelling, stained glass windows and other surviving period gems to ensure a pleasing blend of the old with the best facilities a hotel of today can offer. In the main house, accommodation is available in traditionally designed, individually furnished bedrooms, some with four-posters; rooms in the ground floor extension are contemporary yet elegant, while a self-catering cottage provides all the amenities for an independent stay. Wherever you choose, you'll have a view of the grounds, countryside or coast. With Whitby so close you can expect seafood – trio of salmon, red snapper and king prawns, for example – to feature prominently on the Oak Room restaurant's menu, while lighter lunchtime and early evening alternatives are provided in the Pyman Bar. In addition to seafood, local produce is the foundation of all menus. Guests may visit the hotel's working farm at nearby Ramsdale, where 50 acres of farmland are available for outdoor pursuits and team-building events, so bring wellingtons and a warm coat.

Recommended in the area

North Yorks Moors Railway; Captain Cook Museum; Castle Howard

Estbek House

★★★★ ◉◉ ♔
RESTAURANT WITH ROOMS
Address: East Row, Sandsend, WHITBY, YO21 3SU
Tel: 01947 893424
Fax: 01947 893625
Email: info@estbekhouse.co.uk
Website: www.estbekhouse.co.uk
Map ref: 8, NZ81
Directions: From Whitby take A174. In Sandsend, left into East Row

Rooms: 4 (3 en suite) (1 pri facs) **Notes:** Wi-fi ⊗ in bedrooms ♦ 14yrs **Parking:** 6

Co-owners Tim Lawrence and David Cross run this restaurant with rooms with great skill and enthusiasm, and their attention to detail is evident at every meal and in every one of the bedrooms. Tim, and chef James, lead the team in the open-plan kitchen, and base their menus on local moorland produce and fresh, wild seafood. Not surprisingly, given its location in a pretty coastal village, there is always a large selection of fish, cooked simply and with a choice of sauces, plus seafood creations such as a trio of mornay, halibut in white wine, or whole lobster thermidor with crayfish and brown shrimp. Meat dishes might include Gressingham duck and black pudding, pan-seared and served with slow roasted figs in a balsamic sauce reduction, or loin of local spring lamb. The wine list reflects David's particular interest and expertise, with some unique varieties on offer and an emphasis on antipodean wines. The four rooms make good use of the spacious Georgian architecture, each with its own style and ambience. Contemporary furnishings and modern bathroom fittings blend with original features such as ships' timber beams and unique touches that include original works by local artists and hand-made patchwork quilts.

Recommended in the area

The Cleveland Way; Whitby Abbey; North York Moors

Best Western Dean Court Hotel

★★★★ 77% ◉◉ HOTEL

Address: Duncombe Place, YORK, YO1 7EF
Tel: 01904 625082
Fax: 01904 620305
Email: sales@deancourt-york.co.uk
Website: www.deancourt-york.co.uk
Map ref: 8, SE65
Directions: City centre opposite York Minster
Rooms: 37 (4 fmly) S £105-£145 D £145-£235
(incl. bkfst) **Facilities:** Wi-fi **Parking:** 30 **Notes:** ⊗
in bedrooms

Standing in the very shadow of York Minster, the Dean Court has arguably the best location of any hotel in the city. Inside you'll find contemporary elegance, comfort and style, and genuinely friendly service. Bedrooms are all non-smoking and offer first-class comfort and facilities, with the deluxe and four-poster rooms boasting magnificent views of the Minster. Families are very welcome and a range of services are offered to ensure a stress-free stay, including a toy box for toddlers and a media library offering a wide range of entertainment. Locals speak highly of the food here, served in both the elegant and friendly restaurant, DCH, which has two AA Rosettes and Minster views; and the café-bistro and bar, The Court, a more informal setting with big sofas – just the place for a light meal, cocktails or supper with friends. Privately owned and personally run, the hotel has excellent conference, meeting and private dining facilities, and offers free Wi-fi throughout plus complimentary valet-parking. The hotel offers the opportunity to add extras to a normal stay, from champagne and chocolates to afternoon tea, as well as a wide variety of special breaks, from the Champagne Lovers' break to Christmas and Valentine's Day.

Recommended in the area

York Minster; National Railway Museum; Castle Museum; Castle Howard

Swalesdale, Yorkshire Dales National Park

The Grange Hotel

★★★★ 77% ◉◉ HOTEL
Address: 1 Clifton, YORK, YO30 6AA
Tel: 01904 644744
Fax: 01904 612453
Email: info@grangehotel.co.uk
Website: www.grangehotel.co.uk
Map ref: 8, SE65
Directions: On A19 York/Thirsk road, approx 500yds from city centre
Rooms: 36 (6 GF) **S** £120-£278 **D** £134-£278 (incl. bkfst) **Facilities:** STV Wi-fi **Parking:** 26

This superbly restored Regency townhouse is in the city but feels just like an inviting country house. Open fires in the cooler months in the sumptuous Morning Room and elegant Library and Drawing Room create an ambience perfect for those who wish to relax and unwind. Attention to detail is top priory here including efficient room service in the luxurious bedrooms, which include three with four-posters. The six new guest rooms are air conditioned and feature waterproof plasma TVs at the foot of the baths. The Ivy Brasserie, with two AA rosettes, complements the hotel's stylish character, serving classic brasserie dishes that make good use of the highest quality, locally-sourced, seasonal produce whenever possible. The relaxed and informal New York Grill in the brick vaulted cellars provides an alternative dining venue that offers a superb range of delicious juicy steaks, grills, ribs and burgers. Open for lunch and dinner seven days a week, it proves popular with both guests and local residents alike. There are first class facilities for conferences, meetings and private dining with free Wi-fi provided throughout. The Grange is licensed for civil wedding ceremonies and there is free private parking at the rear of the hotel.

Recommended in the area

York Minster; National Railway Museum; Castle Howard

Conisbrough Castle

Copthorne Hotel Sheffield

★★★★ 79% 🏵 HOTEL

Address: Sheffield United Football Club, Bramhall
Lane, SHEFFIELD, S2 4SU
Tel: 0114 252 5480
Fax: 0114 252 5490
Email: orla.watt@millenniumhotels.co.uk
Website: www.millenniumhotels.co.uk/
copthornesheffield
Map ref: 8, SK38 **Directions:** M1 junct 33/A57. At
Park Square rdbt follow A61 (Chesterfield Rd). Follow
brown signs for Bramall Lane **Rooms:** 158 (23 fmly) **S** £69-£179 **D** £79-£199 **Facilities:** STV Wi-fi
Gym **Parking:** 150 **Notes:** ⊗

This luxurious, boutique-style hotel has well-appointed bedrooms with king-size beds and plasma
TVs with satellite channels. The hotel has a penthouse suite, full disabled access, complimentary
Wi-fi and ample, free, on-site parking for guests. The sleek and modern 18Fifty5 Restaurant offers a
seasonally changing menu; alternatively there is a relaxing bar area serving lights snacks and drinks.

Recommended in the area

Abbeydale Industrial Hamlet; Millennium Gallery; Kelham Island Museum

Millennium Galleries, Sheffield

WEST YORKSHIRE

Helme and The Pennines

Park Plaza Leeds

★★★★ 71% HOTEL

Address:	Boar Lane, LEEDS, LS1 5NS
Tel:	0113 380 4000
Fax:	0113 380 4100
Email:	pplinfo@parkplazahotels.co.uk
Website:	www.parkplaza.com
Map ref:	7, SE23
Directions:	Follow signs for city centre
Rooms:	185
Facilities:	STV Wi-fi Gym

A chic, ultra-modern, city-centre hotel opposite the main line station and City Square. In a city now famous for its busy restaurants, lively nightlife and boutique shops (not to mention Harvey Nichols, whose Leeds store was the first outside London), it fits in as satisfyingly as the final piece in a jigsaw puzzle. Indeed, one of the city's places to be seen is Chino Latino restaurant on the first floor, with its impressive multi-culti menu of modern Japanese, Chinese and Thai food, including 'inside-out' chicken wings; black cod with spicy miso; and an array of sushi and sashimi, and for dessert, florentine of peppered pineapple with mango and coconut cappuccino; or hot chocolate fondant with ginger ice cream. A wide selection of exotic drinks is available in the Latino Bar, or there's Scene! Lobby Bar on the ground floor, which dispenses fine wines, champagnes, cocktails, coffees and light bites throughout the day. Many of the design-led superior and executive guest rooms and suites look out over the rooftops and beyond. All spacious and air conditioned, they lack nothing in the way of modern must-haves like high-speed internet. Eleven meeting rooms and four extensive function rooms are spread over two floors.

Recommended in the area

Royal Armouries Museum; Leeds City Art Gallery; Leeds Grand Theatre & Opera House

Bouley Bay, Jersey

Cobo Bay Hotel

★★★ 82% ◉◉ HOTEL

Address: Coast Road, Cobo, CASTEL, Guernsey, GY5 7HB

Tel: 01481 257102

Fax: 01481 254542

Email: reservations@cobobayhotel.com

Website: www.cobobayhotel.com

Map ref: 13 **Directions:** From airport right, follow W coast at L'Eree. Right onto coast road, 3m to Cobo Bay. Hotel on right **Rooms:** 34 (4 fmly) **S** £49-£99 **D** £79-£190 (incl. bkfst) **Facilities:** STV Wi-fi Gym Sauna **Parking:** 60

A modern, newly refurbished, family-run hotel just metres from one of Guernsey's most beautiful bays. The bedrooms are well-equipped, the most sought after, of course, being those with balconies from which to enjoy the stupendous west-facing sea views and wonderful sunsets. The restaurant is one of only three on Guernsey with two AA rosettes for service and quality of food, not least the fresh, locally caught fish. The Beach Terrace has its own menu. In the health suite you'll find a sauna, exercise bikes and multi-gym machine, while there's an outdoor swimming pool at sister hotel, The Farmhouse.

Recommended in the area

German Military Underground Hospital; La Petite Chapelle; Sausmarez Manor

Castel, Cobo Bay, Guernsey

La Barbarie Hotel

★★★ 81% ◉ HOTEL

Address:	Saints Road, Saints Bay, ST MARTIN, Guernsey, GY4 6ES
Tel:	01481 235217
Fax:	01481 235208
Email:	reservations@labarbariehotel.com
Website:	www.labarbariehotel.com
Map ref:	13

Rooms: 26 (8 GF) (3 fmly) S £57.50-£75 D £91-£126 (incl. bkfst) **Facilities:** Wi-fi ↖ **Parking:** 50
Notes: ⊗ in bedrooms

This fine hotel is named after the Barbary Coast pirates who kidnapped and held to ransom the house's owner in the 17th century. A hotel since 1950, it lies in a peaceful green valley close to some of the lovely bays, coves and cliffs in the south of the island, and retains all of its historic charm, not least in the lovely residents' lounge, with its old beams and open fireplace. The en suite accommodation comes with every modern comfort, and includes some two-room suites with inter-connecting doors, ideal for families with children. Some self-catering apartments are also available, most of which overlook the heated swimming pool. Dining here is serious but far from pretentious – there are excellent choices and fresh local ingredients form the basis of the interesting menus. The fixed-price four-course dinner menu is very good value, while for something lighter you can choose from the bar or poolside menu. The poolside patio is the perfect secluded spot for a lazy lunch or quiet aperitif before dinner. The hotel is ideally placed for walkers, cyclists, horse riders and joggers.

Recommended in the area

Saumarez Manor; Castle Cornet; South Coast Cliff Path

Fermain Valley Hotel

★★★★ 77% HOTEL

Address: Fermain Lane, ST PETER PORT,
Guernsey GY1 1ZZ

Tel: 01481 235666 & 0800 316 0314

Fax: 01481 235413

Email: info@fermainvalley.com

Website: www.fermainvalley.com

Map ref: 13

Directions: Turn left from airport, follow Forest Rd,
turn right onto Le Route de Sausmarez

Rooms: 43 (6 GF) (2 fmly) **S** £90-£145 **D** £120-£230 (incl. bkfst) **Facilities:** STV Wi-fi ⊗ Cinema
Sauna **Parking:** 40 **Notes:** ⊗

Peaceful and secluded yet conveniently situated just five minutes from Guernsey's charming harbour
capital, St Peter Port, the four-star Fermain Valley Hotel offers the perfect place for a relaxing break.
The hotel has 45 exquisitely decorated bedrooms, all unique and designed with comfort in mind. A
long list of thoughtful in-room extras includes bathrobes, fridge, flat-screen TV, Wi-fi, hairdryer, sherry
decanter and complimentary tea and coffee. Some rooms even benefit from private balconies. The
Valley Brasserie offers a French influenced menu and boasts an outside decking area with stunning
views down the valley and out to sea. The hotel also has an indoor heated pool and sauna, a residents'
private cinema showing the latest films, complimentary Wi-fi throughout, and ample facilities for
meetings and functions. The friendly staff are dedicated to providing the very highest standards of
personal service, whether your stay is for business or pleasure. Special offers and breaks are also
available.

Recommended in the area

Castle Cornet; tax-free shopping

Farmhouse Hotel

★★★★ 80% ◎ SMALL HOTEL

Address: Route Des Bas Courtils, ST SAVIOUR,
Guernsey GY7 9YF
Tel: 01481 264181
Fax: 01481 266272
Email: enquiries@thefarmhouse.gg
Website: www.thefarmhouse.gg
Map ref: 13 **Directions:** From airport, left to lights.
Left, left again around runway perimeter. In 1m left at
x-rds. Hotel 100mtrs on right **Rooms:** 14 (7 fmly)

S £110-£190 D £125-£210 (incl. bkfst) **Facilities:** STV Wi-fi ↖ **Parking:** 80 **Notes:** ⊗

Originally built in the 15th century as a working farmhouse, this smart yet informal hideaway sits in
extensive grounds in the parish of St Saviour, and has seen a complete renovation in recent years. Now
established as a leading hotel on the island, it offers luxury guest rooms and suites that have plasma
satellite TVs, free Wi-fi, a fully stocked mini-bar and opulent bathrooms complete with bathrobes and
slippers. The Farmhouse restaurant offers adventurous menus that are full of colours and flavours, and
in summer months guests can enjoy alfresco dining on the poolside terrace or a picnic in the gardens.

Recommended in the area

Bruce Russell & Son goldsmiths; The Little Chapel; German Occupation Museum

Les Vauxbelets, Guernsey

The Club Hotel & Spa

★★★★ ◉◉◉◉ HOTEL
Address: Green Street, ST HELIER, Jersey, JE2 4UH
Tel: 01534 876500
Fax: 01534 720371
Email: reservations@theclubjersey.com
Website: www.theclubjersey.com
Map ref: 13
Directions: 5 mins walk from main shopping centre
Rooms: 46 (4 GF) (4 fmly) S £130-£215 D £130-£215 (incl. bkfst) **Facilities:** STV Wi-fi ⊗ ⚲ Spa
Sauna Parking: 30 **Notes:** ⊗ in bedrooms

This swish, townhouse hotel in the centre of Jersey's capital features stylish, contemporary decor throughout. The fully air-conditioned bedrooms and suites have large, full-height windows opening on to a balustrade, while the beds are dressed with Frette Egyptian cotton sheets and duck-down duvets. All rooms are equipped with safes, flat-screen TVs, DVD/CD players, Bang & Olufsen portable phones and private bars. Granite bathrooms include power showers, robes, slippers and aromatherapy products. Free Wi-fi access is available throughout the hotel. The dining choice includes the award-winning Bohemia Bar and Restaurant, where a typical main course might be roast local turbot with braised frog's leg, minted peas, herb gnocchi and chicken emulsion. Overlooking the outdoor pool is The Club Café, a contemporary New York-style restaurant offering breakfast, light lunches and dinner. Several hours might easily be spent in The Spa, starting with a swim in the salt pool, followed by mud treatment in the rasul (a traditional Arabian ritual cleansing) room, and finally a spell on one of the luxurious loungers. Two luxury meeting rooms with oak tables and leather chairs can accommodate 50 theatre style or up to 32 as a boardroom.

Recommended in the area

German Underground Hospital; Jersey Zoo; Mount Orgeuil

La Corbiere Lighthouse, Jersey

Longueville Manor

★★★★★ ◎◎◎ HOTEL

Address: ST SAVIOUR, Jersey, JE2 7WF
Tel: 01534 725501
Fax: 01534 731613
Email: info@longuevillemanor.com
Website: www.longuevillemanor.com
Map ref: 13
Directions: A3 E from St Helier towards Gorey. Hotel 1m on left
Rooms: 30 (7 GF) S £195-£370 D £220-£630 (incl. bkfst) **Facilities:** STV Wi-fi ⚡ **Parking:** 40

For more than 60 years this charming hotel has been run by the Lewis family, and is currently owned by Malcolm and Patricia Lewis. The refurbished 14th-century manor house is set in its own wooded valley, with 15 acres of grounds including vibrant flower gardens and a lake complete with black swans, yet is only five minutes from St Helier. The hotel is stylishly presented, with warm colour schemes, fine antique furnishings and lavish floral displays. The tranquil location, historic setting and excellent food invite complete relaxation, with a tennis court and a heated swimming pool to enjoy, plus a poolside bar and barbecue. The bedrooms are each named after a type of rose and come with a chaise longue, Egyptian cotton sheets, wide-screen TV and DVD/CD player, cordless phone, fruit, flowers and homemade biscuits. Additional in-room equipment includes a safe, hairdryer, iron and ironing board, and rooms on the ground floor have a private patio overlooking the garden. The hotel's restored Victorian kitchen garden provides abundantly for the dining room, including delicacies from the Victorian glass houses. The restaurant offers a fine dining experience with a Master Sommelier to advise on wines.

Recommended in the area

Royal Jersey Golf Club; Durrell Wildlife Conservation Trust; Mont Orgeuil Castle

SCOTLAND

Rest and Be Thankful Pass, near Arrochar, Argyll & Bute

Banchory Lodge Hotel

★★★ 81% ◉ COUNTRY HOUSE HOTEL
Address: BANCHORY, AB31 5HS
Tel: 01330 822625 & 822681
Fax: 01330 825019
Email: enquiries@banchorylodge.co.uk
Website: www.banchorylodge.co.uk
Map ref: 10, NO69
Directions: Off A93, 13m W of Aberdeen, hotel off Dee St
Rooms: 22 (10 fmly) **Parking:** 50

Steeped in history this Georgian mansion stands in richly wooded grounds alongside the River Dee, one of Scotland's greatest salmon rivers, and offers superior accommodation and high standards of service. Located at the end of a tree lined avenue this is a haven of tranquillity. The homely atmosphere owes much to the traditional decor, fresh flowers, open fires and collection of original paintings. Three of the bedrooms have four posters and there are several spacious family rooms; all are luxuriously furnished and comprehensively equipped, and many have river views. The dining room offers imaginative dishes based on the wonderful produce of Scotland such as the salmon, lamb and Aberdeen Angus beef. By prior arrangement fishing can be arranged, together with fly-fishing tuition from a ghillie and hire of equipment if wished. There are two golf courses in Banchory and shooting is available in season; for those wishing to explore the area this is ideal location for picking up the Whisky Trail, the Victorian Heritage Trail and the Castle Trail.

Recommended in the area

Crathes Castle; Balmoral Castle; Lochnagar Whisky Distillery

Falls of Lora Hotel

★★★ 77% HOTEL

Address: CONNEL, Connel Ferry, By Oban,
PA37 1PB
Tel: 01631 710483
Fax: 01631 710694
Email: enquiries@fallsoflora.com
Website: www.fallsoflora.com
Map ref: 9, NM93
Directions: From Glasgow take A82, A85. Hotel
0.5m past Connel sign. (5m before Oban)
Rooms: 30 (4 GF) (4 fmly) **S** £49.50-£59.50 **D** £59-£147 (incl. bkfst) **Facilities:** Wi-fi **Parking:** 40

This Victorian owner-run hotel enjoys views over the hotel gardens (across the road), Loch Etive and the
Connel Bridge. The ground floor includes a comfortable traditional lounge and cocktail bar with open
log fires, offering more than 100 whiskies. Well-equipped bedrooms come in a variety of styles, ranging
from cosy standard doubles to high quality luxury suite-type rooms. Guests may eat in the comfortable
and attractive Bistro and in the evening there is an exciting and varied menu.

Recommended in the area

Oban Distillery; Iona Abbey; Ben Nevis

Oban Harbour

The Ardanaiseig Hotel

★★★ ⑩⑩⑩ COUNTRY HOUSE HOTEL

Address: by Loch Awe, KILCHRENAN, by Taynuilt,
PA35 1HE

Tel: 01866 833333

Fax: 01866 833222

Email: ardanaiseig@clara.net

Website: www.ardanaiseig.com

Map ref: 9, NN02 **Directions:** In Kilchrenan, left
opp pub (narrow road) signed 'Ardanaiseig Hotel' &
'No Through Road' **Rooms:** 18 (5 GF) (4 fmly)

S £99-£210 D £138-£360 (incl. bkfst) **Facilities:** Wi-fi **Parking:** 20 **Notes:** ⊗ in bedrooms

A peaceful country house built in baronial style in 1834 on a peninsula jutting out into Loch Awe, this lovely hotel is surrounded by glorious gardens and scenery for which the only word is, indeed, awesome. The individually designed bedrooms combine antique furniture with bold decor and carefully selected accessories. Long known as a mecca for food-lovers, Ardanaiseig was awarded a third AA Rosette in 2010 for its loch-side restaurant, where skilfully cooked dishes that make full use of local, seasonal produce are likely to be a highlight of any visit.

Recommended in the area

Inveraray Castle; Falls of Cruachan Power Station; Kilchum Castle

Taychreggan Hotel

★★★★ 76% ⑩⑩ COUNTRY HOUSE HOTEL

Address: KILCHRENAN, Taynuilt, PA35 1HQ

Tel: 01866 833211 & 833366

Fax: 01866 833244

Email: info@taychregganhotel.co.uk

Website: www.taychregganhotel.co.uk

Map ref: 9, NN02

Directions: W from Crianlarich on A85 to Taynuilt,
S for 7m on B845 (single track) to Kilchrenan

Rooms: 18 S £87.50-£168.50 D £115-£277 (incl.
bkfst) **Facilities:** Wi-fi **Parking:** 40

Taychreggan Hotel is a romantic 300-year-old drover's inn situated on the shores of Loch Awe. The comfy bedrooms have breathtaking views of Scotland's longest inland loch from most windows. Guests can enjoy cuisine that will tempt the robust appetite, fine wines and a dram or two from Taychreggan's shamefully large selection of malt whiskies. Snooker, sailing (boats are available on site), fishing rights, clay pigeon shooting and hawk handling are all available. Or you could just relax in an overstuffed armchair looking out across the loch and enjoy a spot of afternoon tea.

Recommended in the area

Inverary Castle; Cruachan Power Station; Oban War Museum

Stonefield Castle Hotel

★★★★ 73% ◉ HOTEL

Address: TARBERT LOCH FYNE, PA29 6YJ
Tel: 01880 820836
Fax: 01880 820929
Email: reservations.stonefieldcastle@ohiml.com
Website: www.oxfordhotelsandinns.com
Map ref: 9, NR86
Directions: M8 From Glasgow towards Erskine
Bridge, follow Loch Lomond signs on A82. From
Arrochar follow A83 signs through Inveraray &
Lochgilphead, hotel on left 2m before Tarbert **Facilities:** Wi-fi **Parking:** 50 **Notes:** ⊗ in bedrooms

In 1837, the Campbell family built this outstanding example of Scottish baronial architecture on the
Mull of Kintyre, overlooking Loch Fyne – and, although stunning views are around every corner in
the west of Scotland, you know immediately why they chose this 60-acre spot. If you walk the short
distance through the rhododendron-rich gardens – they're at their best in late spring – to an isthmus
that connects with Barmore Island, you reach the beautiful loch itself, stretching away to your right and
left. The one-AA Rosette restaurant is all period grandeur and sweeping picture windows (so expect
more inspirational views). The kitchen successfully juggles its cooking output between classical and
modern British, while always ensuring a prominent role for Scottish ingredients, particularly locally
sourced beef and game, and fish and seafood landed at the pretty village of Tarbert nearby. After
dinner, relax in the traditional elegance of the wood-panelled bar, warmed externally by an open log
fire, internally perhaps by a wee dram of locally distilled malt whisky. The tastefully decorated en suite
bedrooms are split between the main house and a purpose-built wing, with, yes, even more panoramas
of the gardens and Loch Fyne.

Recommended in the area

Corryvreckan Whirlpool; Springbank Distillery; Islay

The Balmoral

★★★★★ ⑧⑧⑧ HOTEL

Address: 1 Princes Street, EDINBURGH, EH2 2EQ
Tel: 0131 556 2414
Fax: 0131 557 3747
Email: reservations.balmoral@
roccofortecollection.com
Website: www.roccofortecollection.com
Map ref: 10, NT27 **Directions:** Follow city centre
signs. Hotel at E end of Princes St, adjacent to
Waverley Station **Rooms:** 188 (22 fmly) **S** £320-

£2100 **D** £380-£2100 **Facilities:** STV Wi-fi ⓧ Gym Spa **Notes:** ⓧ in bedrooms
This elegant and luxurious hotel enjoys a prestigious address at the top of Princes Street, with iconic
views over the city and the castle. The bedrooms and suites are stylishly appointed in rich, earthy
Scottish colours and all have impressive marble bathrooms and a range of guest extras. Amenities
include the outstanding Balmoral Spa, extensive private function facilities, a choice of bars and two
dining options. The restaurant Number One, awarded three AA Rosettes, offers inspired Scottish
cuisine, and Hadrian's (AA Rosette), is a bustling informal brasserie with a cosmopolitan menu.
Recommended in the area
Palace of Holyroodhouse; St Giles Cathedral; Royal Mile

The George Hotel Edinburgh

★★★★ 80% HOTEL

Address: 19-21 George Street, EDINBURGH,
EH2 2PB
Tel: 0131 225 1251
Fax: 0131 226 5644
Email: enquires.campbell@principal-hayley.com
Website: www.principal-hayley.com/thegeorge
Map ref: 10, NT27
Directions: In city centre
Rooms: 249 (4 GF) (20 fmly) **Facilities:** STV Wi-fi
George Street, the prestigious address of this elegant hotel, was built in 1775 as part of the city's New
Town boom and today is one of Edinburgh's finest thoroughfares. Originally five separate town houses,
its owners Principal Hayley spent an eye-watering £20 million on it, creating, amongst other things, the
EH2 Tempus Bar & Restaurant, and transforming the en suite bedrooms, all of which feature plasma
TV and movies on demand. The upper ones look across Edinburgh's scenic rooftops. Businesses can
choose from nine conference and events suites, while the magnificent domed Kings Hall is ideal for
weddings and banquets.
Recommended in the area
Edinburgh Castle; St Giles' Cathedral; Edinburgh Zoo

Uplawmoor Hotel

★★★ 80% ⚜ HOTEL

Address: Neilston Road, UPLAWMOOR, G78 4AF

Tel: 01505 850565

Fax: 01505 850689

Email: info@uplawmoor.co.uk

Website: www.uplawmoor.co.uk

Map ref: 9, NS45

Directions: M77 junct 2, A736 signed Barrhead & Irvine. Hotel 4m beyond Barrhead

Rooms: 14 (1 fmly) **S** £60-£70 **D** £85-£95 (incl. bkfst) **Facilities:** STV Wi-fi **Parking:** 40

Instantly recognisable by its whitewashed façade and prominent location in the village, this popular hotel dates back to the 1750s when it stood on the old road between Glasgow and Irvine. Over the years, from being a one-room coaching inn, it has been greatly expanded and upgraded, most extensively in 1958 when Art Nouveau touches, inspired by the designs of innovative Glasgow-born architect Charles Rennie Macintosh, were applied to the exterior. Once a barn, the comfortable restaurant is the only holder of two AA Rosettes in Renfrewshire and, as such, must be a continual delight to the owners, who set as their goal to run 'the best village eating place in Greater Glasgow'. Richly furnished, with a copper-canopied fireplace, it offers fillet steak with haggis among its traditionally Scottish cuisine, but there are contemporary dishes too, such as baked cod with tomato compote and saffron oil. The separate lounge is popular for freshly prepared bar meals. After a night in one of the comfortable modern bedrooms, the full Scottish breakfast may feature local black pudding, or hot porridge oats. In the right sort of weather, visitors can also enjoy the beer garden, which leads to the village park.

Recommended in the area

Burrell Collection, Glasgow; People's Palace & Winter Gardens, Glasgow; Robert Burns' Cottage, Alloway

Loch Ness Lodge

★★★★★ ◉◉ ⌧ RESTAURANT WITH ROOMS

Address: Loch Ness-Side, BRACHLA, IV3 8LA
Tel: 01456 459469
Fax: 01456 459439
E-mail: escape@loch-ness-lodge.com
Web: www.loch-ness-lodge.com
Map ref: 12, NH53
Directions: A9 onto A82 signed Fort William, 9m,
at 30mph sign, lodge on right just after Clansman

Hotel **Rooms:** 7 (1GF) **D** £245-£395 (incl dinner)
Facilities: Wi-fi Sauna **Parking:** 10 **Notes** ⊗ ᵛ⁴ 12yrs **Closed** 2-31 Jan

The location of this hotel, winner of the AA's Guest Accommodation of the Year Award 2009-2010,
takes some beating. Perched on a landscaped hillside above the Loch Ness shore, it bonds traditional
Scottish architecture with more contemporary design. Most of the nature-inspired, well-appointed
bedrooms look out over the loch's mysterious waters to the hills beyond, so keep an eye out for the
monster. Franco-Scottish, five-course evening meals, based on local artisan produce, are served in the
award-winning restaurant, following which most guests head for one of the fire-warmed lounges.

Recommended in the area

Culloden Battlefield (NT); Highland Wineries, Moniack Castle; Falls of Moriston

Urquhart Castle, Loch Ness

Moorings Hotel

★★★ 82% ◉ HOTEL

Address: Banavie, FORT WILLIAM, PH33 7LY
Tel: 01397 772797
Fax: 01397 772441
Email: reservations@moorings-fortwilliam.co.uk
Website: www.moorings-fortwilliam.co.uk
Map ref: 12, NN17
Directions: Take A830 (N from Fort William), cross
Caledonian Canal, 1st right
Rooms: 27 (1 GF) (1 fmly) **S** £50-£135 **D** £95-£145
(incl. bkfst) **Facilities:** STV Wi-fi **Parking:** 60

Just three miles from Fort William and alongside the famous Neptune's Staircase on the Caledonian Canal, this hotel offers high standards of accommodation and panoramic views, which take in not only the canal, but also Aonach Mor and the UK's highest mountain, Ben Nevis. Each bedroom is individually designed and all have spacious living areas, satellite TV, a hospitality tray, direct-dial telephones, and free Wi-fi. The executive rooms also have 32" flat-screen LCD TVs, DVD players, bathrobes, slippers and iron facilities plus wonderful panoramic views of the mountains and the canal. The dining options are Neptune's Restaurant, awarded an AA Rosette, that offers a fine dining experience with a menu based on locally sourced seafood, salmon, venison and game; alternatively the informal split-level Upper Deck Lounge Bar serves seasonally created bar menu choices. In the summer guests can relax in the secluded garden or enjoy a delightful canal-side stroll. The area is, of course, a mecca for outdoor pursuits including climbing, hill walking, fishing and mountain biking.

Recommended in the area

West Highland Museum; Ben Nevis Distillery; Jacobite Steam Train

Glenmoriston Town House Hotel

★★★★ 74% ◉◉◉ HOTEL
Address: 20 Ness Bank, INVERNESS, IV2 4SF
Tel: 01463 223777
Fax: 01463 712378
Email: reception@glenmoristontownhouse.com
Website: www.glenmoristontownhouse.com
Map ref: 12, NH64
Directions: On riverside opposite theatre
Rooms: 30 (6 GF) (1 fmly) **Facilities:** STV Wi-fi
Parking: 40 **Notes:** ⊗ in bedrooms

The Glenmoriston Town House is close to the city centre and enjoys charming views of the River Ness. The hotel's bold contemporary designs blend seamlessly with its original classical architecture. Each of the individually appointed bedrooms is strikingly designed and well-proportioned to provide much guest comfort; each has a flat-screen TV, work desk, cotton linens, hairdryer, tea- and coffee-making facilities and Wi-fi. The stylish bathrooms have power showers, fluffy towels, bathrobes and luxury toiletries. Many of the guest rooms look out onto the river. Visitors here will be spoilt for eating options as both restaurants have been awarded AA Rosettes. The refined French restaurant Abstract, with 3 Rosettes, gives top priority to Scottish produce by creating imaginative seasonal menus and a 7-course tasting menu with wine pairings. To get near the action in the kitchen, and to witness how it all comes together you can book the six-seater chef's table at the pass. The chic Contrast Brasserie with one Rosette and views of the river, is a great place to meet up for lunch or dinner, and in summer you can eat alfresco. Whisky enthusiasts should make a beeline for the Piano Bar with its 250 malts.

Recommended in the area

Culloden Battlefield; Loch Ness; Cawdor Castle

Glenmorangie Highland Home at Cadboll

★★★ ◉◉ COUNTRY HOUSE HOTEL

Address: Cadboll, Fearn, TAIN, IV20 1XP
Tel: 01862 871671
Fax: 01862 871625
Email: relax@glenmorangie.co.uk
Website: www.theglenmorangiehouse.com
Map ref: 12, NH88
Directions: From A9 onto B9175 towards Nigg.
Follow tourist signs
Rooms: 9 (3 GF) (4 fmly) **S** £225-£245 **D** £350-£400 (incl. bkfst & dinner) **Facilities:** Wi-fi
Parking: 60 **Notes:** ⊗

From the moment one is greeted, it's clear that guests are not in for a run-of-the-mill hotel experience. Evenings are dominated by the 'house party', where everyone socialises over malt whiskies in the drawing room, then dines together around one long table. Afterwards comes the big test – is your bedroom in the main house or in one of the cosy cottages in the grounds? Each room has its own character and all the expected en suite comforts. There is also an extra touch – a complimentary dram of (yet more) Glenmorangie. The daily changing menu is created with enthusiasm and to discover why the food here is so celebrated, start by wandering down to the centuries-old walled garden and look at the quality of the vegetables, herbs and soft fruit. Then remember that fresh seafood comes from 200 yards away, world-renowned beef and lamb from the coastal grazing pastures, and ample supplies of game from neighbouring estates. Breakfast includes home-made porridge, fresh fruit, scrambled fresh farm eggs with smoked salmon, tea and home-made preserves.

Recommended in the area

Dunrobin Castle; Falls of Shin; Dornoch Cathedral

Mackay's Hotel

★★★ 75% HOTEL
Address: Union Street, WICK, KW1 5ED
Tel: 01955 602323
Fax: 01955 605930
Email: info@mackayshotel.co.uk
Web: www.mackayshotel.co.uk
Map ref: 12, ND35
Directions: Opposite Caithness General Hospital
Rooms: 30 (2 fmly) **Facilities:** Wi-fi

Many hotels overlook rivers, just as this one, built in 1883, overlooks the River Wick. But what totally differentiates well-established Mackay's from any other is that Ebenezer Street, the 6'9" stretch of road at its narrow end, has been verified by Guinness World Records as the Shortest Street in the World. The hotel's No 1 Bistro has the honour of being the street's only address, which must surely be a talking point for overnight guests as they enjoy their breakfast of Caithness sausages, bacon and eggs, or diners at lunch and in the evening as they tuck into their fish straight from the boats at Scrabster; grilled Wick haggis with neep purée and mashed, locally grown tatties; and pan-fried breast of Scottish free-range chicken with bubble and squeak. The heart of the hotel, indeed of the town, is the well-stocked bar where you can relax with a newspaper or a board game over a pot of one of the many types of coffee or tea, a malt whisky or a glass of wine. The hotel is known for providing a high standard of room service; all rooms are en suite, and are equipped with flat-screen digital TV with Freeview.

Recommended in the area

Wick Heritage Museum; Castle of May; John O'Groats

Craigellachie Hotel

★★★ 81% ◉ HOTEL

Address: CRAIGELLACHIE, AB38 9SR
Tel: 01340 881204
Fax: 01340 881253
Email: reservations.craigellachie@ohiml.com
Website: www.oxfordhotelsandinns.com
Map ref: 12, NJ24
Directions: On A95 between Aberdeen & Inverness
Facilities: Wi-fi **Parking:** 30

How many malt whiskies are there? If nearly 700 is the answer, then they're all here at the Quaich Bar in this impressive and popular, 1893-built hotel in the heart of Speyside, home to more distilleries than anywhere else in Scotland. An in-house whisky specialist conducts nosing and tasting sessions for up to around 20 people, but be prepared to pay anything from £2 to £275 per nip. Bedrooms come in various sizes but all are tastefully decorated and the en suite bathrooms are of a high specification; the Master bedrooms have wonderful views of the River Spey and Thomas Telford's famous 1814 bridge. The Ben Aigen restaurant, a long-term AA Rosette holder, does a mean line in traditional Scottish cooking, making full use of local meats, game and seafood. Start with Buckie potted crab, crisp croutons and pea shoots, followed by seared rump of Cabrach lamb with Arran mustard mash and red wine jus. The hotel's fishing beat on the Spey, right in front of the hotel, is predominantly time-share, but rods can usually be hired.

Recommended in the area

Strathspey Railway; Cairngorm ski area; RSPB Loch Garten

Dalmunzie Castle

★★★ 80% ◉◉ COUNTRY HOUSE HOTEL

Address: SPITTAL OF GLENSHEE, Blairgowrie,
PH10 7QG

Tel: 01250 885224

Fax: 01250 885225

Email: reservations@dalmunzie.com

Website: www.dalmunzie.com

Map ref: 10, NO17

Directions: On A93 at Spittal of Glenshee, follow signs to hotel

Rooms: 17 (2 fmly) **S** £100-£175 **D** £165-£290 (incl. bkfst & dinner)

Facilities: STV Wi-fi **Parking:** 40 **Notes:** ⊗ in bedrooms

Scott and Brianna Poole had been searching for a quintessential Scottish property for years; in 2004 they found Dalmunzie. With circular turrets and pointed roofs, this Scottish Baronial-style, former laird's manor house stands proudly at the head of a 500-year-old, 6,500-acre estate. Magnificent Highland scenery surrounds it, yet Edinburgh, Glasgow, Aberdeen and Inverness are only about two hours' drive away. Peace is guaranteed in the various lounges, library and bar. The bedrooms are spread throughout the castle – in the Hunting Lodge, the Tower, and the Victorian and Edwardian wings. Breakfast is taken in either the sun-room, with Ben Earb visible through its windows, or in the Dining Room, overlooking the front lawn; lunch may be eaten more or less wherever you like. Dinner is a deliberately slow-paced affair to enable full appreciation of the 'traditional estate/country house' cuisine. Ingredients are extensively drawn from the surrounding area, and the menu changes daily. Wine list descriptions are insightful, and the whisky enthusiast can choose from over 80 single malts. The active can try golf, tennis, mountain-biking, fishing, stalking and walking, for which the options are infinite.

Recommended in the area

Balmoral; Glamis Castle; Edradour Distillery

The Four Seasons Hotel

★★★ 83% ◉◉ HOTEL

Address: Loch Earn, ST FILLANS, PH6 2NF
Tel: 01764 685333
Fax: 01764 685444
Email: info@thefourseasonshotel.co.uk
Website: www.thefourseasonshotel.co.uk
Map ref: 9, NN62
Directions: On A85, towards W of village
Rooms: 18 (7 fmly) **S** £55-£90 **D** £110-£150 (incl. bkfst) **Facilities:** Wi-fi **Parking:** 40

Of countless highly desirable hotel settings in Scotland, this is unquestionably in the upper echelons. Looking south west down beautiful Loch Earn, the views are almost too good to be true – they include spectacular sunsets, morning mists and snow-covered mountains. Built in the 1800s for the manager of the local lime kilns, the house has been extended over the years to become today's small but exceedingly comfortable hotel, with several individual sitting rooms, a choice of bedrooms and, out on the wooded hillside at the rear, six comfortable and well-equipped chalets. All bedrooms are spacious, most with bath and shower, and many have uninterrupted views down the loch. The chalets have a double or twin room and a bunk room making them ideal for family use. When eating, choose between the more formal Meall Reamhar Room or the Tarken Room. Both offer the same high standard of contemporary Scottish cuisine, with much, as you might expect, coming from local sources. Rabbit and pistachio terrine, Scrabster king scallops, Angus Limousin beef, and pressed dark chocolate cake are typical of the fare. A large selection of malts is stocked in the bar. Dog owners will be gratified to know that resident canine Sham welcomes his cousins; he'll even tolerate cats, parrots and gerbils, depending on his current humour.

Recommended in the area

Loch Lomond & the Trossachs National Park; Stirling Castle; Famous Grouse Experience

Best Western Gleddoch House Hotel

★★★ 81% HOTEL

Address: LANGBANK, PA14 6YE
Tel: 01475 540711
Fax: 01475 540201
Email: reservations.gleddochhouse@ohiml.com
Website: www.oxfordhotelsandinns.com
Map ref: 9, NS37 **Directions:** M8 to Greenock, onto A8, left at rdbt onto A789, 0.5m, right, 2nd on left **Rooms:** 70 (8 GF) (20 fmly) **S** £40-£175 **D** £50-£185 **Facilities:** Wi-fi ③ Gym Spa **Parking:** 150 **Notes:** ⊗ in bedrooms

Successful Clydeside shipbuilder Sir James Lithgow built this fine-looking house in the 1920s. A hotel since 1975, it stands in 360 acres of landscaped grounds and is high enough above Langbank and the Clyde estuary for clear views of Ben Lomond and the rolling Renfrewshire hills; the distant night-time glow of Glasgow also gets in on the act. Its en suite bedrooms are individually designed and elegantly furnished, and from most you can see across the hotel's 18-hole championship golf course, gardens and surrounding estate. The Crannog Brasserie offers menus that make good use of Scotland's natural produce to offer the highly tempting pork fillet wrapped in bacon with Stornoway black pudding, potato rösti and buttered greens; lamb rump with sweet potato dauphinoise, rosemary and red wine sauce; and pan-seared gnocchi with semi-dried tomatoes, rocket and Parmesan shavings. In the Leisure Club there's a 17-metre swimming pool, sauna and well-equipped gym, while golfers can take advantage of one-night golfing breaks, Sunday Drivers, residential courses and pro-lessons. Many arrive at Glasgow International Airport, which is about nine miles away.

Recommended in the area

Loch Lomond; Clydebuilt Maritime Heritage Centre; Kelvingrove Art Gallery & Museum

The Horseshoe Inn

★ ★ ★ ★ ◉◉◉ RESTAURANT WITH ROOMS

Address: EDDLESTON, Peebles, EH45 8QP
Tel: 01721 730225
Fax: 01721 730268
Email: reservations@horseshoeinn.co.uk
Website: www.horseshoeinn.co.uk
Map ref: 10, NT24
Directions: A703, 5m N of Peebles
Rooms: 8 en suite (1 fmly rooms) (6 GF) **S** £70-£90
D £100-£150
Notes: Wi-fi **Parking:** 20 **Closed:** 25 Dec & Mon & 2wks Jan

Just half-an-hour from Edinburgh, this former blacksmith's (smiddy in the local vernacular) is situated in the quiet village of Eddleston in the beautiful Scottish Borders. It was transformed some four years ago into one of the most appealing restaurants in the area. In the Lodge (formerly the village's Victorian primary school) at the rear of the inn, are the individually designed bedrooms. There are five double rooms, two twin rooms and a family room – each one delightfully appointed and very chic. Co-owner (with wife Vivienne) and head chef Patrick Bardoulet revels in having his own restaurant, where he and his team use the freshest local ingredients to create regularly changing lunch and dinner menus. The result? Award-winning, high quality classical French cuisine, typified by wild grouse fillet soufflé with Scottish mushroom, confit root vegetables and Cassis jus and Valrhona chocolate soufflé, mandarin espuma and mandarin sorbet. Over 100 European and New World wines are offered in both the restaurant and the bar/bistro. Guests come back time and time again to this gem of a place.

Recommended in the area

Edinburgh Castle; Edinburgh Crystal Visitor Centre; Scottish Textiles Museum

Malin Court

★★★ 83% HOTEL
Address: TURNBERRY, KA26 9PB
Tel: 01655 331457
Fax: 01655 331072
Email: info@malincourt.co.uk
Website: www.malincourt.co.uk
Map ref: 9, NS20
Directions: On A74 to Ayr then A719 to Turnberry & Maidens
Rooms: 18 (9 fmly) **Facilities:** STV Wi-fi
Parking: 110 **Notes:** ⊗ in bedrooms

Many guests stay at this modern hotel partly because they are golfers. It adjoins Turnberry, the championship golf course famous for hosting the Open, and there are a dozen other courses within a twenty-mile radius. But if golf isn't your bag, so to speak, there are plenty of other leisure activities, such as walking, fishing, horse riding, pony trekking and sailing. Even if you don't sail, you'll appreciate the beautiful views of the Firth of Clyde down to Ailsa Craig (known locally as Paddy's Milestone), over to the Isle of Arran and, on a clear day, the Mull of Kintyre. The sunsets are not to be missed! With well-equipped, en suite bedrooms providing such views for nothing, it would be quite understandable if guests made little use of the satellite TV and internet connection. The smart Cotters restaurant, whose lunch, high tea and dinner menus blend the modern with the traditionally Scottish, typified by Stornoway black pudding; Ayrshire ham salad; breast of chicken stuffed with haggis; and poached, locally caught cod. A carefully chosen list of traditional and New World wines complements the food, while liqueurs, coffees and malt whiskies are served in the lounge.

Recommended in the area

Culzean Castle & Country Park; Souter Johnnie's Cottage (NTS); Robert Burns' Cottage, Alloway

Lochgreen House Hotel

★★★★ ⍟⍟⍟ COUNTRY HOUSE HOTEL

Address: Monktonhill Road, Southwood, TROON,
KA10 7EN
Tel: 01292 313343
Fax: 01292 318661
Email: lochgreen@costley-hotels.co.uk
Website: www.costley-hotels.co.uk
Map ref: 9, NS33
Directions: From A77 follow Prestwick Airport signs.
0.5m before airport take B749 to Troon. Hotel 1m
on left **Rooms:** 38 (17 GF) **S** £145-£180 **D** £190-£225 (incl. bkfst & dinner) **Facilities:** STV Wi-fi Spa
Parking: 50 **Notes:** ⊗ in bedrooms

Lochgreen House Hotel, the flagship of family-run hotel and restaurant group Costley and Costley, is situated in 30 acres of secluded woodland and gardens. Following a loving restoration it opened its doors in 1991 and is still considered one of the best places to stay in Ayrshire. Located on Scotland's beautiful west coast, it offers magnificent views over Royal Troon golf course and the Irish Sea. From the moment you walk through the doors of Lochgreen you'll experience the highest standards of luxury and elegance found only in an AA four-red-star hotel. A meal in the Tapestry Restaurant, overlooking the fountain garden, really shouldn't be missed. The restaurant is acclaimed as one of the finest dining experiences in Scotland. Executive chef director Andrew Costley, youngest son of proprietor and master chef Bill Costley, has led his team to achieve three AA Rosettes, and his personal supervision ensures every meal is prepared and served to the highest international standards. Menus have a distinct Scottish influence, making optimum use of the excellent seafood, meat, game and cheese that are synonymous with the west coast of Scotland.

Recommended in the area

Culzean Castle; Burns National Heritage Park; Scottish Maritime Museum

The Forth Rail Bridge

Macdonald Houstoun House

★★★ 78% ◉ HOTEL

Address: UPHALL, EH52 6JS
Tel: 0844 879 9043
Fax: 01506 854220
Email: houstoun@macdonald-hotels.co.uk
Website: www.macdonaldhotels.co.uk
Map ref: 10, NT07 **Directions:** M8 junct 3 follow
Broxburn signs, on at 1st rdbt, right at mini-rdbt
towards Uphall, hotel 1m **Rooms:** 71 (10 GF)
(12 fmly) **Facilities:** STV Wi-fi ☺ Gym Spa
Parking: 250

An imposing, 17th-century tower house in 20 acres of beautifully landscaped grounds, where the
doomed Mary, Queen of Scots once lived. The age of the building is knowingly reflected in each
bedroom; some, for example, overlook the courtyard, although common to all is a spacious en suite
bathroom and a generously proportioned bed. The Feature rooms, which overlook the walled gardens,
go one better with a king-size or four-poster. Before lunch, take a mid-morning break with a pot of tea
in one of the three interconnecting rooms of the Vaulted Bar in the cellars, or settle into a wing-backed
armchair with a pint of local cask ale. Panelled walls, shuttered windows and open fireplaces define
the Tower restaurant, to which the AA has awarded a Rosette and whose menu is represented by such
dishes as Scottish sirloin steak; chump of Highland lamb; Gressingham duck breast; seared bream;
and ratatouille ravioli. The more active might wish to swim a few lengths of the 18-metre indoor heated
pool, stay fit on the latest gym machines, play tennis, or just chill out, if you'll forgive the oxymoron, in
the sauna or steam room. Extensive conference and meeting facilities include a courier service.

Recommended in the area

Edinburgh Castle; National Museum of Scotland; Edinburgh Zoo

Highland Cottage

★ ★ ★ ◉◉ SMALL HOTEL

Address: Breadalbane Street, TOBERMORY,
Isle of Mull, PA75 6PD
Tel: 01688 302030
Email: davidandjo@highlandcottage.co.uk
Website: www.highlandcottage.co.uk
Map ref: 9, NM55
Directions: A848 Craignure/ Fishnish ferry terminal,
pass Tobermory signs, straight on at mini rdbt across
narrow bridge, turn right. Hotel on right opposite fire
station **Rooms:** 6 (1 GF) **S** £120-£135 **D** £150-£185 (incl. bkfst) **Facilities:** Wi-fi
Parking: 6 **Notes:** 🐾 under 10 yrs

David and Jo Currie designed and built this small hotel. Both are career hoteliers and bring to it many years of experience. The hotel stands above Tobermory, the Isle of Mull's pretty 'capital', in the town's quiet conservation area, yet only minutes from the hustle and bustle of Main Street and Fisherman's Pier. With just six individually designed bedrooms, staff rarely need to ask guests for their room number. This relaxed policy continues in the rooms themselves, where the Curries have deliberately avoided decor that screams 'Hotel!' All are provided with flat-screen TV with Freeview, DVD, CD player and i-Pod dock, and an en suite bathroom with full-size bath and thermostatic shower, while some have four-posters. There are two inviting lounges – the Sitting Room upstairs, with views across the bay to the mainland; and downstairs the Sun Lounge, an extension of the Dining Room and the ideal place for pre- or after-dinner drinks. Breakfasts are described as 'memorable', dinners as 'splendid'. Whenever feasible, the kitchen uses only the freshest of locally-sourced ingredients, such as scallops from Tobermory Bay, crabs from Croig on the island's west coast, mussels farmed at Inverlussa on Loch Spelve, and venison reared at Ardnamurchan.

Recommended in the area

Duart Castle; Fingal's Cave (Staffa); Whale-watching

The Quiraing, Isle of Skye

Duisdale House

★★★★ 80% ◉◉ SMALL HOTEL

Address: ISLEORNSAY, Isle of Skye, IV43 8QW

Tel: 01471 833202

Fax: 01471 833404

Email: info@duisdale.com

Website: www.duisdale.com

Map ref: 11, NG71

Directions: 7m S of Bradford on A851 towards
Armadale. 7m N of Armadale ferry

Rooms: 18 (1 GF) (1 fmly) **S** £120-£150 **D** £169-

£269 (incl. bkfst) **Facilities:** STV Wi-fi **Parking:** 30 **Notes:** ⊗ ⋈ 5yrs

A romantic hotel in the south of the Isle of Skye with panoramic views across the Sound of Sleat. The
sleek bedrooms, including four-poster rooms, have flat-screen TVs, luxury amenities and either sea or
garden views. Blazing fires and candlelight create the perfect atmosphere for a romantic evening and
there is a well stocked bar and extensive wine list. The chef's skilfully prepared modern Scottish cuisine
is based on the freshest island produce. Complimentary Wi-fi is available and daily sailing excursions
possible on onboard the hotel's luxury yacht.

Recommended in the area

Talisker Distillery; Dunvegan Castle; Portree Town

Toravaig House Hotel

★★★ 81% ◉◉ SMALL HOTEL

Address: Knock Bay, TEANGUE,
Isle of Skye, IV44 8RE

Tel: 01471 820200 & 01471 833231

Fax: 01471 833231

Email: info@skyehotel.co.uk

Website: www.skyehotel.co.uk

Map ref: 9, NG71

Directions: From Skye Bridge, left at Broadford onto
A851, hotel 11m **Rooms:** 9 **S** £120-£150 **D** £169-

£215 (incl. bkfst) **Facilities:** STV Wi-fi **Parking:** 15 **Notes:** ⊗ in bedrooms ⋈ 12yrs

Glorious sunsets are a frequent bonus at this hideaway, set in two-acre grounds with magnificent
views. The bedrooms are designed with rich fabrics and contemporary furnishings. The lounge, with
its squashy sofas and crackling fire, is the perfect place to relax and sample the fine wines and malt
whiskies. Only the finest local ingredients find their way onto the menu in the Iona Restaurant, where
the cuisine's innovative style allows the quality produce to take centre stage. In summer guests can
take a trip on the hotel yacht.

Recommended in the area

Armadale Castle; Gardens & Museum of the Isles; Cuillin Hill; Skye Serpentarium

WALES

Harlech Castle, Gwynedd

St David's Hotel & Spa

★★★★★ 81% HOTEL
Address: Havannah Street, CARDIFF, CF10 5SD
Tel: 029 2045 4045
Fax: 029 2031 3075
Email: stdavids.reservations@principal-hayley.com
Website: www.thestdavidshotel.com
Map ref: 2, ST17
Directions: M4 junct 33/A4232 for 9m, for Techniquest, at top exit slip road, 1st left at rdbt, 1st right **Rooms:** 132 S £99–£369 D £109–£389
Facilities: Wi-fi ⊗ Gym Spa **Parking:** 80 **Notes:** ⊗ in bedrooms

This striking, contemporary building, spectacularly located on the waterfront of Cardiff Bay, is a light and tranquil space that evokes a calm atmosphere. The seven-storey atrium creates a dramatic first impression. All bedrooms are appointed with Italian furnishings, have floor-to-ceiling windows and private balconies that look out over Cardiff and Mermaid Quay; the top three floors have interconnecting master suites. Tempus at Tides Restaurant, adjacent to the stylish cocktail bar, has views across the water to Penarth and offers a menu of locally sourced produce; there's a tempting choice of local Welsh delicacies and a wide selection of ocean specialities. Alfresco dining is possible in the warmer months. The hotel has a first-floor lounge for guests seeking peace and quiet. But for total relaxation seek out the state-of-the-art spa with a wide range of carefully chosen marine, aromatherapy and natural products, a gym and hydrotherapy pools, and for those with time on their hands there is a comprehensive choice of all-day spa and pampering packages. Extensive business, conference and special events suites complete the picture.

Recommended in the area

National Museum of Cardiff; Millennium Stadium Tours; Dyffryn Gardens

Ivy Bush Royal Hotel

★★★ 75% HOTEL

Address: Spilman Street, CARMARTHEN, SA31 1LG

Tel: 01267 235111

Fax: 01267 234914

Email: reception@ivybushroyal.co.uk

Website: www.ivybushroyal.co.uk

Map ref: 1, SN42

Directions: M4 onto A48 W, over 1st rdbt, 2nd rdbt turn right. Straight over next 2 rdbts. Left at lights. Hotel on right at top of hill

Rooms: 70 (4 fmly) **S** £55-£95 **D** £75-£150 (incl. bkfst)

Facilities: STV Wi-fi Gym **Parking:** 80 **Notes:** ⊗ in bedrooms

Once a favoured retreat of Lord Nelson and Lady Hamilton, this friendly family-run hotel has been sympathetically modernised to blend its old-world charm with up-to-date facilities. The accommodation is spacious and well-equipped, and includes some family rooms, a four-poster suite, executive suites and the Merlin Suite with its own whirlpool bath. Dine in style in the restaurant, where the produce is locally sourced and the carte menu changes with the seasons. Welsh black beef is a particular speciality, and carvery lunches are extremely popular on Sundays. For guests looking for a more informal dining experience, the cosy bar and lounge area is open all day, every day, serving a full range of traditional meals. For those wanting to get active during their stay, the gym has all the latest cardiovascular equipment, and you can ease your tired muscles after a workout with a relaxing session in the sauna. The hotel is licensed for weddings and has four meeting and conference rooms with facilities to accommodate up to 200 people.

Recommended in the area

National Botanic Garden of Wales; Aberglasney House & Gardens; Oakwood Theme Park

The Cliff Hotel

★★★77% HOTEL

Address: GWBERT-ON-SEA, Cardigan, SA43 1PP
Tel: 01239 613241
Fax: 01239 615391
Email: reservations@cliffhotel.com
Website: www.cliffhotel.com
Map ref: 1, SN14
Directions: Exit A487 into Cardigan, take B4548
towards Gwbert, 2m to hotel
Rooms: 70 (5 GF) (6 fmly) **S** £59-£85 **D** £70-£150
(incl. bkfst) **Facilities:** STV ⓩ Gym Spa
Parking: 100

Built in 1850 and originally known as the Gwbert Inn, this coastal retreat was renamed the Cliff Hotel in the early 1900s in a bid to become a seaside getaway to rival the holiday resorts of southern England. Whether the name change was enough to persuade holidaymakers away from the south coast and across into Wales, we don't know, but The Cliff Hotel is certainly in a prime sea-facing spot. The 70-bedroom hotel sits in 30 acres of land along south Ceredigion's beautiful coastline, with stunning views of Cardigan Island, Cardigan Bay and Poppit Sands. Most rooms benefit from those views and all are en suite and have tea- and coffee-making facilities. There is a state-of-the-art gym along with a hydro spa, sauna, jacuzzi, steam room, heated loungers, and a beauty therapy suite offering a range of treatments. A day spent on the par 3, nine-hole golf course, which stretches along the cliff top, should give you a good appetite for dinner in the restaurant or the Island Bar. The food is locally sourced and freshly prepared, and a meal here very often comes with the added bonus of watching the sun set over Cardigan Bay.

Recommended in the area

Clifftop walks; golf; dolphin, porpoise and seal watching

Royal Oak Hotel

★★★ 83% ◉ HOTEL

Address: Holyhead Road, BETWS-Y-COED,
LL24 0AY
Tel: 01690 710219
Fax: 01690 710603
Email: royaloakmail@btopenworld.com
Website: www.royaloakhotel.net
Map ref: 5, SH75
Directions: On A5 in town centre, next to St Mary's
church **Rooms:** 27 (1 fmly) **Facilities:** STV Wi-fi
Parking: 90 **Notes:** ⊗ in bedrooms

The wonders of Snowdonia National Park are right on the doorstep of this former Victorian coaching inn, which nestles at the foot of a wooded hillside in the heart of the picturesque village of Betws-y-Coed. Rooms have been designed with the heritage of the hotel in mind, with stylish fabrics and feature beds offering contemporary luxury in a period setting. For a special occasion book one of the four-poster rooms with jacuzzi bathroom. Guests benefit from complimentary membership of the nearby Stations Leisure Complex, while free broadband is available in all rooms and Wi-fi in the lounge bar. The award-winning Llugwy Restaurant offers modern Welsh cooking via a set three-course menu. Dishes might include locally smoked halibut or a trio of Welsh mountain lamb, and, if you're lucky, the bara brith-and-butter pudding with Welsh whisky ice cream. Alternative dining options are the relaxed and modern Grill Bar which prides itself on serving the best local Welsh produce, or the Stables Bistro which has a rather special atmosphere with its regular music nights, plenty of cask ales and alfresco dining.

Recommended in the area

Snowdon Mountain Railway (or a walk to the summit); Conwy Castle; Llechwedd Slate Caverns

Castle Hotel Conwy

★★★★ 79% ◉◉ TOWN HOUSE HOTEL

Address: High Street, CONWY, LL32 8DB
Tel: 01492 582800
Fax: 01492 582300
Email: mail@castlewales.co.uk
Website: www.castlewales.co.uk
Map ref: 5, SH77
Directions: A55 junct 18, follow town centre signs,
cross estuary (castle on left). Right then left at mini-
rdbts onto one-way system. Right at Town Wall Gate,
right into Berry St then High St
Rooms: 28 (2 fmly) **S** £84-£94 **D** £125-£135 (incl. bkfst) **Facilities:** Wi-fi **Parking:** 34

The distinctive building that houses the Castle Hotel hints at its long and fascinating history. Built on the site of a Cistercian abbey, it has welcomed many famous people through its doors, including Thomas Telford (who built the town's famous bridge), railway pioneer George Stephenson, William Wordsworth and the Queen of Romania. The current owners, the Lavin family and partner/head chef Graham Tinsley, have been very mindful of this important heritage while giving the place an attractive facelift. All of the bedrooms have en suite bathrooms and modern facilities. Deluxe rooms have spa baths, one has an ornately carved four-poster bed, and another enjoys a good view of the castle. Graham Tinsley MBE, and his award-winning kitchen team, have gained a reputation for serving excellent Welsh produce. Food is available in both Dawson's Restaurant and the bar, where the atmosphere is relaxed and the emphasis is on locally sourced ingredients. There's a real seasonal feel to the menu, with Conwy mussels featuring in the winter months, and Conwy Valley lamb in spring and early summer. There's also a good selection of vegetarian and organic food on the menu.

Recommended in the area

Conwy Castle; Caernarfon Castle; Snowdonia National Park; Bodnant Garden (NT); Anglesey

Osborne House

★★★★ ⊚ TOWN HOUSE HOTEL

Address: 17 North Parade, LLANDUDNO, LL30 2LP
Tel: 01492 860330
Fax: 01492 860791
Email: sales@osbornehouse.com
Website: www.osbornehouse.com
Map ref: 5, SH78
Directions: Exit A55 junct 19. Follow signs for Llandudno then Promenade. Continue to junct, turn right. Hotel on left opposite pier entrance
Rooms: 6 S £150–£170 D £150–£170 (incl. bkfst)
Facilities: STV Wi-fi **Parking:** 6 **Notes:** ⊗ in bedrooms ⛄ 11yrs

Built in 1832, this Victorian house, which makes an excellent touring base for visiting north Wales, has been restored to a grand design by the Maddocks family, with original art, antiques and beautiful drapes in abundance. Today, this all-suite luxury townhouse provides a gloriously romantic retreat, and guests can enjoy stunning views of the bay and promenade from each bedroom. All of the spacious suites offer unrivalled comfort and luxury, combining antique furnishings with state-of-the-art technology, and free Wi-fi is available throughout. In addition, all of the bedrooms are air conditioned and feature king-size canopied beds and sitting rooms with a large sofa and an original Victorian fireplace; each room also boasts an Italian marble bathroom with double-sided clawfoot bath and monsoon walk-in shower. Dining at the award-winning Osborne's Café/Grill is a sumptuous experience not to be missed. This is an all-day venue with brasserie-style menus and an emphasis on fresh, local produce, and fish is a speciality. In the evening, it is transformed by a multitude of candles, reflecting the gilt-edged mirrors and crystal chandeliers. As an added benefit, guests at Osborne House may also make full use of the spa at the Empire Hotel just 100 yards away.

Recommended in the area

Bodnant Gardens; Snowdonia National Park; Portmeirion Italianate village

St Tudno Hotel and Restaurant

★★★ ◉◉ HOTEL

Address: The Promenade, LLANDUDNO, LL30 2LP
Tel: 01492 874411
Fax: 01492 860407
Email: sttudnohotel@btinternet.com
Website: www.st-tudno.co.uk
Map ref: 5, SH78
Directions: On Promenade towards pier, hotel opposite pier entrance
Rooms: 18 (4 fmly) **S** £65-£90 **D** £90-£210 (incl. bkfst) **Facilities:** Wi-fi ⊗ **Parking:** 5

Right on the Llandudno seafront, this outstanding hotel is personally run by the owner, Martin Bland, who has put together a loyal and caring team to look after guests. There is a delightful sitting room with sea views as well as a leafy coffee lounge and Victorian style bar lounge, the latter renowned for its afternoon teas. The restaurant transports you to northern Italy with its vast murals depicting Lake Como, but it is the food that has the greatest impact of all. With its two AA Rosettes it is clear that you are in for a treat, and this might include a warm salad of langoustines, duck ham and pea shoots with a nut-brown butter dressing, or a composition of game with a honey, blackberry and truffle dressing. The bedrooms are individually styled all are en suite and half have spa baths. All have fine linen, bathrobes and Molton Brown toiletries, a Villeroy and Boch tea service and home-made biscuits, as well as facilities such as Wi-fi and flat-screen TV with a multitude of free-view channels. Even more luxurious suites are also available. There is a heated indoor swimming pool in case the sea temperature is too bracing, and a delightful little garden.

Recommended in the area

Great Orme Tramway; Conwy Castle; Snowdonia National Park

Imperial Hotel

★★★★ 79% ⊕ HOTEL

Address: The Promenade, LLANDUDNO, LL30 1AP
Tel: 01492 877466
Fax: 01492 878043
Email: reception@theimperial.co.uk
Website: www.theimperial.co.uk
Map ref: 5, SH78
Directions: A470 to Llandudno
Rooms: 98 (10 fmly) **Facilities:** Wi-fi ⊗ Gym
Parking: 25 **Notes:** ⊗ in bedrooms

Right at the heart of the famous Promenade, The Imperial can trace its history back to the time when the Victorians first acknowledged the benefits of a seaside break. The guest rooms, including four suites with lounges, offer high levels of comfort; expect large flat-screen TVs, bathrobes, slippers and mineral water as standard. Many rooms have glorious sea views. Eating options include the elegant Chantrey's Restaurant, where accomplished dishes using locally sourced produce are served, and The Terrace where light refreshments are available all day. The Imperial was awarded the AA Hotel of the Year for Wales 2010-11.

Recommended in the area:

Bodnant Gardens (NT); Conwy Castle; Snowdonia National Park

View from the summit of Snowdon

Dunoon

★★★ 81% HOTEL

Address: Gloddaeth Street, LLANDUDNO, LL30 2DW
Tel: 01492 860787
Fax: 01492 860031
Email: reservations@dunoonhotel.co.uk
Website: www.dunoonhotel.co.uk
Map ref: 5, SH78
Directions: Exit Promenade at war memorial by pier onto wide avenue. 200yds on right
Rooms: 49 (7 fmly) **S** £60-£120 **D** £90-£157 (incl. bkfst)
Facilities: Wi-fi **Parking:** 24

Close to the promenade in this well preserved Victorian seaside resort, the Dunoon has a certain old-world grace about it. Hushed and stuffy it isn't, though. In fact, the Williams family, who have been here a good while, make sure it offers a happy antidote to what they regard as anodyne modern living. For example, they treat returning guests like old friends, and first time customers as new ones. Their approach is evident too in the way they have styled the bedrooms, with no two alike, and in their attention to detail, with crisp Egyptian cotton bed linen, and Molton Brown toiletries in every bathroom. The same is true of the restaurant, where silver rings contain freshly pressed linen napkins, and white porcelain is used on the tables. Food and wine are the Williams' abiding passions. Cooking is unpretentious, using fresh ingredients sourced locally as far as the seasons allow, with specialities such as terrine of game, medley of local fish, ragout of Welsh lamb with mint dumplings and asparagus mousse. Their taste in wines is adventurous, with a list that, in their words, 'offers more than you would expect from a modest hotel in the sleepy outer reaches of Britain'.

Recommended in the area

Great Orme; Bodnant Gardens; Snowdonia National Park

Bron Eifion Country House

★★★ 87% ◉ COUNTRY HOUSE HOTEL

Address: CRICCIETH, LL52 0SA
Tel: 01766 522385
Fax: 01766 523796
Email: enquiries@broneifion.co.uk
Website: www.broneifion.co.uk
Map ref: 5, SH43
Directions: A497 between Porthmadog & Pwllheli, 0.5m from Criccieth, on right towards Pwhelli
Rooms: 18 (1 GF) (1 fmly) **S** £95-£125
D £135-£185 (incl. bkfst) **Facilities:** Wi-fi **Parking:** 50 **Notes:** ⊗ in bedrooms

Bron Eifion, a delightful Grade II listed country house hotel set in extensive grounds to the west of Criccieth, enjoys breathtaking views of the sea. Golfers are particularly well catered for here, with five of the best courses in North Wales in close proximity to the hotel; special golf packages can be arranged. Inside, guests will find a tranquil and relaxing atmosphere, with attentive and friendly service, and the interior style highlights the many retained period features. There is a choice of restful lounges, warmed by log fires, and the very impressive central hall features a minstrels' gallery. The en suite bedrooms have been individually decorated to combine luxury and elegance, and tea- and coffee-making facilities as well as flat-screen TV, Wi-fi and hairdryers all come as standard; deluxe rooms also provide bathrobes and slippers. The Garden Restaurant, overlooking the spectacular grounds, is fresh and bright by day, candlelit and relaxed in the evening. The emphasis is on fresh Welsh produce, with dishes such as Llyn Peninsula Seabass, Tyddyn Mawr Welsh Beef and roast rack of Welsh lamb, followed by seasonal desserts, home-made ice creams and pastries. Afternoon tea includes a delicious selection of sandwiches and home-made sweet treats.

Recommended in the area

Portmeirion; Snowdonia National Park; Blaenau Ffestiniog Railway

Penmaenuchaf Hall Hotel

★★★ ◉ COUNTRY HOUSE HOTEL

Address: Penmaenpool, DOLGELLAU, LL40 1YB
Tel: 01341 422129
Fax: 01341 422787
Email: relax@penhall.co.uk
Website: www.penhall.co.uk
Map ref: 2, SH71
Directions: Off A470 onto A493 to Tywyn. Hotel approx 1m on left **Rooms:** 14 (2 fmly) **S** £95-£145 **D** £150-£240 (incl. bkfst) **Facilities:** STV **Parking:** 30

Peacefully set in the Snowdonia National Park overlooking the Mawddach Estuary, Penmaenuchaf Hall is a magnificent Victorian mansion surrounded by beautiful gardens. A very warm welcome awaits here and every effort to made to make you feel at ease. With views towards the mountains, the individually designed bedrooms are luxuriously appointed. 21st-century technology is evident too with satellite TV and internet access included. The elegant conservatory restaurant is a delightful place to enjoy the award-winning cuisine, especially when candlelit in the evening. This is an excellent base for many outdoor pursuits – walking, fishing, golf, mountain biking and white-water rafting.

Recommended in the area Portmeirion; Harlech Castle; Welsh Highland Heritage Railway

The Crown at Whitebrook

★★★★★ ◉◉ ≜ RESTAURANT WITH ROOMS

Address: WHITEBROOK, NP25 4TX
Tel: 01600 860254
Fax: 01600 860607
Email: info@crownatwhitebrook.co.uk
Website: www.crownatwhitebrook.co.uk
Map ref: 2, SO50
Directions: 4m from Monmouth on B4293, left at sign to Whitebrook, 2m on unmarked road, Crown on right **Rooms:** 8 en suite **S** £90-£110 **D** £135-£160
Notes: Wi-fi ⊗ in bedrooms ⭁12yrs **Parking:** 20 **Closed:** 22 Dec-4 Jan

The Crown at Whitebrook lies just five miles from Monmouth in the beautiful Wye Valley. Set in five acres of landscaped gardens, this establishment offers a peaceful haven. The contemporary bedrooms all come with luxury en suite bathrooms, and some have power showers or double-ended baths. Other features include flat-screen TVs and individually controlled heating. The modern restaurant lies at the heart of the Crown. Guests may enjoy an aperitif while perusing chef James Sommerin's award-winning menu.

Recommended in the area

Tintern Abbey; Offa's Dyke; Chepstow Castle; Chepstow Racecourse

Best Western Lamphey Court Hotel & Spa

★★★ 80% HOTEL

Address: Lamphey, PEMBROKE, SA71 5NT
Tel: 01646 672273 **Fax:** 01646 672480
Email: info@lampheycourt.co.uk
Website: www.lampheycourt.co.uk
Map ref: 1, SM90 **Directions:** A477 to Pembroke.
Left at Milton for Lamphey, hotel on right
Rooms: 38 (6 GF) (7 fmly) S £129-£149
D £139-£159 (incl. bkfst) **Facilities:** Wi-fi ⊗ Gym **Parking:** 50 **Notes:** ⊗ in bedrooms

Lamphey Court Hotel & Spa, one of Pembrokeshire's best kept secrets, is a stunning country hotel set in beautiful grounds. The facilities include 39 bedrooms, a beautiful Georgian restaurant and a wonderful conservatory restaurant, bar, lounge, plus function and conference facilities. The hotel has its own spa with gym, spa bath, sauna, treatment rooms for massage, reflexology, hot rock therapy, hair and beauty treatment and much more. There are also two flood-lit tennis courts, and under construction is a new state-of-the-art spa with infinity pool, which is due to open in early summer 2011.

Recommended in the area

Lamphey Bishop's Palace; Pembrokeshire Coast; Tenby & Saundersfoot

Warpool Court

★★★ 81% ◉◉ COUNTRY HOUSE HOTEL

Address: ST DAVID'S, SA62 6BN
Tel: 01437 720300
Fax: 01437 720676
Email: info@warpoolcourthotel.com
Website: www.warpoolcourthotel.com
Map ref: 1, SM72
Directions: At Cross Square left by The Bishops Restaurant (Goat St). Pass Farmers Arms pub, after 400mtrs left, follow hotel signs, entrance on right

Rooms: 22 (3 fmly) S £165-£210 D £240-£330 (incl. bkfst & dinner) **Facilities:** Wi-fi ⊗ Table tennis Pool table **Parking:** 100

A privately-owned hotel in large grounds on St David's peninsula, overlooking the gentle sweep of St Bride's Bay. Bedrooms are well equipped and attractively furnished, and many have sea views. The spacious restaurant, overlooking the gardens and the sea, offers an extensive menu. A heated swimming pool opens from Easter to 31st October and there is an all-weather tennis court.

Recommended in the area

Pembrokeshire Coast National Park; St David's Cathedral; Pembroke Castle

Maes-Yr-Haf

★★★★★ ◉ RESTAURANT WITH ROOMS
Address: PARKMILL, SA3 2EH
Tel: 01792 371000
Fax: 01792 234922
Email: enquiries@maes-yr-haf.com
Website: www.maes-yr-haf.com
Map ref: 2, SS59
Rooms: 5 S £65-£120 D £95-£160 **Facilities** Wi-fi
Notes Closed 11-31 Jan **Notes:** ⊗ in bedrooms
An award-winning restaurant with rooms,

Maes-Yr-Haf nestles quietly in the peaceful rural village of Parkmill, just a gentle stroll from the renowned Three Cliffs Bay. There are five luxuriously appointed en suite double bedrooms, each tastefully furnished with pure cotton linens and the latest technology including flat-screen TV, DVD player and iPod dock. Complimentary Wi-fi is available throughout the building. In the contemporary and spacious restaurant, top quality produce is used to create an inspired modern European menu with a distinctly local flavour. The wine list is carefully selected and there's an excellent range of aperitifs and digestifs.

Recommended in the area

Three Cliffs Bay and Gower coastline; Gower Heritage Centre; Mumbles and Swansea

Three Cliffs Bay, West Glamorgan

The Preseli Hills, Pembrokeshire Coast National Park

County Map

England

1	Bedfordshire
2	Berkshire
3	Bristol
4	Buckinghamshire
5	Cambridgeshire
6	Greater Manchester
7	Herefordshire
8	Hertfordshire
9	Leicestershire
10	Northamptonshire
11	Nottinghamshire
12	Rutland
13	Staffordshire
14	Warwickshire
15	West Midlands
16	Worcestershire

Scotland

17	City of Glasgow
18	Clackmannanshire
19	East Ayrshire
20	East Dunbartonshire
21	East Renfrewshire
22	Perth & Kinross
23	Renfrewshire
24	South Lanarkshire
25	West Dunbartonshire

Wales

26	Blaenau Gwent
27	Bridgend
28	Caerphilly
29	Denbighshire
30	Flintshire
31	Merthyr Tydfil
32	Monmouthshire
33	Neath Port Talbot
34	Newport
35	Rhondda Cynon Taff
36	Torfaen
37	Vale of Glamorgan
38	Wrexham

MAPS

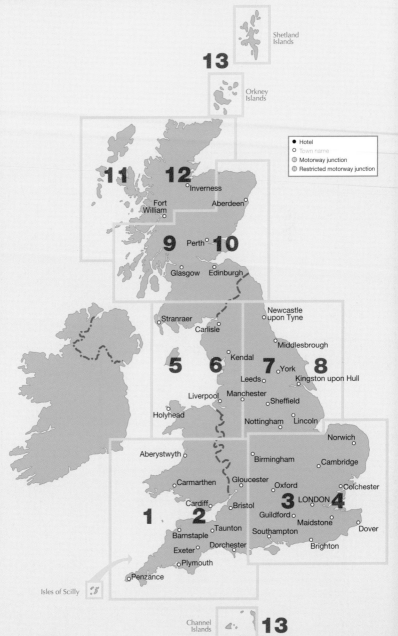

KEY TO ATLAS PAGES

Shetland Islands

13

Orkney Islands

- ● Hotel
- ○ Town name
- ⓜ Motorway junction
- ⓡ Restricted motorway junction

11 **12**

Inverness

Fort William

Aberdeen

9 Perth **10**

Glasgow Edinburgh

Stranraer

Carlisle

Newcastle upon Tyne

Middlesbrough

5 **6** Kendal **7** York **8**

Leeds

Kingston upon Hull

Liverpool Manchester

Sheffield

Holyhead

Nottingham Lincoln

Norwich

Aberystwyth

Birmingham

Cambridge

Carmarthen Gloucester

Oxford

Colchester

Cardiff

3 LONDON **4**

Bristol

1 **2** Guildford

Maidstone

Taunton Southampton

Dover

Barnstaple

Dorchester

Brighton

Exeter

Plymouth

Penzance

Isles of Scilly

Channel Islands **13**

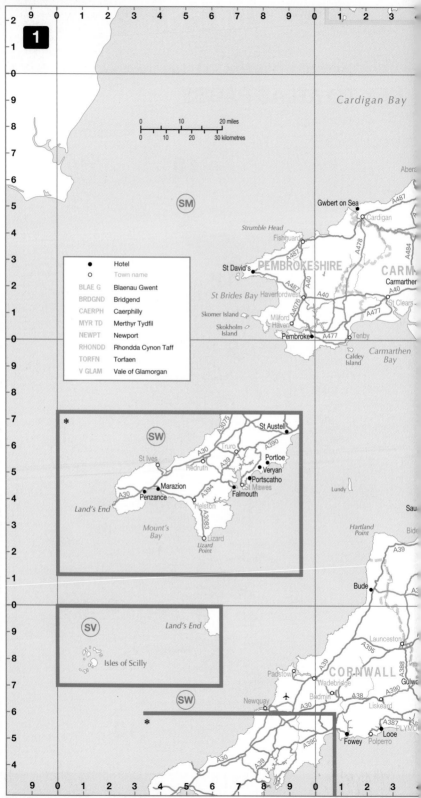

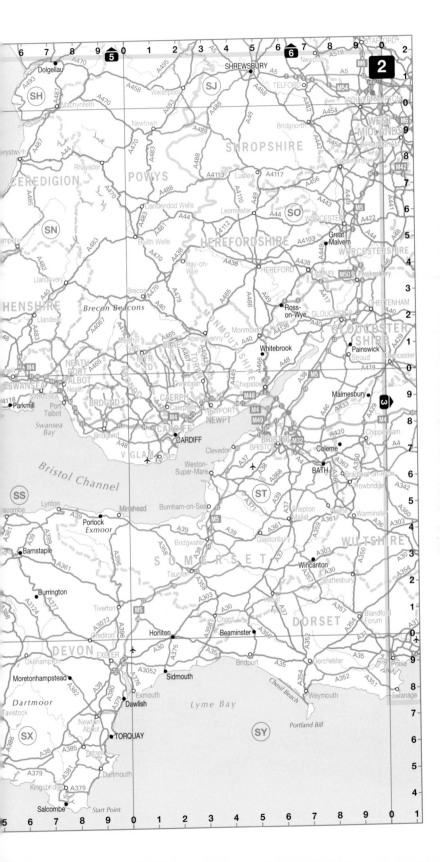

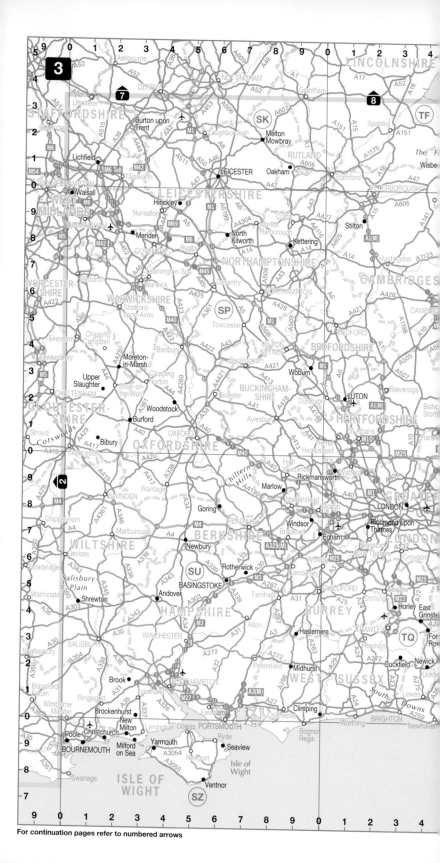

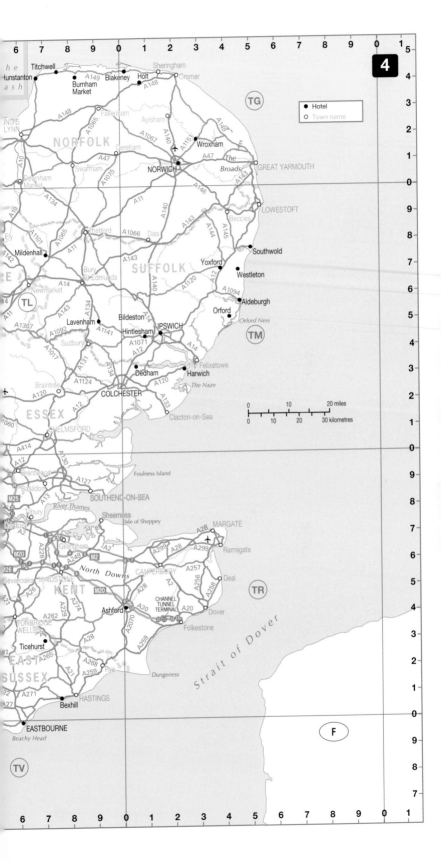

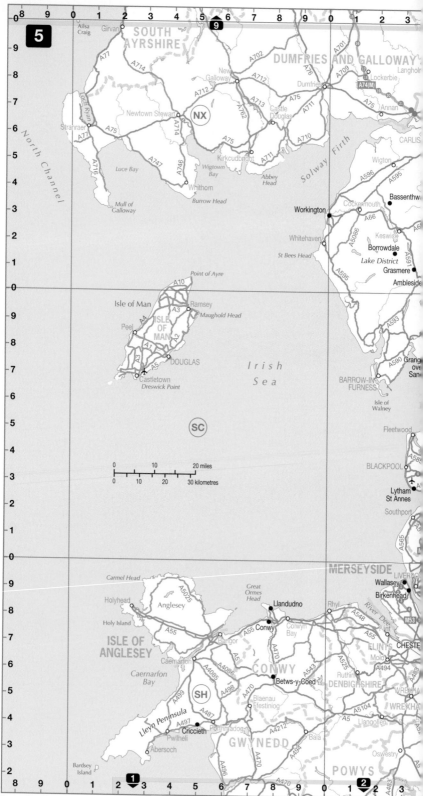

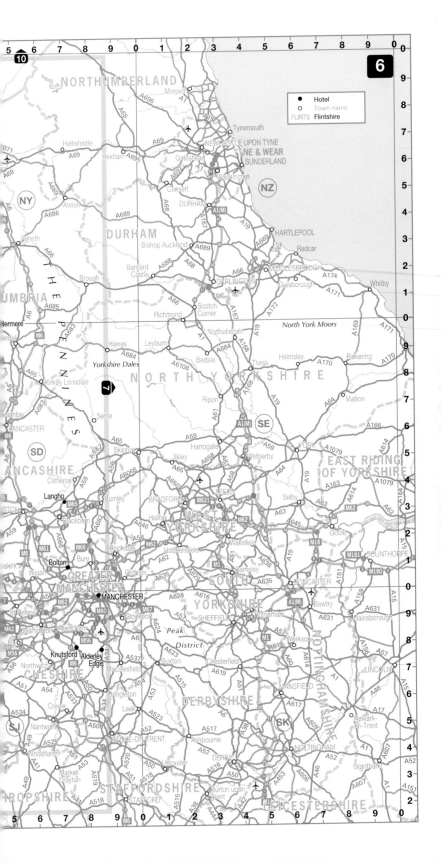

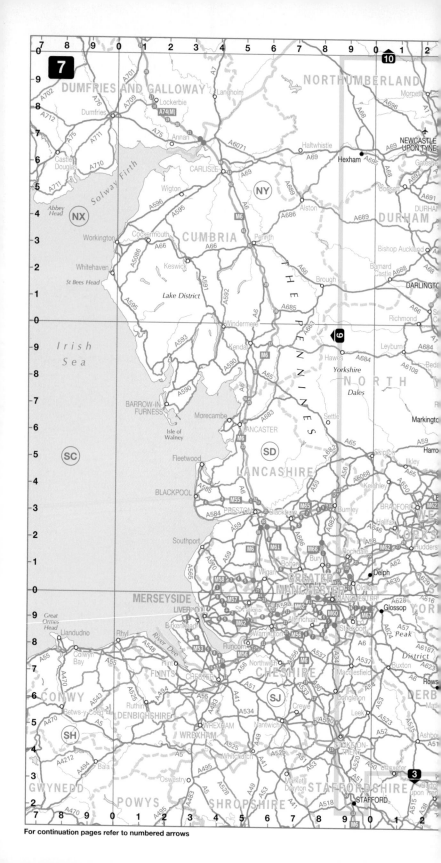

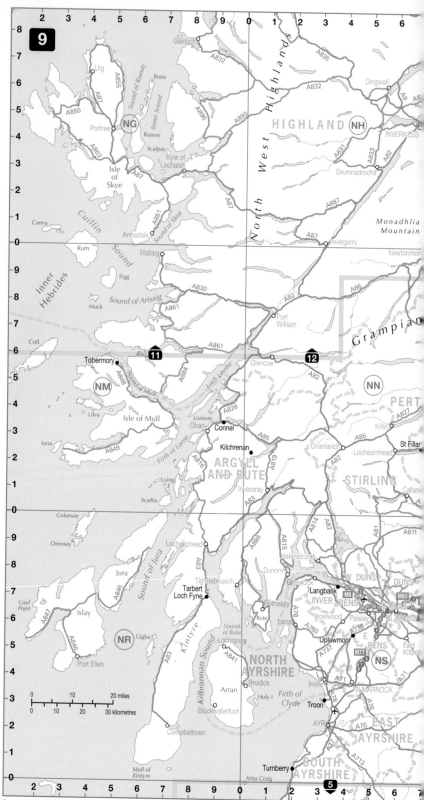

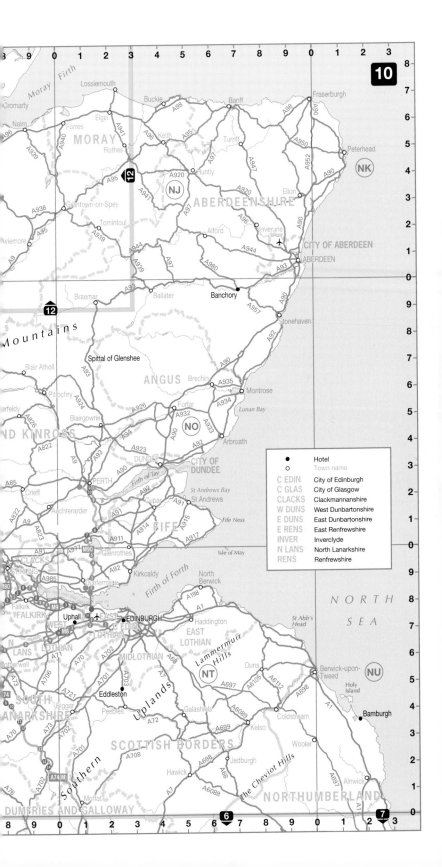

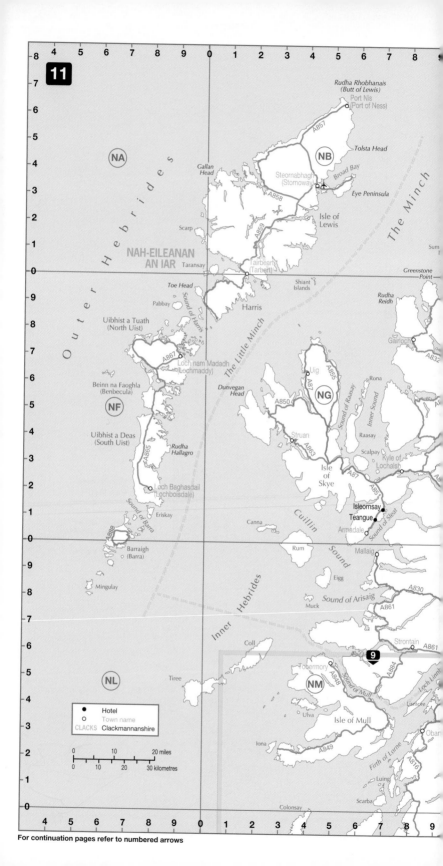

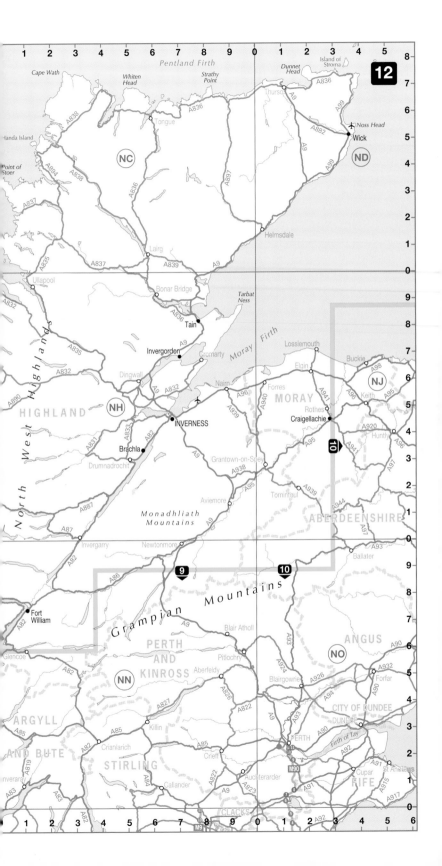

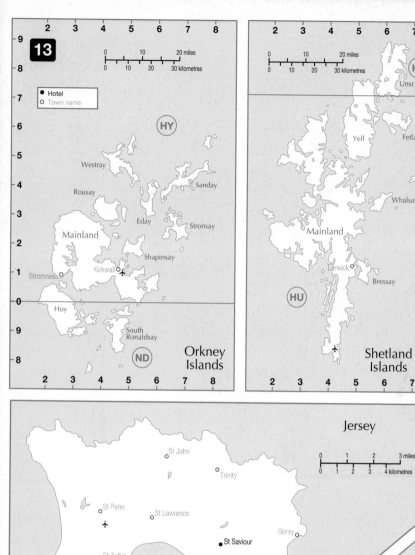

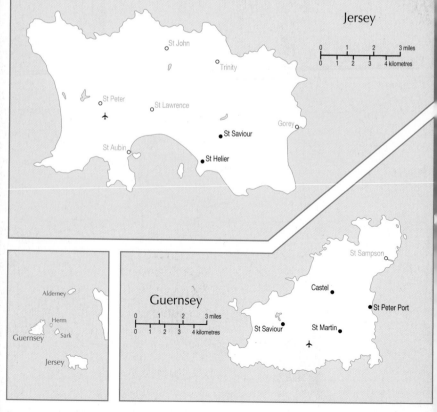

St Ouen's Bay, Jersey

Hotel Index

Hotel Index

Hotel Index

Hotel Index

Location Index

Location Index

Location Index

Credits

The Automobile Association would like to thank the following photographers, companies and picture libraries for their assistance in the preparation of this book.

Abbreviations for the picture credits are as follows: (t) top; (b) bottom; (l) left; (r) right; (c) centre; (AA) AA World Travel Library.

12 AA/S Day; 14/15 AA/D Clapp; 16 AA/M Birkitt; 19 AA/J Tims; 22 TTL Images/Alamy; 24 AA/T Mackie; 26b AA/T Mackie; 27 AA/T Marsh; 30 AA/A Burton; 35b AA/C Jones; 40 AA/A Mockford & N Bonetti; 44b AA/A Mockford & N Bonetti; 48 AA/T Mackie; 50 AA/C Jones; 52b AA/A Burton; 63b AA/N Hicks; 64 AA/A Burton; 69b AA/A Burton; 70 AA; 72b AA/R Coulam; 73 AA/M Birkitt; 76 AA/S Day; 80b AA/K Doran; 81 AA/C Molyneux; 84b AA/A Greaves; 85 AA/A Burton; 92 AA/C Jones; 93b AA/C Jones; 94 AA/M Moody; 96 AA/M Busselle; 98 AA/D Clapp; 100 AA/D Clapp; 101b AA/C Jones; 102 AA/P Baker; 105b AA/P Baker; 107 AA/C Sawyer; 108b AA/N Setchfield; 117b AA/J Tims; 126b AA/J Tims; 130 AA/J Miller; 132 AA/D Clapp; 135 AA/T Mackie; 137b AA/T Mackie; 141b AA/L Whitwam; 142 AA/M Birkitt; 144 AA/R Coulam; 145b AA/J Hunt; 147 charistoone-images/Alamy; 152 AA/J Tims; 155b AA/C Jones; 156 Mark Chapman/ Alamy; 158b Colin Underhill/Alamy; 160 AA/C&A Molyneux; 162 AA/R Duke; 166b AA/J Tims; 167 AA/C Jones; 170b AA/J Welsh; 171 AA/T Mackie; 177b AA/T Mackie; 179b AA/T Mackie; 184 AA/R Turpin; 187 AA/P Baker; 191b AA/J Miller; 193 AA/J Miller; 196b AA/T Souter; 198 AA/L Noble; 199b AA/M Trelawny; 200 AA/R Coulam; 202 AA/D Kelsall; 205 AA/S McBride; 208b AA/D Forss; 209 AA/M Moody; 211b AA/M Moody; 213 AA/C Jones; 216 AA/L Whitwam; 218b AA/L Whitwam; 220b AA/J Morrison; 224 AA/T Mackie; 226 David Kilpatrick/Alamy; 227b Colin Palmer Photography/Alamy; 228 steven gillis hd9 imaging/Alamy; 230 DAVID NEWHAM/Alamy; 231b International Photobank/Alamy; 234b Stephen Dorey ABIPP/Alamy; 236 Simon Heron/Alamy; 238/239 AA/D W Robertson; 241b AA/S Anderson; 246b AA/J Smith; 258 AA/J Beazley; 260 AA/S Whitehorne; 262 AA/A J Hopkins; 264/265 AA/M Bauer; 273b AA/S Lewis; 278b AA/N Jenkins; 279 AA/C Warren; 295 Jon Arnold Images Ltd/Alamy;

Every effort has been made to trace the copyright holders, and we apologise in advance for any accidental errors. We would be happy to apply any corrections in the following edition of this publication.